Care in a Confused Climate

Care in a Confused Climate

Pastoral Care and Postmodern Culture

PAUL GOODLIFF

First published in 1998 by
Darton, Longman and Todd Ltd
1 Spencer Court
140–142 Wandsworth High Street
London SW18 4JJ

Reprinted 1999 and 2001

ISBN 0-232-52281-2

A catalogue record for this book is available from the British Library

Designed by Sandie Boccacci
Phototypeset in 10/12.5pt Plantin by Intype London Ltd
Printed and bound in Great Britain by
Page Bros, Norwich

Contents

Foreword

The salutary message of this book is that pastoral care, as a form of churchly action, will not be genuinely pastoral – as distinct from being mere therapy or counselling – unless it is informed by a whole range of skills, from the theological to the personal. Paul Goodliff's achievement is to integrate trinitarian theology, social analysis and the experience of pastoral practice in a work which throws light at once on pastoral care and the world in which it has to be done. As he shows all too clearly, we do live in an era called 'postmodern' by virtue at least of the kinds of attitudes and approaches to life that are increasingly apparent in our society. While they offer a threat, they also, in questioning old shibboleths, provide new opportunities.

The book also demonstrates the disastrous effects of allowing both social trends and the ideologies of secular counselling to determine what is done in the Church. Although there will, and indeed must, be interaction between the different spheres we call 'Church' and 'world' – for is not the triune God Lord of the world also? – the Church's distinctive mission is to form people in Christ, and that involves taking her orientation from the Gospel as it is embodied in a community of worship and life. Particularly interesting is the argument that the lifeblood of pastoral work is provided by those activities which are most difficult and often invisible: Bible study, prayer and thoughtful – theological – preparation. They are, however, the very things that are neglected by many of those who are impatiently concerned with outward success or hasten to conform their practice to that of 'the world', and who thereby abandon their true birthright. As I read this book, I was continually given fresh insights into the nature of our world and of the Christian life within it. It should provide a valuable resource for those who are engaged in that most difficult of tasks, pastoral work in a divided Church and desperate world.

COLIN GUNTON
King's College, London
November, 1997

Acknowledgements

I am aware that acknowledgements can seem rather like the enthusiastic Oscar winners who, having thanked their agent, director, producer and fellow actors, continue with a list that includes their family, partner and God! While this book was written alone, it has benefited from the advice and stimulation of many, and would not have been possible without the support of others. In deciding where to begin, however, I am reminded of the mosquito at the nudist camp who, faced with the enormity of the task, was at a loss to know where to begin.

While the themes had been gestating over a long period, the first draft was written in a concentrated three months while I was on sabbatical leave from my pastoral responsibilities at Bunyan Baptist Church in Stevenage. The support and generosity, both financially and in spirit, of my congregation, and especially of those who lead the church with me, was a reminder that I 'belong' in this family of God, and feel proud to serve as its minister. I want to thank John, Eric, Laurie and Andy who, as elders, bore an extra burden of responsibility with good grace and wisdom, and my deacons who shared in those extra responsibilities. I also took three months leave from my post as part-time Free Church Chaplain at the North Herts NHS Trust, and I must thank Jane, Barbara and Marion, fellow chaplains, and most especially, Michael Belfield, who increased his Free Church Chaplaincy duties to cover mine, and to Jane Bandcroft, my manager, who allowed me leave. The Baptist Union of Great Britain gave me a sabbatical grant, and I hope that in helping other pastors, this book will prove a wise investment for them. The librarians at Regent's Park College, Oxford, and Queen's College, Birmingham gave me access to their resources, while the Senior Common Room at Regent's Park welcomed me as a sabbatical minister.

The advice and stimulation of conversations with my friend Alistair Ross has always been special, particularly so in the writing of this book, and he and Judy, and their children Hannah and Toby, welcomed me into their home while I studied at Queen's, and Nick and Leslie Smith gave me hospitality while at Oxford. Thank you. Others read and commented on certain chapters and I am grateful to Joan King and Geoff Colmer for their encouragement and critique. John and Sonia Hall and John Taylor helped with case studies for building pastoral teams.

On the broader scene, many of my convictions about pastoral care owe their genesis to mentors and colleagues: Douglas McBain, Mike Wood, Paul Beasley-Murray, fellow tutors in counselling at St John's, Nottingham, and the planning group for the Swanwick conferences in pastoral care and counselling among them. What passes for theology in this book is a poor reflection on the tutoring of Professor Colin Gunton and his colleagues on the postgraduate course in systematic theology, but I look upon those two years at King's as amongst the most significant in my life and I am grateful for that opportunity. I am especially grateful to Professor Gunton for agreeing to write the Foreword, and for this generous assistance thank you.

The encouragement of David Moloney, commissioning editor at Darton, Longman and Todd, has made my first brush with the publishing world a happy and fruitful one.

My wife, Gill, gave me her unstinting support and an eye for the 'typo' and the grammatical glitch, and my sons Andrew, Nicholas and Stephen had less of me than they deserved; my parents first showed me what care looked like and it is to my family that I owe most in the writing of this book, and it seems appropriate that it should, therefore, be dedicated to them.

How to Read this Book

I wonder if all writers flatter themselves that their readers want to read everything in their book. There are far too many books in my library that are part read, unread or waiting to be read for me to presume that everyone who has this book will read it all. Practitioners will, perhaps, skip to the second part; those attracted by the postmodernism in the title might stop halfway through. Of course, I believe everyone will benefit from reading it all! However, I have wanted to help different kinds of reader by guiding them to different parts of the book, and this introduction and the opening chapter will help you decide what to read first.

The contents of this book fall naturally into two sections. The first offers an analysis of postmodernism, a theological response to it, some discussion about postmodern ethics and pastoral care, and a theological and pastoral call for community. The second section calls for four urgent tasks of pastoral care in the light of the socio-cultural changes sweeping the West as it is poised on the verge of a new millennium.

Some of the material in the first part is by its very nature hard to grasp. I have attempted to make it as accessible as possible, but, in a true postmodern spirit of choice, the more difficult sections have been set in boxes, and function as extended footnotes embedded in the text. These sections could be skipped by those not versed in continental philosophy or the mysteries of systematic theology without any loss to the essential argument. However, other readers, particularly students of pastoral theology, will benefit from the greater depth of analysis in those sections, and I hope that every reader will at least attempt some of the boxed sections.

PART ONE

Patterns in Postmodern Culture

Introduction

Most modern societies notice change more than tradition, the new more than the enduring. Nowhere is this seen with greater clarity than in the West as the Millennium approaches. The old traditions of modernity are being replaced by postmodernism, both in the wider culture as well as in the Church. The transition is resisted in church and culture alike, not without good reason, for in some of its most prominent ways postmodern religion appears to be the enemy of truth, while the wider postmodern culture is closely allied with a fragmenting and alienating society.

Pastoral care is inevitably affected by both arenas of change, Church and society, and to define the priorities for pastoral care, as we shall do in the second part of this book, we must first explore the shape and landscape of postmodern culture. In this first part, therefore, we shall first look briefly at the way in which pastoral care has changed in the course of our century. The major exploration of the postmodern cultural landscape follows. Particular attention will be given to ethical issues and a Christian response to the relativism and plurality of postmodern culture. Holding ministry together in a world that is falling apart is no easy challenge, and so the prescription for the future health of pastoral care will be rooted in a Trinitarian faith and in a radical engagement with our culture, both in dialogue and in costly, compassionate caring.

CHAPTER 1

Holding Ministry Together in a World that is Falling Apart

Overview

The pastoral care of people as whole persons, the cure of souls, the *cura animarum*, as it is still sometimes called, has been the great task of generations of Christian leaders, be they priests, ministers or pastors. In the ordination service of deacons in the Church of England, the deacon's 'general duty' is 'to do such pastoral work as is entrusted to him'. Likewise at his or her ordination to the priesthood, the priest is to 'set the Good Shepherd always before him as the pattern of his calling, caring for the people committed to his charge'.[1] In my own Baptist tradition, the ordination prayer includes the words 'in pastoral care and leadership may he be filled with the compassion and vision of Christ'.[2] The pastoral care of people lies near the heart of what many clergy would see as their prime task. Yet I believe that fulfilling that task today is more difficult than has been the case for centuries, and at the very least it is harder to fulfil now than at any time since the bleak years of the 1930s with the economic misery of the Depression and the uncertainty of the European scene.

Primarily this is so because of the rapid social and cultural changes that we generally call postmodernism, with its attendant secular and eclectic world views. In place of the older, modernist view of reason as the basis of understanding, there is now uncertainty over the way to discern what is real, what is true. Our culture is increasingly pluralist, eclectic and ephemeral. The impact of the revolution in communications brought about by the microchip is pervasive and continual, with new ways of communicating over the Internet creating a global and unlimited pool of knowledge and communication. The older moral certainties, both those that are rooted in the Judaeo-Christian tradition, and those that are more humanistic, seem to be diminishing in their control, replaced by an amorality that is unfixed, ever in flux. Change is so rapid, and the implications of that change so inimical to the values that have sustained our Western modernist culture, that the task of pastoral care has become bewildering, multifaceted and complex.

Fifty years ago pastoral studies were hardly taught to ordinands, and texts like Charles Forder's *The Parish Priest at Work: An Introduction to Systematic Pastoralia*[3] encompass the needs of individuals in seventeen pages, with but the briefest of nods in the direction of psychology. It would be difficult today to find a competent pastor who does not have some basic knowledge of popular psychology (albeit limited to some unconnected knowledge of terms such as the unconscious, defences or archetypes), and many would be familiar with counselling and psychotherapy, if not themselves trained in those professions.

Writing in the preface to S. K. Knight's Cambridge Pastoral Theology Lectures of 1925–1926, entitled *Fulfilling the Ministry*,[4] Bishop Herbert Hensley Henson says, 'The conditions of pastoral ministry have been revolutionised within recent years, so completely revolutionised that the classical treatises on the subject are too remote from modern life to be very helpful.' He goes on to note that 'the circumstances in which the parish clergyman must now fulfil his ministry are changing so rapidly that even an experience so recent as that of Dr Knight has become already in some degree irrelevant'. To read S. K. Knight today, seventy years after those lectures were delivered, is to inhabit a different country. He wishes to 'adapt to present conditions Richard Baxter's method of pastoral visitation'. Baxter[5] set aside two days a week for the purpose, announced on the preceding Sunday where he was visiting, and requested the whole household to be present at the hours he named! Even Knight says that it is impossible these days for the clergy to claim so well-recognised an authority as Baxter's. Most of the visits that I make to non-church folk, say in the case of a funeral or infant dedication, are deemed of such little worth that unless I request it (which I always do) the television remains on full volume and I conduct my conversation initially in competition with daytime TV! If things were changing rapidly in Hensley Henson's 1930s, how much more so in the late 1990s.

One of the characteristic signs of postmodernism, the culture of our age, is rapid change, far more rapid than in the 1930s, and the breadth of understanding generally acknowledged to be of importance in the training of pastors and the practice of pastoral care include not only the disciplines familiar to S. K. Knight and Charles Forder (homiletics, church administration, the conduct of public worship and the occasional offices, teaching adults, youth work, hospital and school visiting, general pastoral visiting and the constant need for study in the areas of theology, church history and philosophy), but aspects quite unfamiliar to them (psychology, counselling theory and practice, social change, information technology, management theory and the management of people and organisations, a working knowledge of world religions and the multiplicity of New Age as well as older cults), and developments in the church scene that are demanding both of mind and emotion (such as women in ministry, homosexual relationships, the Toronto blessing and its ilk, new styles of worship and youth church/rave worship).

No wonder clergy are leaving the Church at a pitifully high rate and new vocations in some of the traditional denominations are at a very low level, too low to replace those who are leaving prematurely or retiring. We expect our pastoral leaders to be polymaths, renaissance men or women, competent in a wide range of disciplines and possibly expert in one or two, willing to work the equivalent of twice the maximum EC working week for a stipend that is the equivalent to a basic-scale teacher's, but with little prospect of enhancement over the years, and still to care professionally for whoever comes their way in Church or community.

Even that more recent stalwart amongst handbooks of pastoral care for the Evangelical and Free Church market, R. E. O. White's *A Guide to Pastoral Care*,[6] which was still being recommended to my generation of ministerial students in the mid-1980s, appears hopelessly anachronistic today. With its focus on the tasks of pastoral care, such as regular and disciplined visitation, preparation and conduct of the wedding and the funeral; its relatively superficial awareness of counselling practice; and its view of 'typical problems' that presuppose an almost universal acceptance of the norms of the traditional family amongst evangelical Christians, it is clearly the product of a society that has all but disappeared. The 1950s Scottish Baptist world of R. E. O. White has so clearly changed that the models of pastoral care that he advocated are now, at worst, redundant, and, at best, severely in need of reshaping for a world that has changed in many ways beyond recognition.

Definition of Pastoral Care

We have been discussing pastoral care without adequate definition, I fear. Before looking at the substance of this exploration of pastoral care and postmodernism there needs to be some clarity in this definition. In recent years the definition by Clebsch and Jaekle has become seminal. For them pastoral care

> consists of helping acts, done by representative Christian persons, directed towards the healing, sustaining, guiding and reconciling of troubled persons whose troubles arise in the context of ultimate meanings and concerns.[7]

Quite apart from the now rather quaint 'ultimate meanings and concerns' with its nod towards Paul Tillich, rather than 'religious' or 'spiritual', there are some serious shortcomings to this definition. Stephen Pattison[8] argues that 'representative persons' could be too clerical and denies the role of the laity, 'troubled' belies a problem-centred approach, 'persons' is too individualistic, while the wider Christian community and its traditions are not seen as a resource, nor does it take into account that Christian pastoral carers should be responsive to needs which do not arise in the context of 'ultimate meanings and concerns'. In its place Pattison defines pastoral care as

> that activity, undertaken especially by representative Christian persons, directed towards the elimination and relief of sin and sorrow and the presentation of all people perfect in Christ to God.[9]

In his own critique of this definition, Pattison notes that 'activity' can focus upon what is done rather than the kind of person who offers pastoral care (Alistair Campbell's danger of pastoral carer simply being a highly trained professional) and that for care to be pastoral it must be Christian. This means the carer will often be someone who has been 'appointed' in some way so as to be representative of the wider Christian community, though that does not necessarily mean an ordained minister. In this way the pastoral ministry is paradigmatic of the pastoral care carried out by all members of the community. How is that Christian element to be maintained in a way that recognises the importance of insights from beyond the Christian community? Pattison argues that pastoral carers should maintain a 'Christian vision, a spiritual life and a sense of being rooted, grounded in and orientated towards God'. Thus the means by which pastoral care remains truly Christian lies in the subjectivity of the pastoral carers' spiritual experience rather than in any strongly objective mode of expressing care, dogmatic affiliation or the articulating of Christian presuppositions.

More recently, in the Preface to the magisterial *Dictionary of Pastoral Care and Counselling*, its editor Rodney Hunt

> . . . regards pastoral care and counselling as the theologically informed ministry of religiously faithful persons to individuals and families. More specifically, *pastoral care* is considered to be any form of personal ministry to individuals and to family and community relationships by representative religious persons (ordained or lay) and by their communities of faith, who understand and guide their caring efforts out of a theological perspective rooted in a tradition of faith.[10]

Again the individualistic bias, so familiar to modernist and post-modernist sensibilities, is present, albeit weakened by the role of 'communities of faith'. However, this definition seems to be closest to the realities and aspirations of Christian pastoral care, and it is the one adopted here. Thus it differentiates *Christian* pastoral care from other forms of care in the community, emphasises the place of the carer as the one whose religious faith makes care *pastoral* care, but lacks the most helpful aspect of the Clebsch and Jaekle definition, namely the categorising of outcomes of pastoral care as healing, sustaining, guiding and reconciling.

Thus I might redefine pastoral care myself, acknowledging the debt to others, as *the healing, sustaining, guiding, personal/societal formation and reconciling of persons and their relationships to family and community by representative Christian persons (ordained or lay), and by their faith communities, who ground their care in the theological perspective of that faith tradition and who personally remain faithful to that faith through spiritual authenticity.*

Pathways through the Book

This book attempts to map the cultural changes that constitute postmodernism and, with one hand grasping the traditional tasks of pastoral care and the other hand holding the cultural and social changes that are transforming the context in which we practise pastoral ministry, adjust the shape of pastoral care so that we can hold ministry together in a world that is falling apart. In this opening chapter I want to set out the broad picture, with themes that will be developed in successive chapters in greater depth.

We shall first consider how the cultural climate has affected the practice of pastoral care from a historical perspective, giving us clues to how far the current cultural changes are likely to alter pastoral care practice. While the account will begin with the immediate post-First World War period, when the task of pastoral care began to be explored in the work of, for instance, Forder and Knight, as discussed above, the focus will be upon changes over the past forty years since the impact of the pastoral counselling movement began to be particularly felt in the churches.

Secondly I shall introduce an exploration of the cultural changes that the tag 'postmodernism' describes: what is the newly emerging culture like, in both the Church and the world?

Some would doubt whether the very nature of postmodernism allows a coherent account of it, since its very plurality and fragmentation precludes a single 'postmodernism'. However, being aware of the question 'whose postmodernism?', I shall attempt to map the culture of postmodernism from its philosophical contours of post-structuralism, Jean-François Lyotard's 'incredulity towards meta-narrative', and so forth, through its social, economic and political consequences, to its 'popular' and its religious manifestations.

Thirdly, we shall evaluate postmodernism in the light of the Christian faith, and ask if the fragmented culture can, unlike Humpty Dumpty, be put back together again. Postmodernism declares that there is no objective knowledge of truth, especially moral or metaphysical truth, outside of particular traditions embedded in particular communities. This presents a dilemma and an opportunity for the Christian faith. A dilemma, because traditionally Christian faith has been founded upon a notion of universal truth and it has been at odds with any moves towards relativising that universality. Thus the more fundamentalist of sectors in the church see postmodernism as its implacable foe. However, the very plurality of postmodernism could also create new opportunities for the Christian faith to be understood on its own terms, rather than on the terms of the post-Enlightenment project of modernism, and postmodern pastoral care can be one of the ways in which its validity can be demonstrated. In the new cultural landscape pastoral care is perhaps the most important means of mission.

The problematical issue of postmodern ethics will be the focus of Chapter 5, in dialogue with the modernist counselling notion of the value-free therapeutic encounter, where the therapist 'suspends' his or her judgment. The notion of the value-free therapist is entirely mythical, and I shall argue for a bold reclamation of an overt Christian ethic on the part of pastoral carers and counsellors. The work of Alasdair MacIntyre, especially his *After Virtue*[11] and *Whose Justice? Whose Rationality?*,[12] will also be explored as we engage in the quest for an appropriate means of doing ethics in pastoral care, and the critique of pastoral care by Don Browning, emphasising the moral context of pastoral care, will be discussed.

In Chapter 6, the postmodern fascination with community will be explored in relation to the community of faith which is the proper locus of pastoral care. I shall pay particular attention in the socio-political realm to communitarianism, especially as espoused by Amitai Etzioni.[13] I shall also examine the emphasis placed upon the doctrine of the Trinity, which is the theological grammar for the new postmodern theological turn. Its out-working in the areas of the doctrines of the Church (ecclesiology) and of the Spirit (pneumatology) will be given precedence, as Graham Ward argues in *Theology and Contemporary Critical Theory*,[14] that these areas address questions of ways of being and the nature of communities of being.

In Part Two, we shall first explore some critical metaphors for pastoral care:

(i) pastoral care as gift,
(ii) as proclamation,
(iii) as service, and
(iv) as sacrament.

Following this we shall argue for certain pastoral care priorities for the Church to pursue in response to the cultural transformations taking place, in the belief that in both its mission and its pastoral care the Church must address itself to how the world actually is, rather than how it would like the world to be, or remembered it used to be. Amongst those priorities are building Christian community; the nurturing of human relationships, especially those in the postmodern family in all its diversity; the healing of the wounded soul arising from, for instance, abusive family relationships; and the nurturing of authentic Christian faith in our sceptical and secular age. Thus Chapter 8 considers the task of building Christian community; Chapter 9, creating relational health; Chapter 10, healing the wounded soul; and Chapter 11, nurturing and sustaining faith.

Finally, after discussing the resources that enable and sustain pastoral care, and issues of spirituality, training, care for the carers, theology and companionship, we shall turn to some practical matters concerning the establishment of pastoral care teams in the local church community.

Pastoral Care in the Secular Community

Pastoral care, of course, is not confined to the Church. There is now pastoral care in the workplace, secondary schools often replace 'form groups' with 'pastoral groups', and personal tutors with pastoral responsibilities replace the former form teachers of my teaching days. For most people the traditional dispensers of pastoral care, the clergy and especially the parish priest, have been largely replaced by the new world of 'trained listeners', the counselling fraternity. With 460 training courses and some 20,000 people participating in some form of counselling training in the UK at the moment, the growth in this aspect of pastoral care has been extraordinary, particularly when compared with the figure of under 10,000 people training at Theological Colleges and Bible Schools in 1995,[15] many of whom will not be training for the role of pastoral carer in its traditional sense, but preparing for overseas missionary work, undertaking theological studies, evangelistic training or a whole raft of non-residential training programmes not necessarily leading to pastoral leadership. In short, there are perhaps 250 Baptist ministerial students, under 2000 Anglican, 350 Roman Catholic seminarians, probably about the same number of Methodists and United Reformed students. All told, probably not more than 3000 people are training for the regular pastoral ministry, 15 per cent of the figure for those training to be counsellors.

We might not want to go as far as Stephen McGinty, writing in the *Sunday Times* of 5 January 1997, when he says 'Counselling has become Britain's new religion,' but certainly the average person in Britain today looking for pastoral care will turn to their GP or find a counsellor before contacting the local parish priest or Free Church minister. This change has been amongst the most potent in reshaping the map of pastoral care in the modern and now postmodern world. We shall need to explore the place of pastoral counselling in the map of pastoral care that we will be drawing.

Alongside the 'new religion' of counselling (and I write as a counsellor and tutor in counselling, as well as a pastor and Hospital Chaplain) has been the loss of nerve on the part of some clergy, the traditional dispensers of pastoral care, in the central features of their role. The pastoral theologian Eugene Peterson writes of the crisis affecting American clergy, echoing a trend that Kenneth Leech[16] identified in the 1970s in Britain.

> American pastors are abandoning their posts, left and right, and at an alarming rate. They are not leaving their churches and getting other jobs. Congregations still pay their salaries. Their names remain on the church stationery and they continue to appear in pulpits on Sundays. But they are abandoning their posts, their calling. They have gone whoring after other gods. What they do with their time under the guise of pastoral ministry hasn't the remotest connection with what the church's pastors have done for most of twenty centuries . . .
>
> The biblical fact is that there are no successful churches. There are, instead, communities of sinners, gathered before God week after week . . . The pastor's responsibility is to keep the community attentive to God. It is this responsibility that is being abandoned in spades.[17]

Peterson argues that the three disciplines of prayer, attention to Scripture and spiritual direction are 'so basic, so critical, that they determine the shape of everything else'. In their place, as Leech argued a decade before, clergy have put counselling and social work, selling their birthright for a mess of pottage. More cynically Bernice Martin describes the 'therapeutic clergyman':

> One role drawn from the modern professions, that of pastoral therapist, does have ready appeal . . . So clergy learn less Greek, Latin, Hebrew and classical theology but more social science. They become a species of semi-professional therapist, with a roving brief, generic case workers for the parish with a mildly spiritual aura.[18]

This particular development in the shape of pastoral ministry illustrates the need to hold together both the pull of the past and its traditional practices and the present, with its secularising processes, if pastoral ministry is to be true to its calling and relevant to its cultural and social arena. The challenge is to see if Christian pastoral carers can remain true to the pattern of traditional pastoral ministry and embrace the newer disciplines of pastoral counselling.

Pastoral Theology: The Dialogue of Belief and Praxis

Stephen Pattison writes of his passion for pastoral theology as a 'place where religious belief, tradition and practice meets contemporary experiences, questions and actions and conducts a dialogue which is mutually enriching, intellectually critical and practically transforming'.[19] He uses the analogy of a lake to 'gain a sense of the depth, complexity, richness and dynamism of pastoral theological activity'. The lake is susceptible to a variety of uses, as is pastoral theology, and out of the lake flow two rivers: one is 'significant action', and the other 'significant words and thoughts'. The creation of a book is clearly the latter kind of enterprise, but it is my hope that out of this book will flow a response of action and practice. However, for that action to be transformational it must be the product of pastoral reflection and theological cogency.

This book is not, therefore, primarily a 'how to do pastoral care' manual, neither is it simply an academic treatise on the nature of pastoral theology, although I hope that there will be elements of both genres in this book. Rather, it is my intention to be synergistic, not only in the classical theological sense of the cooperation of the human and divine will, but also in the sense of producing a synergetic dialogue between postmodern culture, pastoral theology, the traditions and Scriptures of the Christian faith and the practice and experience of pastoral care. This is akin to Pattison's critical, creative conversation between his own beliefs and ideas, the beliefs, perceptions and assumptions arising from the Christian community and the contemporary situation.[20] For him, that conversation should be, among a number of characteristics, transformational (involving a practical wisdom that helps people distinguish how they should act or be; akin to Aristotle's *phronesis*), confessional and unsystematic rather than the creating of a systematic theology, apophatic (living close to the dark and the experience of the hidden face of God), flexible, provisional, pluralist, practical, dialectic, communal and aware. I hope this conversation will be like that vision!

CHAPTER 2

A History of Pastoral Care in the Late-Modern Period

Overview

The history of pastoral care in this century has been well documented, and I do not want to simply cover ground that has been described elsewhere.[1] What concerns us here are the influences which have shaped the development of pastoral care.

Pastoral Theology and the Influence of the New Psychology 1920–1960

In the period up to the late 1950s the 'new psychology', beginning with a trickle, and ill received by the churches, grew into a flood that has come to dominate the human sciences in the latter half of the century. An older form of pastoral care that initially took little note of these developments[2] came to be replaced by forms of pastoral care that were dominated by insights from the psychological movement broadly called psychotherapy.

Initially the ideas of Freud were advanced in Britain by his advocate Ernest Jones[3] and by 1920 there was sufficient interest to establish the Tavistock Clinic in London and the Cassels Hospital in Kent. The psychotherapeutic models of treating the mentally ill gradually spread through the psychiatric community as well as outside it in the alternative medicine community, although there have always been areas of the psychiatric profession which give it little intellectual credence. The early days using Freudian psychoanalysis soon became a broad movement embracing a great variety of different theoretical perspectives, from the ideas of Jung and Adler to behaviourism and the work of Melanie Klein and Anna Freud.

Meanwhile, popular culture was increasingly influenced by psychology and psychotherapy. In the 1920s it was the most popular of the sciences in the press and in ordinary conversation, a position it has but rarely lost. At present psychology is the most popular degree course for undergraduates in Britain, though presumably relatively few proceed to practise as psychologists either within the health service or beyond.

In 1930 the situation faced by those concerned with the treatment (or lack of it) of the mentally ill was radically changed by the Mental Treatment Act. Until that time little was provided by way of treatment, other than a secure and relaxed atmosphere, open air treatment (sitting in the open air rather than in the ward) and psychotherapy. The Mental Treatment Act made possible the admission of patients on a voluntary basis, with an emphasis on prevention as well as cure, but more significantly, psychiatrists needed something to do, and by the end of the 1930s a whole range of newer treatments that owed little to the 'talking cure' were developed, i.e. drug therapies, electroconvulsive treatment and the start of psychosurgery. This enhanced the status of the psychiatrist, now firmly a member of the medical profession, unlike psychotherapists. Ross identifies three areas in which these changes had important implications for pastoral care.[4] First, in trying to establish itself as a credible branch of medicine, psychiatry distanced itself from areas of non-scientific thought, including pastoral care and psychotherapy. Secondly, psychiatry considered itself the prime provider of the 'cure of souls' for the mentally ill, but without concern for their spiritual welfare; and thirdly, organic psychiatry developed a strong antipathy to psychoanalysis and psychotherapeutic ideas, which pastoral care was beginning to take seriously.

Behind this widening chasm of understanding lies the familiar dichotomy in the modernist distinction between the public realm of scientific fact and the private realm of unsubstantiated private opinion. Psychiatry sees itself as the standard bearer of the former, while pastoral care is viewed as an area to be confined to the latter, because of its religious beliefs and identification with the unsubstantiated claims of the psychotherapeutic meta-narrative.

The Church, perhaps in part aware of its diminishing status and seeking to halt or slow that diminution by an embracing of a pseudo-scientific credibility, adopted the 'new psychology' as a tool to enhance the work of the pastoral carer (usually the ordained minister), often in a quite uncritical manner. For some it became another skill adopted in the dilettante manner so beloved of the English clergy. Others adopted a more rigorous approach and saw in psychotherapy other means of healing the sick, in an area of life closer to their central spiritual areas of concern than, say, orthopaedics or general medicine. Psychology enhanced their role as those charged with the cure of souls. There were also those who reinterpreted the Christian faith in the light of psychoanalytical ideas, and were ready to 'welcome whatever new facts psychology has to teach us; and if these new facts should seriously affect any traditional assertions of theology, we must be prepared to revise our theology in accordance with new revelations of truth'.[5] This embracing of psychology over the claims of theology was anathema to others, however. It was incompatible with Christian faith and should accordingly be rejected, especially as it smacked of the liberal *rapprochement* with the modernist worldview which Evangelicals and more conservative elements of the Church viewed with dismay.

These continue to be the four main responses that pastoral theology makes to psychotherapy and the psychological insights of a hundred years of its existence. The resulting approaches to pastoral care either:

(i) reject the insights of psychology[6], or
(ii) modify them in the light of a prior commitment to theological principles[7], or
(iii) view them in a somewhat ill-considered or unsystematic way as tools to be used among others, or

(iv) wholeheartedly embrace whatever set of psychotherapeutic ideas seem most plausible to the practitioner.

The first half of the twentieth century, then, saw a range of responses to the new insights of psychology, especially a welcoming of them as a way of relating faith to the modern man or woman, reinterpreting the Gospels in psychological perspectives and giving a new credibility to a declining authority. By the 1950s, J. T. McNeill could say of the way in which psychology had been generally adopted by the Church and society that 'the territory of the old-time guide of souls' had been absorbed 'by the empire of medical science'.[8] With the increasing professionalisation of psychotherapy, the psychological skills of clergy became marginalised, resulting in the switch of profession for some from pastoral care to psychotherapy.

The general condition of pastoral theology until 1960, therefore, was influenced considerably and negatively by psychotherapy. The old school of handbooks on the practice of ministry were replaced by new perspectives. These saw pastoral care as a branch of psychology, rather than seeing psychology as providing insights that might, in some cases, be helpful in the practice of pastoral care, but, in other cases, be incompatible with theology that remained rooted in the orthodox traditions of the Church.

The Period from 1960: The Growing Influence of Pastoral Counselling

During the 1960s and 1970s significant influences from the United States reshaped the practice of pastoral care in Britain. There was a growing tendency to equate pastoral care with pastoral counselling and to adopt the values and practices of Rogerian client-centred psychotherapy in particular. These trends were visible from the 1930s, but were more widely adopted from the 1960s.

In the United States two significant developments had seen pastoral care transformed into pastoral counselling. First was the development of the Clinical Pastoral Education movement (CPE). E. E. Thornton traces the history of the movement from its beginnings in 1925 ▶▶

when Boisen, Keller and Cabor adapted the methods of professional education in psychiatry, social work and medicine respectively to the training of those exercising pastoral care. Its most influential early figure was Seward Hiltner, the doyen of the new pastoral theology in the States. The process of supervision around which the accreditation of practitioners revolves is of central significance, and uses the 'verbatim' account of particular pastoral encounters to train its practitioners. Thornton describes the aims of CPE as:

(i) the formation of a pastoral identity in seminarians and clergy,
(ii) the development of interpersonal competence (influenced by Rogerian therapy and encounter groups),
(iii) the integration of theology and ministry with a distinctively open stance to the theological trends of the day (Tillich in the 1960s, process theology in the 1970s, narrative theology in the 1980s, and postmodern theology currently), and
(iv) spiritual guidance, currently providing a more recent corrective to the overemphasis upon psychotherapeutic understandings in earlier expressions.

Attempts to develop a movement equivalent to the American CPE in Britain in the late 1960s were met with opposition, not least from Bob Lambourne, an influential critic of the easy assimilation of counselling into pastoral care. He argued that such an organisation would not promote pastoral care which was 'lay, voluntary and diffuse in the community'.[10] In place of a monolithic organisation a range of training courses has developed, which seek to train both laity and clergy in pastoral counselling skills: the Westminster Pastoral Foundation and its offshoots, with a psychodynamic approach to counselling, the Clinical Theology Association, which introduced many clergy to counselling in the decades before counselling courses were widely available, and various more local services such as Care and Counsel, influential amongst Evangelicals in the 1980s, the Church Army Counselling Service, the St John's College, Nottingham, Diploma in Pastoral Counselling and so forth, all of which provide training as well as a service to the community. The Association for Pastoral Care and Counselling, an arm of the British Association of Counselling, also grew in its influence through its journal *Contact*, the longest-running and most widely respected British journal of pastoral care.

The second North American development was the professionalisation of pastoral care along the lines of secular psychotherapy. Thus, it is common for pastoral counselling by clergy to be office-based, with fees charged and limited client contact. There is professional oversight in the American Association of Pastoral Counsellors. It is this professionalisation that Peterson argues so strongly against.

Similarly, in Britain, one can detect a professionalisation of the pastoral task undertaken by the clergy. Not that professionalisation of itself is wrong. God grant us pastors who conduct their ministry with a dedication and pursuit of excellence that is properly professional. But in this regard, the developments in North America a decade or two ago, whereby the ministry of pastoral *care* was transformed into a ministry primarily of pastoral *counselling*, are finding their echo in Britain in the 1990s. An organisation to oversee Christian pastoral counselling, its accreditation and training, was established in the Association of Christian Counsellors. More and more clergy undertake pastoral counselling as part of their ministry and adopt the methods and values of the wider counselling and psychotherapeutic world. The wider culture, in short, moulds the practice and values of pastoral care.

There has been something of a reaction to the dominance of counselling in pastoral care in America, notably by Thomas Oden.

In the 1960s Oden was concerned to integrate theology and Rogerian therapy. The client-centred therapy of Carl Rogers was then in considerable vogue in the States, and Oden set himself the task of discovering the theological assumptions of Rogerian psychology in relation to the theology of Barth.[11] He did not seek simply to collapse the categories of therapy into theological categories, but to 'expose the theology which is already present in the approach of psychotherapy'.[12] The psychotherapeutic process, Oden argues, is based on Christian assumptions about worth, love and empathy. This correlative ▶▶

method, which explores the relationship between incarnation and empathic understanding, forgiveness and acceptance, grace and permissiveness, divine love and unconditional positive regard, sees psychotherapy as a soteriology without Christ, and ultimately failing to restore humanity's relationship with its creator. At this stage Oden, and another influential American pastoral theologian, Don Browning,[13] epitomise the correlative approach, accepting psychotherapy with all of its religious limitations, and wanting to claim it for God.

The more recent developments in Oden's theology, however, are more critical of the acceptance of pastoral counselling as the primary way of doing pastoral care in the United States. He criticises the central values explicit in contemporary psychotherapies that have been absorbed into pastoral care. These are: the primacy of the autonomous individual, a tendency towards naturalistic reductionism which sees nothing beyond scientific, empirical data, and a narcissistic hedonism by which the individual always seeks what is best for him or herself. He criticises the impact of modernist assumptions and values upon the pastoral theology and care of contemporary American practice. He believes that the ideology of modernism should be rejected and that an attempt should be made 'to recover classical ecumenical orthodoxy amid postmodern cultural consciousness'.[14] He demonstrates the neglect of the classical Christian pastoral writers (such as Augustine, Gregory the Great, Luther and Calvin) in the writings of the 1960s and 1970s by Howard Clinebell, Seward Hiltner, Wayne Oates and Paul Tournier, in favour of Freud, Jung, Rogers, Berne and Fromm, and calls American pastoral care back to its classic roots, albeit within a postmodern context. Others have joined Oden in this call for a more consciously Christian content to pastoral care. Don Browning has called for a recovery of the moral content to pastoral care[15] and Donald Capps has sought to recover the pastoral use of the Bible.[16]

The American pastoral care scene is moving in a number of directions: away from an over-identification of pastoral care with pastoral counselling and from a focus on crisis and problems, to more general needs of individuals. There is a new emphasis upon the traditions of the Christian Church as a vital resource for pastoral care and upon the Christian community as the context for pastoral care involving not only clergy, but laity as well. This involves a move away from the former preoccupation with specialised counselling undertaken by the clergy, and a new emphasis upon the social and political context for pastoral care.[17]

In Britain, developments reflect the postmodern emphasis upon the 'other', those elements of society and culture which under modernism were accorded a secondary status (women as opposed to men, homosexuals as opposed to heterosexuals, blacks and Asians as opposed to Caucasians, first world as opposed to third world). Thus feminist criteria and values inform Elaine Graham's work,[18] and in recent issues of *Contact* there are articles on bereavement counselling for African Caribbean people in Britain,[19] African sexuality,[20] and the position of people with learning difficulties.[21] In common with the wider theological world, there are new perspectives on pastoral care issuing forth from the 'other' cultural perspectives (that is, other than white, middle-class, educated and male). This is a dimension of post-modernity now significantly influencing pastoral care.

Stephen Pattison argues that the postmodern theology of Don Cupitt is suggestive for and consonant with contemporary pastoral care, with its emphasis upon human life in the present time, the affirmation of embodied human existence, women, creation and the transforming possibilities of words, metaphors and stories. 'If, living in a postmodern world, the fragmentation and incompleteness of pastoral care allows the possibility of trying to see what it might be to be a postmodern pastor relating better to others who also live in fragmented and incomplete worlds, then a partial defect may be turned to very considerable relevance and advantage.'[22] Pattison at least is willing to embrace the postmodern world in the name of more appropriate pastoral care, even if a doubt remains over the appropriateness of building that pastoral care upon a theology which has taken leave of God.

We have already seen that the influences from the United States, where pastoral theology and pastoral care as a distinct discipline are more widely taught and more highly professionalised than in Britain, tend to migrate across the Atlantic. Some of the concerns that I have about the practice of pastoral care in Britain are already being voiced in the States. Will we heed them, or will the influence of postmodernism pull pastoral care in the direction of greater individualism, moral vacuum and eclectic, New Age spirituality? Such spirituality is rooted neither in the classic Freudian metanarratives that so enamoured a previous generation of pastoral counsellors, nor, more importantly, in the orthodox and historic Christian faith and practice.

CHAPTER 3

Fragments and Fragility

Overview

Introduction

These fragments have I shored against my ruin.

T. S. Eliot, *The Wasteland*

What on earth is postmodernism? The word is used so widely these days that some now refer to it as the 'dreaded P word'. A thumbnail sketch of its contours would have to include seven features.

1. The rejection of all the big stories that attempted to explain everything: the 'metanarratives' or grand theories such as Marxism, or, indeed, Christianity. Such all-encompassing visions are impossible, says the postmodernist.
2. In their place comes a fragmented view of the world. There is no social unity, only the power of choice. Even our lives are not a unity, but rather an unrelated series of selves constructed as appropriate to the multitude of settings we find ourselves in. We shall see later in this chapter how Madonna, the American actress and singer, illustrates this.
3. The new religion is consumerism, and its temples are the shopping centres where now more than 50 per cent of Britons shop on a Sunday (when only 10 per cent might be found in church). Image is everything in this competitive world, and everything is marketed in the same way: health care, education, consumer goods, entertainment, even religion.
4. The old reliance on science as the activity which established 'truth' is weakening. Indeed, there is no such thing as objective truth for the postmodernist, as the old distinction between object and subject is dissolved. Everything is relative and there are no fixed points of reference.
5. The world is now a global culture, with Coca-Cola the most widely recognised word in history. The world invades our living room, and there is no privileged position for Western rationalism. This global culture is popular culture, and the demise of 'high culture' is a symptom of this change. Diana, Princess of Wales, was a global figure of popular culture, and her death a phenomenon of global mourning.
6. Elements of previous cultures that modernism set aside, such as mysticism, cosmology, intuition and emotions, are all wel-

comed back by the postmodernist. Perhaps the most visible example of this is in architecture, and is discussed in greater detail later. In religion, paganism, the New Age and Eastern faiths are welcomed alongside the Western expressions of Christianity, and even here the revival of interest in Celtic Christianity could be seen as postmodern, with its use of symbolism and its concern for creation.

7. Finally, there is the demise of the optimistic hope for progress and development that characterised modernity. In its place is a loss of hope, one significant reason amongst others for the fact that while we are much wealthier in the West than we were fifty years ago, we are also a great deal unhappier, if statistics of mental health and social breakdown are taken as measures of a society at ease with itself.[1]

All of these have profound effects upon the task of pastoral care, and not just the obvious aspects of despair and fragmentation. The revaluing of the past creates opportunities for older styles of pastoral care to be revalued also (and Thomas Oden has been significant in revaluing the Fathers of the Church as pastoral guides). When metanarratives are rejected, how do we as pastoral carers start to integrate our faith and practice? When postmodernity dissolves rigid compartments and welcomes interdisciplinary practice, what new opportunities are there for pastoral carers in health care and educational settings, and how should church-based carers work with other professionals, such as psychiatrists or social workers?

To understand postmodernism we must first understand its mighty precursor, modernity. Recently I have become fascinated by the detective story: the TV version of *Inspector Morse*, Helen Mirren's Detective Superintendent Jane Tennison in *Prime Suspect*, and Patricia Cornwell's Dr Kay Scarpetta fascinate me. The detective story is one of the clearest icons or symbols of modernity. This one phenomenon could not have been possible before this period of modernity. Think for one moment about what happens in a detective novel: a tragedy occurs, usually someone's murder. The police involve the detective to solve this crime. The philosophical assumption behind this is that all problems are solvable by human reason. The novel begins with disorder (death) and moves to order (the solving of the puzzle). Thus progress is the ability to leave one's animal instincts behind (which cause death) which allows society to continue on its own ordered way (when the criminal is captured). But where did modernism come from?

The Roots of Modernity

The cultural period of modernity (in which we are still in part living, since postmodernism is by no means all triumphant nor ubiquitous) is often equated with the late-seventeenth to eighteenth-century Age of Enlightenment, but its roots go deeper than that. Some of the factors which made modernism possible are: the rise of a capitalist economic system, the beginnings of modern science with Francis Bacon (1561–1626) and the earlier Copernican revolution, the great geographical discoveries of the Americas and East Asia in the fifteenth and sixteenth centuries, and the development of technological answers to the problems of humankind. Depending upon which factors you include, the modern world was born somewhere between the beginnings of the Italian Renaissance (often dated from 1470) and the Enlightenment's origins in the late seventeenth century, with the crucial phase taking place between 1750 and 1850.

The Renaissance was the period in which the previous major cultural shift had taken place. Characterised by a new interest in the classical languages, culture and literature (humanism), a shift took place in the relationship between God, the world and humankind. In the medieval period, God was central to people's view of the world (evidenced by the extraordinary flowering of religious art, and particularly the architecture of the High Gothic). Now humanity took centre stage; man was now the measure of all things. Leonardo da Vinci's drawing of a male figure encompassed by a square and a circle epitomises this change.

The Enlightenment gave birth to another radically transformed paradigm of human society and a new understanding of what it is to be human: a confident belief in the ability of humanity to progress towards a utopia of rational, humanistic and autonomous harmony. Gone were the preoccupations with the supernatural, ecclesiastical authority, and the transcendent power of God. In its place was a preoccupation with *this* world, which involves a belief in the secular rather than the sacred, the power of the individual's mind and rationality to institute change and progress, the fruits of scientific and technological endeavour and the triumph of a rational humanity that has been liberated from superstition and is now directed towards the future. Modern humanity was self-confident and self-governing, *homo autonomous*.

The single most important factor remains the Enlightenment project. The fact we call it a 'project' displays our postmodern critique and scepticism towards its success, but its focus upon the priority of reason as the foundation of knowledge is still its most important character. The heroes of this project were René Descartes (1596–1650), John Locke (1632–1704), and its greatest exponent, Immanuel Kant (1724–1804).

The immediate socio-political environment for these philosophers was the horror of the Thirty Years War (1618–48), a complex series of struggles originating in religious conflicts between Protestants and Catholics, but quickly embracing wider political factors that engulfed most of Europe. The Thirty Years War unravelled the Constantinian settlement that had put the Christian faith and the Church at the intellectual and political heart of Europe for a millennium. By its conclusion in the mid-seventeenth century, the religious map of Europe that we see today was drawn, but the cost had been untold misery, death and starvation. No wonder thinking men in the seventeenth century had lost faith in the ability of religion to give adequate answers to man's problems, just as many in Britain today would not view the partisan struggles in Northern Ireland as a sign of the healthy state of religion at the end of the twentieth century. In reacting to the failure of religion, the Enlightenment thinkers looked for a new foundation for knowledge and progress in the power of human rationality, as epitomised by Descartes' *cogito ergo sum*, 'I think therefore I am.' Reason would replace the old dogmas, superstitions, traditions and authorities, and this spirit, the spirit of the French Revolution, would be embodied in new political and social conditions.

Upon these foundations of reason would be built the progress towards the utopia of a prosperous and fulfilling society, as ▶▶

scientific knowledge was translated into technological developments used to control our environment and ensure food and goods for all, and fuelled by a market-led rising standard of living. The future was scientific, technological and economic, although its social structures differed from place to place. In the West, the socio-economic pathway was to be the free-market capitalist system, while the communist world favoured a centralised state-controlled market. The great ideological divide between individualism and communalism predates the Cold War era of the twentieth century, but its settlement in favour of individualism is the most significant political change of the late twentieth century. The collapse of the communist vision epitomised in the destruction of the Berlin Wall is a very postmodern event!

There are some key elements to the shape of modernity that need to be explored in greater depth.

The Scientific World View

Modernism is irrevocably wedded to the practice of the scientific method. The scientific revolution of the seventeenth century involved a commitment to the empirical method, whereby knowledge of the world around us is gained by experimental exploration of observed data and confirmed through the testing of theory by experiment. The use of human rationality, not superstition or religious dogma, is the foundation of this method. Its methodology was first applied to the physical sciences, but in the nineteenth and twentieth centuries it has spread to the human sciences of sociology, economics, geography and politics. It has come to dominate the study of the Scriptures in the historico-critical method. Human behaviour is as susceptible to the empirical scientific method as the inanimate universe, if more complex and seemingly prone to chance.

Economics and Consumerism

The fruits of the scientific revolution were translated into consumer goods by the development of the mass market, fuelled by large-scale capital investment. Many still believe that the continuing growth of the global market is the key factor in enabling the poor to become richer, while the already-rich West remains the power house of the global economy. Economics have been transformed by modernity from a branch of ethics regulating the fair distribution of goods in a harmonious community (economics is rooted in the Greek *oikonomia*, the law of the household) into a quasi-science, dealing with what is quantifiable – the money supply, interest rates and the laws of supply and demand.

> The geographer David Harvey in his Marxist critique of postmodernism echoes Marx, himself a great early modernist writer who owed much to Enlightenment philosophy, in his description of the way in which goods come to be represented by money: 'Even though money is the signifier of the value of social labour, the perpetual danger looms that the signifier will itself become the object of human desire.'[2] The power and nature of the market enables us to be blind to the methods of production and any injustice in them, for we are separated from the means of production. The very pervasiveness of the market propagates the values of consumerism and legitimises the selfishness and conflict, injustice and exploitation which result from the market and makes them into virtues.

The market has become something of a quasi-religious cult. It now determines how schools and hospitals are managed, it pervades all of life. The British political Left in New Labour have come to accept its significance like born-again Thatcherites, and postmodernism seems to have done little to weaken its power. Indeed, as Harvey explains,

> postmodern concerns for the signifier rather than the signified, the medium (money) rather than the message (social labour), the emphasis on fiction rather than function, on signs rather than on things, on aesthetics rather than ethics, suggests a reinforcement rather than a transformation of the role of money as Marx depicts it.[3]

Privatisation

In the culture of modernity there are two worlds: the public world of civic involvement, debate and scientific fact, and the private world of personal opinion, religious and moral beliefs. The social processes related to this divide are complex, and include the alienation that is the product of industrialisation and particularly urbanisation[4] and migration. It would be crass to suggest that the Kantian dichotomy between public and private has led to the social changes attendant on urbanisation, but the two processes do mirror each other. There has been a tendency to retreat from the public world of the city as well as retreat from public discourse about religion. We withdraw from the threatening public realm into our own private world where we can feel safe, and it is deemed 'unprofessional' for, say, a teacher or lawyer to discuss 'personal' matters, such as faith or religion, with a client (similar proscriptions apply to pastoral therapists). Recently, beside a busy London street in the middle of the rush hour, as cars queued at a road junction, a woman was brutally attacked. No one left the privacy of their car to assist her, even though the struggle was clearly visible for some minutes. In the privatised world of modern Britain we pass by on the other side. We are an audience fearful of personal involvement.

Power and Politics

The era of modernity sees the rise of the nation state as an institution dependent on secular power rather than ecclesiastical authority. Both the Western democracies and the Marxist socialist states are the products of the modernist views of human nature. The impact of the Enlightenment upon the institutions arising from the French Revolution is clear. There was to be a radical separation of Church and state, similarly enshrined in the American constitution, and in the place of the old authorities was to be created a state founded upon the principles of *liberté*, *egalité* and *fraternité*; the 'self-evident' truth that 'all men are created equal . . . endowed by their creator with certain unalienable rights, that among these are life, liberty and the pursuit of happiness.'[5] The results of that impact are, however, ambiguous, as Gunton remarks:

> Modernity is not a monolithic phenomenon, but a range of practices and attitudes . . . from one point of view we could take the French Revolution as a typical expression of the modern quest for freedom and progress, yet France was in certain respects modernising more quickly before the Revolution than during its course. From one point of view, the Revolution was predicated on freedom, while as a paradigm for repression and the absence of freedom it put into the shade the behaviour of the *ancien régime* that it sought to replace.[6]

If secular democracy has come to be seen as the only form of virtuous political system in the late twentieth century, enshrining individual freedom (the power of political choice of every citizen in the nation state, irrespective of gender, race or creed, and their freedom to self-expression and thought), its ambiguities are also becoming clear. For instance, the great political debate of the 1990s in Britain over Europe could be seen as one of modernism (the nation-state as sacrosanct) versus postmodernism (the transnational super-state of 'Europe'), and the proper locus of political power. Similarly, many of the intra-national conflicts of our day concern the formation of small nation states from modernist-inspired amalgams of conflicting ethnic groups, seen pre-eminently in the break up of the former Yugoslavia after the death of Tito and the corresponding loss of power needed to hold together the competing ethnic groups of Serb, Croat and Bosnian.

The Loss of Creaturely Dependence upon God

Modernity deliberately takes leave of a creaturely dependence upon God. It rebelled against God in the name of the many. No longer was humankind dependent upon revelation to unveil the realities of the world, but could find these things out for itself through the empirical process of the scientific method. With this taking leave of God we also lost a providential idea of history: that is, history as the arena of God's providential care (the belief that God acts in and through all of life). The great English Catholic convert and cardinal, John Henry Newman, wrote in

1870: 'What Scripture especially illustrates from its first page to its last, is God's Providence, and that is nearly the only doctrine held with a real assent by the mass of religious Englishmen.'[7] Contrast that with the widespread ignorance of providence by even the most religious of Englishmen and women today.

In his analysis of the shape of modernity, Colin Gunton argues that taking leave of God in the name of the assertion of rights of the many, has paradoxically achieved the opposite: the subversion of the many by new and in some cases demonic versions of the one. In contrast to the variety which should be the outcome of the assertion of the rights to freedom of the individual, there is rather a flat homogeneity, where fashion dictates we all dress alike, listen to the same music and so forth. It is therefore not freedom that results from the eviction of God from the public square, but a form of displacement of the freedoms of the many to the powers of the few, be they the rulers of the modern totalitarian state or the insidious homogeneity of consumer culture governed by impersonal market forces. Gunton quotes Robert Pippin: 'modernity promised us a culture of unintimidated, curious, self-reliant individuals, and it produced . . . a herd society, a race of anxious, timid, conformist "sheep" and a culture of utter banality.'[8]

Because modernism does not conceive of human beings relationally, but rather as free individuals, there is a disengagement from the world. It becomes the object of our enquiry and we presume a privileged position regarding it, unlocking the possibilities of its destruction and exploitation. We behave towards the world as if we were God, and things lose their particular and distinctive being, subjected instead to universal and rigid patterns of thought and behaviour.

A second dimension of modernism described by Gunton is the problem of the loss of the proper relatedness of particular things and people. We live in a this-worldly culture, ascribing priority to time over eternity, space over infinity, now over a future heaven. Modernity throws off traditions which are seen as stifling freedom and replaces fate or providence with the efficacy of human endeavour. We are what we make of ourselves.

There is a frantic and busy rush about modern life, in a society that is dedicated to leisure aided by machines that save labour. This paradox is described by Harvey as 'time-space compression . . . characterised by speeding up the pace of life, while so overcoming spatial barriers that the world sometimes seems to collapse inwards upon us'.[9] The loss of living *sub specie aeternitatis*, in the light of eternity, means we have to create the future ourselves. Modernity is obsessed with its own future in place of a proper anticipation of God's future. This is seen in as mundane an area as the proliferation of credit. No longer willing to wait until savings can be spent, people buy goods on credit and pay for them later. The result is that the present is never enjoyed for itself as the time we have now, but viewed as the springboard for the future. If 'time is God's way of keeping things from happening all at once' then modernity wants to obliterate time whilst being obsessed with the clock. 'Modern culture is marked by a pathological inability to live in the present, while at the same time, as in the consumer culture, it is unable to live anywhere but the present.'[10]

Many of the characteristics of the modernist project remain firmly in place: knowledge is power; the scientific endeavour continues apace, albeit with less self-confidence about its messianic role; and we remain wedded to technological progress, though more for leisure than the alleviation of human misery, and certainly more for the ability through military means to grasp power than to ensure human well-being. We remain convinced of the power of the free market to ensure the economic well-being of the great majority (of Western, affluent people, that is; the fate of the poor two-thirds world is somehow excluded from those benefits), and the trust in organised religion in the West continues to decline.

The Crisis in Modernity

The utopia that modernism promised has been cancelled due to a shortage of drivers and leaves on the line. The self-confidence of the nineteenth century has been lost in the trenches of Flanders; the concentration camps of the holocaust and the Gulags, Rwanda and Bosnia; the bombing of Hiroshima and

Nagasaki; the increasing casual violence of everyday existence; and the systematic destruction of the Earth through pollution. The myth of progress is losing its power.

The foundations of modernity include a radically self-determining freedom which cannot bear the weight of significance placed upon it. The location of evil for the modernist lies externally to the individual in lack of education, progress or reason. The Judaeo-Christian tradition places it internally to the individual, as made clear in the words of Jeremiah: 'The heart is deceitful above all things and beyond cure,'[11] and Jesus: 'For out of the heart come evil thoughts.'[12] That tradition knows the fragility of human nature is quite unsuited to bearing the weight of the modernist programme.

The brash self-confidence of modernity was replaced by anxiety, existential *angst* and despair. The demise of the Soviet system has not lessened the despair of the loss of the Vietnam war for the United States, and the old tribalisms in the Balkans brought a return of the concentration camp and ethnic cleansing to Europe after fifty years. Modernism has not been able to solve the Middle East crisis nor the centuries-old divide in Ulster. Modernity is crumbling and in terminal decline and anxiety is a predominant mood. As Middleton and Walsh put it, 'it feels as if our whole culture has the willies,'[13] and in Langdon Gilkey's words, 'everything seems to slip: our landscape, our institutions, our values, our way of life – and so the security and meaning, the sense of being at home in a world we can understand and deal with that they brought.'[14]

Undoubtedly there have been enormous benefits from the modernist programme. I am certain that from a physical health point of view I would not want to live in any other period, and despite the continuing crisis of funding a public health service, for most people it functions admirably. The Apple Macintosh computer on which I am writing this enables me to do more than the mainframe computers of my university days would have done, and in five years this will be a creaking antique! At school I used a slide rule and logarithm tables, which my children think is extraordinarily quaint. Between them, the West and Soviet versions of modernism spread the culture worldwide, so that for the first time in human history we can talk of a global culture, and Coca-Cola is its calling card.

However, there are widespread signs that doubt about the social and spiritual implications of modernity is now endemic. The enterprise has failed to deliver and a crisis is upon us. In the place of wisdom is the overwhelming flood of information. The scientist, once the stormtrooper of the modernist enterprise, is now viewed with distrust. What shape has the postmodernist culture taken?

Postmodernism: A New Babel

The relation of postmodernism to modernism is problematical. Some see it as a new era, a necessary critique of modernity, while others view it as a new phase of modernity (perhaps 'high' modernism, or 'late' modernism): 'postmodernism is modernity come home to roost.'[15] Is it simply a revolt within modernism against a certain kind of 'high modernism' such as the architecture of Mies van der Rohe, or is it a radical break with modernism?

> Does it have a revolutionary potential by virtue of its opposition to all forms of meta-narratives, the 'big pictures' that describe a whole way of understanding the world (including Marxism, psychoanalysis and all forms of Enlightenment reason) and its close attention to 'other worlds' and to 'other voices' that have for too long been silenced (women, gays, blacks, colonised peoples with their own histories)? Or is it simply the commercialisation and domestication of modernism, and of the latter's already tarnished aspirations to a laissez-faire, 'anything goes' market eclecticism?[16]

David Lyon suggests that postmodernity may be an ironic comment on the impossibility of saying anything about our world today in one word.[17]

We shall begin our exploration of postmodernity by making a distinction between postmodernism and postmodernity. Because many of the expressions of postmodernity are 'cultural' – music, art, literature, architecture – the term 'postmodernism' will be used for this cultural movement. The broader range of changes, philosophical and social as well as cultural, we will call 'postmodernity'. Now we can describe some features of the postmodern landscape.

Architecture

Charles Jencks was the first to popularise the term postmodernism[18] by applying it to architecture, and we begin here for no better reason than that chronological priority. Arnold Toynbee had used the term much earlier to describe the new historical cycle which started in 1875 with the end of Western dominance, the decline of capitalism and Christianity and the rise to power of non-Western cultures.

Jencks defines postmodernism as 'double coding: the combination of modern techniques with something else (usually traditional building) in order for architecture to communicate with the public and a concerned minority, usually other architects.' Postmodernist architecture is itself grounded in modernist techniques, but seeks to be less inhuman than the 'machines for living in' of the great modernist heroes, le Corbusier and Mies van der Rohe (espousing values of truth to materials, logical consistency, straightforwardness etc.), with the lack of defensible space for occupants of housing, high-rise isolation and so forth.

The collapse of Ronan Point in 1968 and the intentional destruction of the blocks of housing at Pruitt-Igoe, St Louis, in 1972 signify the collapse of the modernist architectural dream, and with it the ideology of progress which offered technical solutions to social problems.

In their place is a playful use of references to other eras and cultures. James Stirling's Neue Staatsgalerie in Stuttgart, 1977–84, has echoes of the Pantheon and the Acropolis and includes 'fallen' classical stones like deliberate ruins. The building is actually a steel frame construction and the stones are mere cladding. This is revealed in the 'ruins' and speaks of the lost innocence of an 'age which can build with beautiful stone so long as it is skin deep and hung on a steel skeleton'.[19] Stirling is saying that we live in a complex, multivalent world, combining past and conventional beauty and current technical and social reality. Stirling's most controversial work in Britain is the Clore Wing of the Tate Gallery. ▶▶

Other postmodern architects include Robert Venturi, architect of the Sainsbury Wing of the National Gallery (which Prince Charles called 'a building of which we can be proud', as opposed to the modernist design of Peter Ahrends, which he called 'a monstrous carbuncle on the face of a much-loved and elegant friend'), Philip Johnson, Charles Moore and Arata Isozaki. Many of the most recent College buildings in the ancient universities of Oxford and Cambridge pay deferential respect to the existing architecture in a postmodern way, such as the Edward Cullinan Architects' library at St John's, Cambridge, built in 1994, or the new building at Downing College, Cambridge designed by the neo-classical Quinlan Terry. At the opposite end of the prestige spectrum, most new speculative greenfield domestic housing is essentially a pastiche of Georgian and Victorian styles. Small boxes for living in which nod towards grander and older buildings are built in their thousands in Britain each year.

There needs to be a distinction made between postmodernism and the continuing modernist style in its late or high form. The architecture of Richard Rogers, for instance, is often mistakenly called postmodern, whereas it might be more accurate to describe the 'inside-out' style of the Lloyd's Building in London or the Pompidou Centre in Paris (1971–7) as late modern, with their emphasis upon open space, industrial detailing, form following function and structure. The same could be said of Norman Foster's Hong Kong Shanghai Bank (1982–6). They have none of the whimsical playfulness or deliberate referencing of genuine postmodernism. It reminds us that not everything is postmodern because it is current.

Art

The fractured and psychological allegories of Ron Kitaj, Carlo Maria Mariana or Peter Blake, with his blend of monumentality and banality, all pay homage to previous artists with an ironic cosmopolitanism. The collision and superimposition of different ontological worlds is a major characteristic of postmodern art which it shares with the world of visual advertising, where an arresting image is paramount. Elsewhere, the use of images of images (especially those from advertising, Andy Warhol's screenprints of Campbell's soup cans or of Marilyn Monroe, or Robert Rauschenberg's use of Coca-Cola bottles) is an attempt to emphasise rhetoric.

Advertising has embraced postmodernism with a desire to undermine the cultural codes whereby advertising images are seen as 'unreal' while the visual images of photo journalism are seen as 'real life'. The campaign by United Colors of Benetton, for instance, takes strong photo images, unrelated to the commodity it is selling (basically, fashion knitwear) and creates desire for the goods, not by selling their desirability, for they rarely are illustrated, but by advocating a spurious 'social conscience' (it is politically correct to wear these clothes). Thus images of a white baby suckling at the breasts of a (faceless) black woman imply racial harmony, actually undermined by the black woman's facelessness, or the dying AIDS patient with his distraught family implying compassion towards those who suffer from this disease, but which actually makes us voyeurs.

Literature

In literature there is the same pluralist concern with different cultures. Umberto Eco's postmodern detective story in *The Name of the Rose*, John Fowles' pastiche of the Victorian novel with multiple endings in *The French Lieutenant's Woman*, and Milan Kundera's *The Unbearable Lightness of Being* all betray post-modern concerns with sign. The magic realism of Kundera and Jorge Luis Borges dissolves the boundary between fiction and science fiction, allowing radically different realities to collide and interpenetrate. Postmodern characters seem confused about the world in which they live.

In a poll of the most popular books of the twentieth century, the first four all included an element of the blurring of reality and magic (although they are thoroughly modernist books, with perhaps the exception of Tolkien), from the most popular, J. R. R. Tolkien's *Lord of the Rings*, through the next two most popular, George Orwell's *1984* and *Animal Farm*, followed by Joyce's *Ulysses*. Numbers 8 and 10 in the poll were postmodern books, Gabriel Garcia Marquez's *One Hundred Years of Solitude* and the recent *Trainspotting* by Irvine Welsh. Maybe the first three represent the books we read in that teenage period when we discover adult books for the first time, and the magical discovery lends a special charm to them, or maybe we are now living in a culture which prefers to mix its reality with a little postmodern fantasy.

Film and Television

Science fiction takes a number of postmodern turns. The traditional science fiction movie has humans battling with invading spaceships full of aliens: a recent example would be the blockbuster *Independence Day*, a throwback to an older genre. The celebration of science in the older, modernist genre turns to a nightmare vision, such as in *Blade Runner* where a futuristic world of space platforms orbits a world of urban squalor. The hero must track down renegade androids which act like humans in a world where humans act like machines. Other films make an ironic postmodern pastiche of the whole genre: *Mars Attacks!*, for instance, with its schlock-horror and deliberate stop-motion animation that mimics the work of Ray Harryhausen.

The quintessential postmodern television programme is the series *The X-Files*. It juxtaposes the scientific modernist, Dana Scully, with her postmodern, open-minded FBI partner, Fox Mulder. The truth about alien abductions, the Roswell incident and the rest, is 'out there', but somehow never quite within reach, always blocked by shadowy figures from an unknown source: the Government? multinationals? Who knows? It trades on the cultural sense of anxiety, fragmentation of reality and uncertainty regarding truth. It has spawned a whole genre of TV shows about aliens, but remains pre-eminent among them. Just as in the fictional world of magic realism, the reality of everyday life is intersected with the magical. In *Groundhog Day*, a man relives the same day over and over again until he gets the girl; in *Field of Dreams* (based on a novel by the postmodern author W. P. Kinsella), Kevin Costner builds a baseball diamond in a cornfield for the late 'Shoeless' Joe Jackson.

Big Stories and Slippery Words

The philosophical critique of modernity that took place in France in the 1960s to 1980s was a reaction against the certainties of the modernist project and its confidence in objective truth. The myth of progress was exposed, whether through evolution, social improvement, education or techno-science. In its post-structuralist variety the relationship of words to an extra-linguistic reality is denied. Words derive their meaning from their relationship to other words, and refuse to bear a relationship to fixed truth. Indeed, there is a profound scepticism towards objectivity, truth and reality.

This is a particularly difficult area of discourse, and you may find the following section hard going. The philosophy of post-structuralism is often deliberately obscure and voiced in dense language. As the joke puts it: 'What do you get when you cross a Mafioso with a deconstructionist? An offer you can't understand.'

In this section the unpacking of the philosophical roots of postmodernity can be seen through its exponents, Jacques Derrida, Michel Foucault, François Lyotard, Emmanuel Levinas and Jean Baudrillard, and their immediate predecessors, the exponents of Structuralism such as Lévi-Strauss and Roland Barthes.

Structuralism

The modernist project was predicated upon the assumption that the knowing subject could arrive at truth and reality by a correspondence of his thoughts to that external reality. I can know the world 'out there' through the function of rationality. The loss of confidence in this correspondence begins with the study of linguistics and especially the multidisciplinary movement of structuralism in the 1960s to 1970s.

> The common feature is the belief that phenomena of human life are not intelligible except through their interrelations, and those relations conform to constant laws of abstract structure. Superficially different social practices or myths, for instance, could be shown to have the ▶▶

same pattern of meaning and relationship. Thus Lévi-Strauss argues that a wide variety of kinship institutions derive from basic structures of communication and are based upon the working of the human mind. The foundations of this move from a simple relationship of words to objects lay in the work on linguistics by Ferdinand de Saussure (1857–1913), who argued that language is a system of signs, each sign composed of a signifier (a word or sound pattern) and a signified (a concept). The relationship between the signifier and the signified (*signifiant* and *signifié*, word and concept) is arbitrary. Individuals are as much formed *by* language as they form language, since the ever-changing nature of language is not controlled by individuals, but changes over time independently of the speaker's will. It is, rather, a social institution and all individual approaches are inadequate.

In the 1960s the socio-cultural implications of de Saussure's work on linguistics were drawn by Claude Lévi-Strauss in anthropology, Jacques Lacan in psychoanalysis and Roland Barthes in semiotics. Just as it was erroneous to study speech acts in isolation from the system of conventions which gave them currency, so it was judged to be inadequate to study social and cultural facts independent of the social or cultural system that gave them currency. Language becomes a system of signs and both it and society need deciphering according to their differences, a theme we will encounter again in postmodernism.

The structuralists opened the way for postmodernism by emphasising the arbitrariness of the linguistic sign and its interdependence on other signs marking the end of the possibility of fixed, absolute meaning. Meaning now derives from the collusion of sign clusters whose signification changes as the clusters interact with each other. The structuralists are still the children of the Enlightenment, however, in their belief that such significating systems could be mapped, and in this context structuralism could be seen as a transitional phenomenon between modernism and postmodernism. It was the next generation of post-structuralist and postmodern thinkers who seriously damaged this epistemological optimism with their exposure of the underlying capriciousness of language and the play upon power by the institutions that exploit it.

The Post-structuralists

Jacques Derrida, Michel Foucault and Emmanuel Levinas question the structuralist presuppositions that social and language systems can be mapped.

Jacques Derrida (1930–) argues against the structuralist's privilege of speech over writing and denies that the writer has created a work with fixed meaning. He explores the unconscious rhetorical aspects of writing, arguing that attention to the incidentals often subverts the intention of a text. In the margins and between the lines lie the echoes of what was suppressed and not said. This means a text is never stable or fixed, but always open to endless interpretation and reinterpretation that stretches to a receding horizon within which meaning is endlessly deferred. This combination of what is not said, but which echoes around the text, and deferral of meaning, is termed *différence* by Derrida. The result is a fundamental destabilisation of fixed meaning. It seems very strange to those brought up in the Western tradition, which assumes a simple and real correspondence between what is real in existence and the language we use to grasp it. This 'metaphysics of presence', to use Derrida's phrase, claims to reflect and represent reality so accurately that it imitates that reality.

It is this substantial convergence of reality and its articulation in language that Derrida and the other deconstructionists attack. They claim we can never get to the reality that is prior to language or concept. Rather, words do not represent objects or concepts in a reality outside of language, but are always self-referential. Thus, it is impossible to get at a 'reality' beyond language, there is no 'truth' beyond language, and language has no fixed meaning.

Deconstruction has transformed the dominant ways of thinking in all the humanities and social sciences, but has paradoxically affected philosophy least, perhaps because it has most to lose in the practice of deconstruction of the pairs of opposites that have dominated Western tradition: culture/nature, spirit/matter, writing/speech, real/ideal, external/internal etc., since the privilege each former term has over the latter is destroyed. With Derrida, *différence* becomes the prototype of what is outside the scope of the Western metaphysical system, because it is the latter's very condition of possibility. The implications of this are the granting of interior status to those who are different ▶▶

to the norm. Thus, because in the West the norm is for people to have white skin, the racist relegates anyone who is not white to an inferior position by anything from slavery to quiet ignorance. Deconstructionists say that the sort of approach seen in racism is the approach to otherness, to difference, and is symptomatic of the whole enterprise of Western thought and especially modernity. What is rejected is the autonomous, self-consciously knowing subject, an epistemology of certainty, representation of reality, universality and comprehensiveness that has been the modernist project. In its place is a human subject inseparably involved with the unconscious, the irrational, shaped by social relations, language and culture.

Michel Foucault (1926–84) has explored those differences in terms of power and control, especially in the way science and reason are used as instruments of power in areas such as medicine and the definition of madness and criminology. He perceived all social relations to be fundamentally relationships of power and was sceptical about the innocence of reason. Research into a particular human disorder, such as mental illness or sexual disorder, appears to be motivated by a philanthropic spirit, a desire to cure, but it resolves into an oppressive search for control and power, expressed through legislation and coercion.

In his *Folie et déraison: Histoire de la folie à l'âge classique*,[20] Foucault studied the way the difference between reason and madness is established in the age of Descartes and the way that the mad person, who was not confined to any institution before 1600, becomes an excluded person, by the middle of the sixteenth century. During the seventeenth and eighteenth centuries the madman is reduced to silence, becoming an anti-social figure with the homosexual, the libertine and the debauched. Thus, by researching the way that practices evolved, it is the material effects that are uncovered rather than the essential meaning of things (which do not exist anyway), and what makes a certain 'regime of practice' interesting is not its intrinsic importance, but what in the present makes the past interesting. History is always written from the perspective of the present, and has no fixed meaning, but takes on shifting meaning in the light of the present, in a similar way to the absence of fixed meanings ascribed to words in Derrida's deconstruction.

Postmodernity

If the post-structuralists argue for a new way of understanding language and social constructs, the broader postmodern themes are epitomised by Jean-François Lyotard and Jean Baudrillard.

In his report to the Quebec government on the state of knowledge, Lyotard describes a growing incredulity towards legitimating metanarratives[21] or the *grands récits* of the Western tradition. A metanarrative is the supposedly universal, absolute truth that is used to legitimise certain projects. Thus the Marxist metanarrative argues for the freedom of humankind by the emancipation of the working class, the capitalist understands the world in terms of the creation of wealth and economic growth, the Darwinian metanarrative enshrines evolutionary progress, and the Freudian metanarrative stresses the dominance of the unconscious mind.

These overarching world views or stories that 'explain' the way things are, especially the scientific metanarratives of modernity, are no longer tenable, says Lyotard, because they cannot encompass the sheer diversity of local interests. The priority must be given to difference, not homogeneity. What is left is an open multiplicity of competing and incommensurable language games. We should not seek to judge any one language game by the values, truth claims or presuppositions of any other, for none has a priority or privileged position. To argue for the upholding of one particular metanarrative as universal – such as the values of reason and the Enlightenment project as a foundational discourse – is to be guilty of a totalitarian standpoint, and intolerance of the sheer plurality and difference in the postmodern world.

Jean Baudrillard (1929–) argues that the boundary between art and life has broken down and both have collapsed into the universal simulacrum or imitation where there is no distinction between signs and what they refer to. His neo-apocalyptic view sees our age trapped in an endless network of artificial sign systems, epitomised by the computer, that are accepted as reality by a rampant consumerism. Everything becomes undecidable because all is simulation, the beautiful and the ugly, left and right in politics, the true and the false in the media. This hyper-reality effaces the difference between the real and the imaginary.

In a more general way, we can now explore the new post-modern landscape. What is our culture looking like?

Disneyworld Reality

One way of looking at the postmodern world is as a culture which blurs reality and artifice: Jean Baudrillard's 'age of simulacrum', the virtual-reality age. For instance, tourism flourishes on the heritage industry, to the extent that the actual development of the countryside in Britain (often areas of high unemployment and poverty as real as any urban priority area) is halted by the perceived loss of heritage amenities, as if large swathes of rural Britain were simply a huge heritage theme park.

The enormous developments in information technology create the technology for the cybertech revolution. The *Independent on Sunday* asked:

> Will any of our culture be recognisable in twenty year's time? How many people will still read books, listen to live music, or visit theatres or art galleries? . . . how will anyone keep track of the endless proliferation, the eternal babble of cyberspace? Will anything remain of the old shared certainties – broadcasting, literature, heritage, a national consciousness? Or will life as we know it fragment beyond repair, as information overload takes its toll?[22]

People now meet one another on the World Wide Web, conduct affairs, act out fantasies in once unthinkable ways. In early 1996 a husband divorced his wife because he claimed that his wife was 'adulterous' even though the act was only ever in her mind and on the PC screen. 'The Internet has become the planet's most volatile meeting ground, an alternative landscape of virtual intimacy.'[23] Where intimacy begins, sex generally follows, except here it is not 'physical', but linguistic. Cybersex involves the exchange via the Internet of descriptions of physical actions between people composed in real time, and, yes, 25 per cent of those polled in a recent survey of net users said they had faked orgasm!

> The postmodern notion of the self as a malleable entity, as an amoeba of multiple personality, has become eerie fact. Hence the compulsion to mate online: the slipperiness of this new self is so disturbing that the mind rebels – by becoming obsessed with the single irreplaceable thing with which one moves through life.[24]

For some, the online romance aches to take real-life form, but the 'reality' is often not as 'real' as the online fantasy. The word takes flesh, but disappoints.

With the film *Jurassic Park*, the creation of the visual effects is dependent upon computer technology and the results are amazing 'hyperreal' images of the dinosaur inhabitants of the fictitious island theme park. Yet Stephen Spielberg, the film's producer, utilises Crichton's book because of its critique of the metanarrative that science means progress. The ability of science to recover the dinosaur DNA, replicate it and grow actual living (and, as it turns out, reproducing) creatures does not mean it is wise to do so. The collusion of human greed, chaos theory and a tropical storm ultimately bring disaster, the failure of both the science and the heritage 'theme park' culture that exploits it. Postmodern culture does not 'believe' in science, but is dependent upon it; it turns reality into a Disneyworld fantasy, but finds it ultimately tedious. It cannot go back to the old certainties, but is unhappy with the new paradoxes. No wonder it is a disoriented society.

The Queen of Appropriation: Madonna as an Icon of Postmodernism

The collapse of reality into art articulated by Baudrillard is perhaps most visible in the life of the most prolific woman singer in history, Madonna. She has perfected the rootless transformation of image to image into a lifestyle. She is variously, a feminist icon, a sex symbol and a mainstream actress. Even motherhood is exploited for the image. Martin Amis has called her 'the self sufficient postmodern phenomenon . . . A masterpiece of controlled illusion.'[25] She achieves that illusion by total control over her shows, from writing the songs to choreography and production, and by dissolving the line where art ends and reality begins, through the abolition of a 'private' life. In the film of her tour, *In Bed With Madonna*, nothing happens off camera. Her then lover, Warren Beatty, says 'Why would she want to say anything off camera? . . . she does not want to live off camera.' In this regard alone she is very postmodern. Image and reality, the collapse of the private person into the public and the domination of her life by the image all point in stark ways to the trends elsewhere. In politics it matters what Tony Blair's hair is like, and style consultants dictate the clothes politicians wear as for many what we wear is more important than who we are.

The rapidity of cultural change is also demonstrated by Madonna. As I write, her most recent transformation has been into Eva Peron, but before this came the virgin, the Catholic bad girl, the naked sado-masochistic sex worker and the 1920s gangster moll. Similarly, we are always moving from image to image, swapping one mask for the next. The constant change takes place with a wink and a playful irony that we have already seen is a feature of postmodern architecture.

Since there are no overarching stories, no metanarratives, we have to create our own world, and that world is ephemeral, always changing, never fixed, any more than language is fixed or static. We are always trapped in our own subjectivity, never committing to an absolute reality, and the image becomes our prison. There being no substance behind the image, the ingredients of the image are available to be borrowed by anyone, just as Madonna plunders Christian imagery of the First Communion dress and the statue of the Virgin, the prayerful stance, without any commitment to the substance of the Christian faith.

Postmodern Politics: Local Metanarratives and Legitimised Violence

Postmodern politics might be called the triumph of style over substance, the soundbite over policy, the package over the actuality. Ronald Reagan was the first postmodern politician, suggests Anderson, 'because he understood the power of free-floating symbolism, rooted in nothing at all'.[26] The spectacle was so good that the American voters re-elected a man who increased the public debt (which is not what Republicans get elected for), created a social spending crisis, fostered a culture of anxiety through the so-called 'Star Wars' programme (the title of a very postmodern movie, you notice) and waged war on democratically elected governments in Grenada and Nicaragua. The American public loved him, the theatre was so good. But then, he was nothing much more than an actor posing as some good ol' boy who really did know best, perhaps the best training there could be for a postmodern President!

While the collapse of the Cold War brought with it the recession of the threat of global war, local violence is still endemic to the postmodern world. Violence is seen as a legitimate way of bringing about a united Trotskyite Ireland by the IRA, the defence of Israeli settlements in land seized by warfare, the creation of a greater Serbia or the defence of animal rights. The juxtaposition of different and conflicting cultures breeding violence is illustrated in the fatwa issued against the novelist Salman Rushdie which is still in place as I write. It is an affair of two mutually incomprehensible world views. Muslims object to Rushdie's blurring of boundaries between fiction and real history, which they say enshrines the Prophet Mohammed's revelation. Liberal Westerners defend Rushdie's right to treat Islam as simply another postmodern grand narrative, with no claim to absolute truth. Rushdie said in an interview on the day of the fatwa: 'Doubt, it seems to me, is the central condition of a human being in the twentieth century. One of the things that has happened to us is to realise how certainty crumbles in your hand.' If Rushdie is a typical postmodern writer, then the fatwa is a typical postmodern defence of an absolute position. Fundamentalism is the panic interface of postmodernism. Western rationalists cannot understand how such an intolerant position can be sustained 'rationally'.

What Are We?

A key aspect of the significance of postmodernism for pastoral care is the way in which it understands the character of human nature, and particularly the way in which it transforms the Enlightenment paradigm.

The American Declaration of Independence, with its confidence in the equality of all people, gives voice to the Enlightenment understanding of humanity. By virtue of the common possession of reason, there is a universality about all human beings. Indeed, there is something fundamentally 'human' about the species *homo sapiens*, a characteristic that makes all humans ontologically uniform. 'Humans are independent, self-reliant, self-centred and self-integrating rational subjects. This is a fundamentally heroic understanding of human subjectivity. We are who we are by . . . determining for ourselves who we will be.'[27] Man becomes a law unto himself.

We see this expressed in modern art, and particularly that of the second half of this century. From the Renaissance onwards, most art connected with its audience through some shared narrative or motif, such as biblical narrative (for example, the Madonna and child), or the representation of landscape or familiar household items. To be sure, 'simple representation' has never been the hallmark of great art, and there is always something of the values and aspirations of a culture embodied in its art. Think of the Dutch celebration of the artifacts that were the fruit of its great age of expansion in the seventeenth century, or the Italian celebration of the cult of the Madonna in the High Renaissance. They communicate to a wide audience because of the concepts shared in their cultural context.

In the nineteenth century the sense of shared values still applied, albeit with new subjects, as the ordinary and the commonplace came to be viewed as appropriate themes, although not without a struggle, as the scandal of Manet's *Olympia* or *Le Déjeuner sur l'Herbe* illustrated. It was not the use of the nude that shocked, but the context. The young naked girl in *Olympia* (1865) is not idealised womanhood, but a particular woman, clearly a courtesan receiving her client, who is the viewer of the picture. Manet's contemporary, Baudelaire, had called for the artist to find the poetry in modern life, the eternal in the transitory, and *Le Déjeuner sur l'Herbe* (1863) with its naked woman and two clothed men, deliberately refused to depict historical fiction or to idealise the subject, but confronted eroticism as real and commonplace.

The art of Modernism in the early years of this century, for instance the Vorticists' celebration of the speed of the plane or express train, continued to provide a way in for the viewer, but increasingly a ▶▶

chasm opens up as the artist draws less and less on a common vocabulary and increasingly draws upon his or her own internal world. In a recent *South Bank Show* documentary on the English artist Sir Howard Hodgkin, Sarah Kent, art critic for *Time Out*, said 'there is a fundamental problem for artists in the twentieth century because there is no shared language. They are not making images of the Madonna and child nor are they painting the aristocracy. So all they have at their disposal is themselves and that is a terribly lonely position to be in.'[28] This problem of a failure to find a shared language is at its most acute in late modernism, amongst the abstract expressionists, Pollock, Rothko and De Kooning etc., and conceptual art such as Carl Andre's infamous Tate Gallery bricks. In becoming a law unto himself, the seeds of incommunicability are sown.

In many ways postmodern art is more 'accessible', since it often returns to an ironic form of representational art: pop art and super-realism, for instance. We can see people that are recognisably people, images that are familiar from everyday life, yet we do not connect with the meaning. For accurate representation we have the camera, so what does this new realism speak of?

We have used modern art as a way of describing how modernism understands the human condition, yet in the very universalising of human nature based upon reason, the seeds of unreason are sown. Postmodernism is not convinced that there is a universal human characteristic based on reason. Instead it emphasises the variety of human nature, its construction by class, local culture, ethnicity, socialisation and gender. There is no self-constructing ego governing human nature: it is a modernist fiction. Just as reality is a social construct via language, so notions of what constitutes humanity are also constructed by language. We do not use language to understand the world around us; language 'uses' us. How we understand human nature is the result of language and it is no longer human subjects that are autonomous, but it is language that is autonomous, a law unto itself, pre-existing any one subject.

If we cannot rely upon the modernist rational subject, any more than we can rely upon rational discourse about that subject, then we are 'submerged in a postmodern identity crisis of immense proportions'.[29] The question 'who are we?' cannot be answered, and we either slip into the chaos, the collapse of the centre that W. B. Yeats saw in the early years of the twentieth century,[30] or we embrace the multitude of roles that the centre-less self allows. The creation of those different selves, the reconstruction of our self-understanding, is shaped above all by the media, and television especially. We take on the image that the media dictates, we live in the mood that it fosters. Those selves are not embraced serially, one after another, like a series of affairs, but simultaneously. Like the person suffering from multiple personality disorder, we are 'multiphrenic', to use Middleton and Walsh's phrase, or to put it biblically, we are Legion.[31]

Perhaps a partial answer to the question 'who are we now?' lies in the predominance of the consumer market. Consumer culture views freedom as 'free to choose' and reclassifies many roles as 'consumer' and 'client', not just in the traditional areas of the consumption of material goods. Students are now 'consumers' of education and parents must have the 'right to choose' the school they want for their children. Of course, this means the right of an articulate middle class to manipulate the school system to the advantage of their children, boosting the performance of the schools they perceive as 'good' and leaving less articulate social groups to use the less advantaged schools that remain. Patients are consumers of health care, churchgoers consumers of religion, and the free market must be allowed to prevail in 'consumerland'. The resultant loss of long-term commitment by the postmodern 'Generation X' feeds the ephemerality and fragility of postmodern culture. Where the free market is fostered then a spirit of relativism, of 'anything goes', will result, with the morality of the marketplace: if there is a demand for it, it must be good.

One wit has redesignated humankind as *homo tesco*, whose motto is *emo ergo sum*: 'I shop therefore I am'. Our place of worship is the shopping centre, and our reason for shopping is not simply to consume the goods, but to find fulfilment in the act of shopping. Recent observations on the shopping habits of people in the twice-yearly sales demonstrates that for some it is the gaining of a bargain, the sense of getting something at a reduction, that gives a 'buzz', not the utility or enjoyment of the article itself. At its extreme the addictive nature of postmodern culture is given shape in the creation of the shopaholic, who needs the regular fix of a shopping spree to ward off the sense of meaninglessness of existence and to keep the inner demons of boredom or depression at bay.

The New Babel

Since the totalitarian metanarratives no longer hold sway, postmodern culture has no way of choosing between the fragmented sub-cultures and their different language games and worlds. Relativism has escaped, like a genie, from the private bottle in which modernism had confined it, into the public realm. Science? Whose science? Reason? Whose reason? The sub-cultures that proliferate find it increasingly difficult to understand one another, be they feminist, Islamic or New Age. This profusion of difference, this affirmation of otherness, does help make a place for those who were formerly denied a place precisely because they were 'other'. The greater tolerance towards homosexuals is one obvious change, new concerns for the rights of the disabled another. However, a danger is the breakup of the old nation states into warring factions, as Bosnia or Rwanda tragically remind us.

The biblical story of the tower of Babel[32] points to this condition. By technical ability the inhabitants of the city at Shinar built a city with a tower that represented an attempt to usurp God's position. They want to 'make a name for ourselves' and not be scattered. They have an overarching metanarrative, you might say, that technical ability confers godlike status and power. Familiar? The action of God, who alone has the power to confer a 'name' on people, to raise up or to cast down, is to bring a confusion of language. This confusion could be said to be the postmodern condition.

The old modernist agenda allowed for private beliefs in their right place, in private, but did not allow their intrusion into the public realm of rational discourse. Reason had a privileged position to alone describe reality. As Middleton and Walsh put it, 'liberalism allows a proliferation of sideshows as long as they do not infringe on the centrality of the Big Top. In a postmodern culture, however, there are nothing but sideshows. . . . Whereas modern liberalism allowed (in principle) for a plurality of private worlds in which people could hold a diversity of religious or personal beliefs, postmodernity insists that all worlds are equally private.'[33] The sideshow culture gives equal weight to the frivolous, the banal, and the grandiose, on the assumption that they all have something important to tell us about the real, pluralist, cosmopolitan environment we now live in. What this boils down to is that quintessentially trivial crazes such as the Hula-Hoop or the Cabbage Patch Doll are as inherently interesting as an economic fad such as monetarism.

The sheer differences expressed in postmodern culture are celebrated rather than questioned, as society collapses into a kind of tribalism where we live in cities of increasingly isolated social groups or tribes – middle-class double-income couples live next door to no-income, benefit-culture families, agricultural entrepreneurs find themselves in conflict with animal rights protesters, and the forces of business struggle to understand the strength of beliefs of 'ecowarriors' protesting the construction of a new road.

The New Science

The heart of the modern world view is an understanding of science as the means of explaining the world *par excellence*. Born in large part out of a Christian world view, as Hooykas has shown,[34] like the cuckoo in the sparrow's nest, it outgrew its nurturing environment. Scientific reason took the place of the centrality of the Christian faith that was the medieval mind's most obvious characteristic. The faith that science can solve our problems is no longer widely held, although it continues to be strongly held by some. For many in the postmodern world, the dream of progress has become the nightmare of destruction. Science has given us medical advances and an unparalleled opportunity to live, but removed our right to die with dignity. It has given us unprecedented wealth at the cost of global warming and increased cancers, from ultraviolet radiation seeping through the hole in the ozone layer and other pollutants. Food is plentiful and cheap in the West, but hardly a year goes by without another food safety crisis, be it BSE, *e-coli* food poisoning or the hundred and one forms of food-processing that render eating in part a toxic activity.

Arthur Jones points out that within science itself the indeterminacy of the new physics (relativity, quantum mechanics and chaos theory), has blown apart the scientific materialism of three centuries.[35] Much popular science remains trapped in the world view of a mechanistic universe, but there are significant new currents flowing. Mystery is returning (as in Fritjof Capra's 'holistic' science), and matter is replaced by organisation, complexity and plurality. There is a 're-enchanting' of the world going on. Furthermore, the study of philosophy of science has demonstrated that its claim to be uniquely objective cannot be sustained. Science is undertaken in 'communities of faith' almost as resistant to new ideas as any fundamentalist sect, operating within frameworks of belief that must be exposed, and Michael Polanyi's work on the instrumentality of knowledge has shown all knowing, all epistemology, is in some regard faith-filled.[36]

Postmodern science takes up many of postmodernism's motifs: the plurality of knowledge, scepticism towards science as a totalitarian metanarrative and science as a social enterprise with its own language games. (Thomas Kuhn, for instance, argues that the history of science is not a smooth progression of knowledge, but a series of ruptures as old paradigms break down and new ones replace them.[37]) No pure accessibility to the world of nature is possible except through the models that science devises as its own language game.

What we have been describing is a profound cultural shift in which art, truth and history are relativised and robbed of depth. There is an ephemerality or shallowness about postmodernism, Baudrillard's *jouissance*, that distinguishes it from modernism. As Huyssens says, '. . . in an important sector of our culture there is a noticeable shift in sensibility, practices and discourse formations which distinguishes a postmodern set of assumptions, experiences and propositions from that of a preceding period.'[38] If the Enlightenment rebellion against the tired and hypocritical political and social stances of seventeenth-century Christian faith gave rise to modernism, perhaps it is the manifest failure of modernism to deliver the just and wholesome society it promised through the wise use of rationality that provided the soil in which postmodernism flourishes. Our next task is to offer something of a brief Christian critique of postmodernism, so that our stance towards it becomes clearer. Are we unrepentant modernists who bewail the new culture, or should we become born-again postmodernists? As we shall see, neither position is advisable if we are to remain true to the Christian faith.

We began with detectives, icons of modernity, putting reason to use in the pursuit of justice and relying upon the fruits of scientific research to support their findings. Indeed, Dr Kay Scarpetta is fundamentally a scientist, trained as a pathologist. What would postmodern detectives look like? They would probably use tarot cards and a spiritualist medium to find the lead!

In Summary

Postmodernism says goodbye to big stories or metanarratives that are grand explanations of truth (the Enlightenment), history (Marxism), or faith (Christianity). In their place are a multitude of local stories, often conflicting, but celebrating their illogicality and diversity. This fragmentation applies to our cultural, social and religious realms where the consumer reigns. Everything becomes an item for consumption: education, health care, knowledge and religion make consumers of parents and children, patients, students and worshippers.

The distinctions between high culture and mass culture become blurred, or perhaps it is just that mass culture, through television, radio and film, has become predominant. Older cultures become 'heritage' to be preserved because they are to be consumed. Jane Austen and Charlotte Brontë become big business for the film and television media, and their 'world' becomes part of heritage Britain (especially Howarth, the Brontës' home). The past is revalued and aspects of culture which modernism rejected – magic, myth, cosmology and feeling – are absorbed into the postmodern melting-pot. The confident culture of modernism, optimistic, utopian and progressive, has been replaced with a diffident, often hope-less and anxious spirit about our age.

CHAPTER 4

What Do We Think of Humpty Dumpty?

Overview

The children's nursery rhyme is a warning to all fragile eggs: fall off walls at your peril. Can the armies of the King put the Humpty Dumpty of modernism back together again, or should we consign him to the landfill site of history? Indeed, how wedded to modernism should Christians be, and how warm should our embrace of postmodernism be?

Being 'for' or 'against' postmodernism makes no sense unless we subject modernism to the same criteria of judgment. The question we must ask of both cultures is to what extent do they conform to the world-view of the Christian faith, especially in the areas of creation, anthropology and salvation.

The Christian World-view

We must first be clear about the Christian world-view that, as a Christian believer, I take to be the truth and against which I compare modernism and postmodernism.

Creation

This world is the direct result of the creative handiwork of an infinite, personal, communal (Triune), and good God.[1] The universe generally follows the laws of physics by which God established the way matter behaves and consists, but remains contingent upon the sustaining power of God, who called it into being.[2]

Anthropology

On the Earth, humans are the only creatures to bear a likeness to God. I take this to mean that we have a spiritual capacity and in our essential need of, and capacity for, relationships we carry the image of the Holy Trinity, Father, Son and Holy Spirit. We were called to bear a special responsibility for the good ordering of the world as God's vice-regent.[3]

Our ability to do so has been drastically diminished by a moral twistedness and fall that invests each human being with a tendency to live an autonomous life, separate from a relationship with God.[4] This independence from God is sinful, and it results in alienation from God,[5] from others, from the created realm and from ourselves, and extends to affect the whole created realm.[6] The sinfulness is not so severe that it cannot be redeemed,[7] and we retain a capacity for moral judgment, if not the potential to follow that morality absolutely. We have an aptitude for rational thought, but it cannot disclose all truth, for there are areas of the reality of things that require God to reveal what reason alone cannot discover.

Salvation

The fall from a condition of absolute dependence upon God, illustrated in the story in Genesis of the fall of humankind, is not the final word. God in Jesus Christ is redeeming humankind and restoring the purposes for which he created humankind in the first place. The death of Christ opens up the possibility for a new beginning for humankind by undoing the twisted power of sin and releasing individuals into a new relationship of dependence upon God, bringing a desire to follow in his ways and membership of a redeemed community.[8] God is the one who calls and saves, although it takes a response of trust and faith on the part of the individual, accompanied by a turning away from the old sinful autonomy and rebellious ways (repentance),[9] for that call to be heard and that invitation to new life to be accepted. Our freedom to respond remains intact throughout, although to what extent our freedom is impaired by sin and our response of faith is preordained is the subject of continuing controversy within the Christian faith.

This, I suggest, is the traditional and orthodox understanding of the Christian faith,[10] sometimes called theism. Debates within Christianity continue to rage concerning the manner of creation, the precise extent of human free will, and the means by which Christ's atoning death achieves its efficacy, but these are second-order debates. The central core of the Christian faith, what C. S. Lewis called 'mere Christianity', has a continuing resistance to fundamental change. There are postmodern forms of faith that deny creation, the existence in reality of a personal transcendent and loving God and the existence of anything like the Gospel story of Jesus Christ,[11] but to the majority of Christians in the world today, this would be unrecognisable as authentic Christianity, and I would not take these expressions as normative of faith.

The Christianity–Modernism Debate

Christianity has by no means been immune to the influences of modernism. Indeed, two of the most characteristic forms of Christian expression, the Liberal and the Evangelical, are to a large extent creatures of the modernist project, the former embracing the rationalist metanarrative, the latter, in a different way, utilising it in part to oppose the Liberal.

The typical scientific modernist would hold radically differing views to orthodox Christianity:

- There would be a sceptical silence about creation since, even if God did set things off in the first place (deism), he has now disappeared off the scene and left a closed universe of cause and effect. Human beings are similarly the result of biological cause and effect, nothing more than organic machines.[12]

- Knowledge is limited by the empirical data we gather from our senses. Human beings are autonomous, self-governing and endowed with a capacity to choose between competing courses of action through the use of reason.
- The result of those choices should be a harmonious and just society, especially when conducted under the influence of the market forces within a Western democracy. Modernists would deny the baleful influence of sin and its limitations upon the ability of the individual to choose the good.
- The rational approach to life is the enlightened approach and has no place for superstition, although religious beliefs are possible within the bounds of private opinion.
- Human society is progressing towards an improving future under the influence of reason and its exercise by rational and autonomous human beings.

We can see clearly that those Christians keen to defend modernism in the face of the attack of postmodernism are defending a strange bedfellow indeed, with radically different world views to its orthodox expression. But then, the latest 'enemy' always makes the last look almost homely!

In his critique of modernity, Colin Gunton lays part of the blame for modernity's 'loss of the concept of truth, and with it, all the connotations of objectivity and universality that it once had for much of Western intellectual history'[13] at the door of Christian theology's tendency to view God in a monolithic way, rather than in the more dynamic model of the Trinity. It is against this inadequate tradition that modernity reacted, with all that followed by way of fragmentation of culture and loss of coherence of truth. The kind of Christian vision that I want to contrast with both modernity and postmodernity will, therefore, not simply be a reformulation of the very inadequacy that created the problem in the first place, but one which takes notice of weaknesses in the older tradition, and seeks to 'reinvigorate the concept of truth, without, however, ignoring the weaknesses of that against which much modern thought has reacted'.[14] Here, Gunton is my guide. In his 1992 Bampton Lectures he explored in depth the roots and characteristics of modernity and argued for Christian theology's indispensable role in finding a way out of the postmodernist dilemma.

> Gunton argues that the quest for an absolute rational truth, which was the Enlightenment project, led instead to a suspicion of the very idea of truth and, in turn, to a new and insidious (because unrecognised) absolute belief: there is no absolute truth. There is a logical inconsistency here: to assert 'there are no absolutes' is itself an absolute statement. What is needed in the debate between modernity's stress on the absolute universality of truth and postmodernity's stress on the particular is a theological perspective, because the Christian faith has at its best held both in tension, especially in the doctrine of the Trinity.
>
> However, a proper doctrine of creation would see the exercise of human rationality as a fruitful activity, because the world is the kind of place where rationality will achieve a measure of understanding, but only a measure. It is not absolute but limited, because of human sinfulness, in the achievement of its quest to discover what Gunton calls 'open transcendentals', those features by which being displays itself, i.e. ways of conceiving what really is everywhere and always.

Christians, though most would not understand the term, are believers in transcendentals. We believe that there are transcendental truths about the world (it is created good by a good God, for instance), about human nature (we are made in the image of God) and about the future (there is a purpose to creation, an end and renewal of all things in Christ). Kant and the Enlightenment project claimed that the quest for the forms by which the fundamental features of the cosmos could be understood from timeless ideas was a failure, and so we must not return to pre-Enlightenment failures. Rather, we must look for ways of understanding the world that are open, limited, but real, by virtue of the fact that God is the creator of the world and has made it susceptible to such enquiry.

The Trinity as the Grammar of Theology

The doctrine of the Trinity, the uniquely Christian understanding of God, is critical. The world is like it is, and human nature is like it is, because God has a triune nature. In the history of the doctrine there has tended to be an emphasis upon either the Oneness of God (particularly in the Western tradition) or the Threeness of God as Father, Son and Holy Spirit.

> It is in Gregory of Nazianzus,[15] as well as the other Cappadocian Fathers, that we find a more dynamic way of understanding the tension between the One and the Three. Gregory writes: 'No sooner do I conceive of the One than I am illumined by the splendour of the Three; no sooner do I distinguish them than I am carried back to the One.'[16] Hilary of Poitiers (315–368) in the West argues similarly for the importance of the distinct persons in God, so that the error should not be made of supposing that God is solitary.[17] Later Western developments also echo the emphasis upon the threeness of God. So, Richard of St Victor in the twelfth century argued that the three persons are necessary if God is truly to be conceived as love.[18]

In our search for a way of understanding the world in the critique of modernism and postmodernism, the Christian answer is that we must begin with God and the way the world is created by him. Thus, if the world is God's creation, because he is three, there will be a corresponding plurality about the world which cannot be subjected to the modernist bar of scientific rationality alone. It is a fundamental misunderstanding of the way things are to submit all questions to the foundation of rationality, because there is a plurality that cannot be reduced to the one scientific means of enquiry. It is precisely this which postmodernism has demonstrated so clearly, and in doing so it has to be welcomed by Christians.

> Religious questions cannot be answered by simply applying some universal scientific criteria, as Richard Dawkins would claim, with disastrous mistaken consequences. However, the Oneness about God will mean, *pace* the modernists, that there is a fundamental unity ▶▶

to existence that is not merely the amalgam of endless indeterminacy and plurality. It allows the possibility of different areas of discourse, science, ethics or art, for instance, to stand without one area being elevated above the others, yet still being linked together. The unity and diversity of human cultural enterprise are given equal significance, and together the richness of creation and human sociability can be celebrated rather than reduced.

The doctrine of the Trinity will help us particularly to transcend the historical polarity of individualism and collectivism in which one has submerged the other. In collectivism, the individual's rights and aspirations are subjected to the needs of the whole society, with all of the attendant human rights abuses illustrated in Stalinist Russia or Maoist China. On the other hand, the individualism so beloved of liberal democracies raises self-fulfilment to the status of a virtue, when the exercise of the individual's freedom to self-fulfilment and happiness was always tempered by a recognition of the needs of others in classic Christian ethics. Indeed, it is self-sacrifice which is the virtue, not the selfish self-fulfilment of much contemporary ethics. In pastoral practice, as we shall see later, the current psychotherapeutic absorption with self-fulfilment must be qualified by the concept of the relatedness to others bringing obligations as well as benefits. The client who seeks a divorce because that is the means of personal self-fulfilment should also recognise the costs to other family members of that decision. The needs of the one and the needs of the many are held in creative tension.

In his plenary address to the 1996 Swanwick conference to pastoral carers and counsellors, Nigel Wright argued for the doctrine of the Trinity to be the grammar by which we understand pastoral practice, and particularly the notion of *perichoresis*, or mutual indwelling, 'a concept heavy with spatial and temporal conceptuality, involving movement, recurrence and interpenetration'.[19] In its patristic[20] origins, the concept was a way of articulating the interdependence and interrelatedness of the members of the Trinity, for instance, how the Father is the Father by virtue of there being the Son. For God to exist does not mean an absolute simplicity, but a unity derived from ▶▶

a dynamic plurality of the three persons in relationship. One member is not possible without the other two, but there exists for ever the eternal dance of the three in one. The particularity of the persons of the Trinity prevents the unity from collapsing into three of the same, but the unity of the three by virtue of the bond of love which is God's nature prevents inter-godhead civil warfare breaking out! In short, the three persons of the Trinity exist only in eternal relatedness, not simply coinhering (the older Latin means of expressing this relationship and suggesting a static relationship), but in a dynamic constituting of one another's being.

The understanding of the Trinitarian God has important implications for pastoral practice in the fostering and sustaining of relationships appropriate to our created status. Alastair Campbell's pithy definition of the task of pastoral care as 'in essence, surprisingly simple, having one fundamental aim: to help people to know love, both as something to be received and as something to give',[21] is important for these implications.

The notion of *perichoresis* illustrates the concept of open transcendentals that we spoke of earlier, as a way of speaking about reality which is neither simply absolutist nor simply pluralist. It is a concept that is clearly human, speaking about God by way of the analogy of movement in space and time that is akin to a dance, and so is limited by our creatureliness and sinfulness. We dare not raise it to the status of the definitive statement about God. Yet it is also developed through revelation of God's nature through Christ, and so is not merely human speculation about God that is confined to rational thought alone. Because God as the Father, the Son and the Spirit, present and active in the world, is involved in space and time, he cannot be conceived of as *simply* timeless and spaceless. The analogy of *perichoresis* is appropriate to the being of God, and therefore an appropriate way of speaking about humanity constituted upon God's image and thus about the care of people.

Furthermore, if this God is God, he is the source of all meaning and truth, and all meaning and truth will in some way bear his fingerprint and be marked by its relationship to its creator.[22] Thus, if human beings particularly bear the image of

God, to be authentically human will be to be perichoretic beings, interrelated, in community. Thus a notion of human *perichoresis* affirms that persons mutually constitute one another, as John Macmurray saw.[23] (John Macmurray is, incidentally, the philosopher who has most influenced Tony Blair and New Labour.)

> Other people are no longer there to be feared or dominated but rather to be sustained and constitute us in mutual loving and be sustained and constituted in turn. Macmurray's views have considerable implications for a world in which we lament a selfish individualism that destroys human community or a consumer collectivism in which the individual is simply lost. We are made for community rather than individualism or collectivism, with all that that implies for social ethics.[24]

I have laboured this point because I want to lay some firm grounds of methodology upon which both to offer a critique of modernism and postmodernism, and construct a way of doing pastoral care which is appropriate to the postmodern culture in which we live, and which will be the substance of the latter part of this book. Unless we lay such grounds, pastoral practice is likely to follow the latest trend or fad uncritically, and cease to be *pastoral* care, while a naive return to pre-modern practice (that is, of the period before the modern era, or pre-Enlightenment) is as likely to fail now as it did then, if not more so.

The Validity of the Postmodern Critique

We began by questioning the response to postmodernism that will govern its relation of pastoral care. Should we welcome postmodernism as a necessary corrective to the mistakes of modernity, or is the cure more destructive than the malaise? We outlined the core beliefs of the Christian faith and contrasted them with modernity's world-view, noting how differently the two view important ways of understanding the world. Rather than simply restate in a louder voice the truths of Christianity, we followed Colin Gunton in a critique of both modernity and traditional Christianity's deficient understanding of the key issues for modernity and postmodernity (or late modernity as Gunton would view it). In so doing, we discovered that a perichoretic understanding of the Trinity provides us with a way of understanding the key problem of postmodernity: the relation of the particular to the transcendental truths that have long been the concern of Western philosophy and religion, and which postmodernity denies exist. In the following sections, we shall see how key doctrines of the Christian faith provide us with ways of understanding the world of human existence and therefore of pastoral care, in many ways. These include understanding human relations in community, the way in which the creative Spirit allows for the unique particularity of all things, and thus recognises their value and possibility of relationship with the other, and the place of worship, especially the Eucharist, as a means of celebrating 'being in communion' as a pastoral care activity.[25]

But what of our delayed critique of postmodernism? Certainly, its judgment that two hundred years of modernism has failed to deliver what it promised is accurate. We seem further than ever from a just, wholesome society freed from crime, poverty or disease. In the late 1990s the gap between rich and poor is wider than ever, diseases such as tuberculosis, which were all but eradicated from the West, are reappearing in newer, more virulent forms, while rickets is now prevalent amongst the children of our poorest homes. Our culture appears to be dominated by the trivial, and such is the decline in the standards of teaching mathematics that some university departments of mathematics now routinely require four years to teach undergraduates what previous generations only took three years to assimilate. The brave new world seems rather timid in its reluctance to step forward into the limelight.

Nick Fox says it is important 'that Christians should not attack the wrong target'.[26] The critiques of Derrida, Foucault and Lyotard have simply shown that modernism's project was doomed to fail from the start: humans cannot know everything by using scientific reason alone. We should not reject the postmodern critique merely because it is uncomfortable for some of traditional Christianity's so-called certainties.

In biblical criticism, for instance, the insights of the deconstructionists emphasise the priority of the reader over the writer and the absence of an absolute interpretation of the text. The use of the Old Testament by the New Testament writers has long proved difficult to reconcile with the rules of hermaneutics beloved of Evangelicals. The intention and context of the Old Testament seems of secondary importance to those New Testament writers who employ it in defence of the point at issue! The fundamentalist reading of Scripture is no longer tenable, even though it is widely practised. There is a new dynamism about the relationship of text to reader that perhaps is more faithful to the notion of the Spirit as Lord of the Word, rather than the Spirit as prisoner of a particular hermeneutic. Karl Barth (whom Hans Kung views as the precursor to postmodern theology) saw that very clearly in his threefold form of the Word of God.[27] Calvin emphasises the action of the Spirit in the understanding of the Word[28] and adds a necessary corrective to certain forms of biblical fundamentalism, while, contrary to postmodernists, allowing for a dynamic of relationship to the Spirit that means we are not therefore just the victims of a relativism and pluralism that denies the existence of any meaning at all.

In postmodernism's celebration of diversity, there is perhaps another welcome corrective to the totalitarian abuses of power that Foucault analyses. In the privilege of men over women, Western over Third World, able-bodied over disabled, modernism has been abusive of its privileges, and the Church has often either remained silent, and guilty by its silence, or it has been actively engaged in those abuses. Postmodernism, in its defence of the 'other', the underdog, the disadvantaged, is surely pointing the way to the proper mission of the Church if it is to follow in the way of Jesus Christ. Celebrating difference is a key feature of St Paul's doctrine of the Church as the Body of Christ[29] and he emphasises the importance of honouring those who seem least worthy of it according to secular values of power.

The Problems With a Postmodern Christianity

However, there are areas of profound disagreement with postmodernism: its scepticism towards a reality outside language must be countered by our Christian belief in the God who is really there, and furthermore, is not silent. God is not simply a construction of the human language game, although we do well not to raise the status of human statements about God to divine authority. The incarnation speaks of a God who communicates in a human life partly through language, and thus our understanding of the status of language should begin with Christ, rather than with postmodern scepticism.

Postmodernism sees truth claims arising from within a community, but has no way of attributing wider significance to those claims beyond that community. All truth is therefore relative, and to ask if any one truth construct, any one community's claims upon truth are a more accurate description of what 'really is' is an impossible question. Christians would want to counter this with the claim that there is indeed One who stands outside of the web of human narrative, and who is Truth, and therefore we are able to claim a privilege to knowledge on the basis of revelation. We follow Jesus Christ who did not say 'I am a Way, a truth for those who choose to see things that way' but 'I am the Way, the Truth, and the Life.'[30] It is this scandal of particularity that contradicts postmodern relativism.

Simply to embrace the postmodern heterogeneity does not take seriously the crisis of our age, even though there are aspects of postmodernity that are helpful in pulling down both modernity's idolatrous superstructure and Christianity's false starts. Yearning for the good old days, attempting to hold the line against postmodernity's encroachments, is equally doomed to failure. This policy of retrenchment fundamentally fails to see how each age is culturally conditioned and ambiguous. There is no golden age to return to, and certainly not the immediately previous one, with its admixture of modernity and genuine faith. The gospel is always being forwarded to a new address because the culture to which it is addressed never stays in one place. Neither an abandonment to the postmodern *zeitgeist*, nor a conservative retrenchment, will meet the challenge of the day.

Graham Cray's suggestion that the response should be one of argument for a recreating of the Christian world-view with humility, which is above all Trinitarian (Gunton's open transcendentals), offers a demonstration of how we can live in community and in hope. It gives the opportunity for a fresh discovery of the Scriptures as a metanarrative that is anti-totalising (in contrast to the totalising metanarratives of modernity), and shows what it means to be human according to the pattern of Christ and the encounter with the Spirit of God that liberates and empowers with love. With this mission in mind, we shall see that at every turn there is a significant role for pastoral care as the vehicle for the message. If the postmodern world will not take heed of the gospel message, it just might take note of the quality and sheer vitality and authenticity of the care with which the Christian community embraces a hurting and disintegrating world in the name of Christ. The epitaph for this postmodern generation might be 'We were going to change the world, but now we can only go to the shops.' The time has come for the Church to quit turning the faith into another consumer commodity and to start changing the world once more.

CHAPTER 5

Pastoral Care and Postmodern Ethics

Overview

In contemporary counselling practice much emphasis is given to the need for the counsellor to 'suspend judgment', to 'bracket out' his or her own moral values in order to attend more carefully to the client. This is commonplace, but can be illustrated by two texts used widely in the training of Christian counsellors. Michael Jacobs, a psychodynamic counsellor, advocates an avoidance of 'moralistic judgments' amongst his guidelines for responding to clients, so that the listener can 'elevate moral thinking and decision-making to an adult level, and away from the parental disposition which the "wayward child" aspect of the speaker might engender in the authority figure.'[1] Gerard Egan is, like Jacobs, a Christian writing more for the secular than the religious counselling market. He argues that 'helpers should not use information as a subtle (or not too subtle) way of pushing their own values'[2] and illustrates this with examples of clients with unwanted pregnancies. Helpers should not immediately give clients information about abortion clinics, and conversely, if the client wants an abortion, but this is contrary to the helper's values, then the helper is to admit that they cannot provide help for her in this area. This is only one aspect of a contemporary mistrust of any moral guidance in the counselling room, and has subtly been imported into the wider practice of Christian pastoral care. Like a tarantula in a crate of bananas, it is an unwelcome and potentially dangerous guest in an otherwise wholesome cargo.

The nonjudgmental ethics of secular psychotherapy threatens to swamp any distinctively Christian ethic expressed in pastoral care. This is not a crisis in pastoral care only, but part of a wider crisis in ethics in the postmodern world, and it is to this wider crisis that we must turn first if we are to discover ways in which ethical judgments can be made in the practice of pastoral care.

Adrift on a Sea of Uncertainty: Postmodern Ethics

The crisis in postmodern ethics is a symptom of the wider crisis in meaning and truth that is the theme of Chapter 3. At a popular level, it takes the widespread form of belief that as long as an action does not harm anyone else, then it is morally acceptable. 'It's not harming anyone,' its exponents proclaim. The ethics of the feel-good factor are closely linked to this: what *is* right is what *feels* right (emotivism). At a deeper level is the relativism which denies the possibility of making objective moral judgments, since there is no way of knowing about the basis upon which those objective judgments can be made, apart from the radical subjectivity of the individual. What is true for me is not necessarily true for you, and who is to say that both of us are not right? Don Cupitt puts it this way: 'truth is human, socially produced, historically developed, plural and changing.'[3]

This crisis of subjectivity and relativism has been closely dissected by Alasdair MacIntyre in his seminal *After Virtue* (discussed later in this chapter), and we shall turn to this analysis in a moment. Before we do so, we should note some of the broad features of this moral landscape. At an international level, the West's awareness of the imposition of its cultural norms on many colonial, Third World cultures over the past two hundred years, and the shame now felt by its intellectuals because of this, has resulted in a doctrine of the equality of all cultures and the denial of universal values. Whereas inhumanity, oppression and cruelty are vigorously opposed in a few, economically advantageous cases (such as the invasion of Kuwait by Saddam Hussein in 1991), in the majority of situations the West has done little to act in defence of 'universal' values of humanity, justice, or the rights of minorities. The catalogue could include Rwanda, Nigeria and Sudan, to name but a few in just one continent. This is a condoning of new forms of racism and totalitarian brutality in the name of 'cultural diversity' and 'freedom'. The West has lost its intellectual nerve to promote the values of justice, human rights, freedom of speech and political freedom in the world beyond some empty rhetoric, immediately countered from within its own ranks as 'culturally insensitive' or politically incorrect.

In defence of 'freedom', modern liberalism is in fact selective in its tolerance, with a bias towards those who are pluralist and relativist. Any who argue for a universal truth, a trans-cultural ethic, especially if it is based upon religious conviction, are pilloried as 'fundamentalist bigots'. 'Intolerance is the only vice recognised, and an indiscriminating openness to different "value-systems" the only virtue.'[4] Modern tolerance of plurality becomes strangely intolerant of any who voice opinions that question that tolerance. As Gunton puts it, 'radical relativism implies an imperious claim for its own truth which is viciously intolerant because it is undiscussible in the terms of the ideology in which it is propounded.'[5] Western culture breaks into parts that can scarcely communicate with each other.

At a political level, the old arts of rhetoric, *disputatio*, or discussion, are replaced by the politics of the demonstration, the mob, and the bear garden. It is the soundbite that counts, not rational argument. Particularly when in Britain the centre ground is so crowded by both moderate right-wing and centrist left-wing parties, debate is replaced by accusation and counter-accusation played out for the journalists who, through the media, shape the opinions of the electorate.

The Importance of the Will in Contemporary Ethics

The characteristic view of human beings in contemporary ethics emphasises the importance of the will. To be free is to have the unrestrained use of the individual's will: the will to choose, to act, to speak. In moral judgments it is my will that I exercise, a will that has become dislocated from its relationship to a universal moral order. Part of the problem can be laid at the door of the eighteenth-century Enlightenment philosopher Immanuel Kant, who emphasised the role of reason in guiding the will.

The task of the will, for Kant, was to be guided by reason into formulating the ethical laws by which human life could be conducted, but it was a will which had no root in anything beyond the human, no reference to anything beyond itself. What had previously been an attribute of deity became the sole prerogative of humanity, and with it the resultant fragmentation of human culture, including ethics.

> An attempt to wrest from God the prerogatives of absolute freedom and infinity leads to the inversion of Pentecost and what is in effect a new Babel. 'Postmodernism' represents that Babel perfectly, because when each speaks a language unrelated to that of the other – when language is not the basis of the communication that shapes our being – the only outcome can be fragmentation. In that sense, postmodernism is modernity come home to roost.[6]

This loss of the transcendent results in our inability to discern the 'value' of values.

The Contemporary Response to the Crisis in Ethics

Contemporary culture attempts to respond to this crisis in a number of ways. Philip Goodchild outlines four of them:[7]

1. There is a denial of the postmodern condition altogether and a continuation of the modernist project that seeks the true nature of the transcendent authority able to legitimise our highest values. Where in the realm of human moral judgments can we find a proper foundation upon which to legislate?
2. The cultural confusion of our day is opposed by attempting to reconstruct a tradition and community in which thought and action will be given their own meaning and value. Here transcendence is found in the source and the purpose of a given community, but is limited to that community. Can we build an ethic that is specific to a Christian community, or an Islamic community, that works for that community without making grandiose claims to being the ground for every one else's community?
3. The impact of a century of unprecedented cruelty and suffering calls for a listening to the voice of the victims and action, at whatever cost to oneself, to alleviate their suffering. Here the basis of morality is theodicy and transcendence is encountered in the need of the sufferer. How can I be vulnerable to the suffering of others?
4. A pragmatic and deconstructive response is offered, where no appeal is made to transcendence at all, but each action is assessed according to its consequences with no fixed strategies of legitimisation. We are bombarded with so much information that we see both sides of every argument and which side we ultimately choose to support is the result of those forces of socialisation which in fact shape all human truth. There is no basis for moral judgment and the result is cynicism.

> Any number of schemes of justice and forms of rationality now serve as warrants for a multitude of beliefs and practices; there is no longer any firm consensus as to what constitutes an absolute. Indeed, nearly 7 out of 10 Americans no longer believe there are any absolutes at all.[8]

The moral ambiguity that characterises our age is generally deplored by the Christian community, yet it offers no unequivocal, clear way of responding. There are those who argue for a return to a pre-modern founding of ethics on revelation. What is right is revealed in Scripture, with a claim to universality in all ages and places. Others argue for a foundation of principles derived from the Christian story and exemplified in the life of Jesus Christ: the primacy of unconditional love and acceptance, forgiveness and justice. Others argue for an ethic that is heavily emotivist, 'love God and do what you like'. Based upon a notion of the immanent inspiration and guidance of the Spirit being preferable to a more prosaic dependence upon the letter of the Scripture ('the letter kills but the Spirit gives life'), this is prone to relativism and emotivism. Advocates of each of these responses would argue that theirs is the right way forward for a recovery of a strong Christian ethic and its translation into the 'answer to the moral ills of our age', but such certainties are naive and take too little account of the scale of the problem.

Having explored the landscape of postmodern ethics, we move on to a more detailed consideration of a thoroughgoing rejection of all modern moral philosophy and its replacement by the Aristotelian notion of virtue, that might point the way forward to an ethic for pastoral care: Alasdair MacIntyre's *After Virtue*.

After Virtue: A Way out of the Crisis in Postmodern Ethics?

For Alasdair MacIntyre, ethics are not presented as a sort of spiritual exercise for the morally scrupulous, but as the way that we actually all live our lives in society. Once an atheist, but now a Roman Catholic, he has criticised the way that ethics have been conducted since the Renaissance and Enlightenment and describes the moral wilderness that is our culture.[9]

MacIntyre argues that in society at the moment moral arguments have three characteristics. First, they are interminable, not just because they go on and on, but because they have no terminus, no common ground upon which the logical claims of competing positions can be weighed. In debates over abortion, or the justice of armed conflict, the rival premises are such that we have no way to evaluate their claims because they are incommensurable. In the abortion debate, one side argues for the permission of abortion on the grounds of women's rights over their own bodies, while the other side, advocating the prohibition of abortion, argues on the basis of the universal prohibition against the taking of human life. There are no ways in our society to establish how to decide between such rival claims.[10]

Secondly, moral arguments are impersonal in tone, presupposing the existence of impersonal criteria independent of the relationship between the two parties in a moral debate.

Thirdly, the plurality (although that term is 'too imprecise' for MacIntyre) of our culture means that a number of different historical roots are used. In the abortion debate, the first position employs notions of rights which originate with Locke, while the second has its roots in the moral law of Thomas Aquinas. The language in which we discuss morality no longer makes sense, and not only do the parties in moral controversies argue from incompatible premises, they hardly recognise how incompatible those premises are. The advocates of 'universal law' simply do not understand the premise of 'relative rights', and vice versa.

MacIntyre dismisses emotivism, with its pompous verdict that every attempt to provide a rational justification for an objective morality has failed, the Enlightenment project in its Kantean, Humean and Utilitarian expressions, and the morality of Nietzsche. He dates the first expression of the characteristic modern moral dilemma of incompatible arguments to the appearance in 1842 of Kierkegaard's *Enten-Eller*, and demonstrates how the Enlightenment project had failed. In *Enten-Eller*, Kierkegaard poses the choice between the ethical way of life and the aesthetic, but because they are first principles, no ultimate reasons can be adduced to support them. The important action is to choose. Kierkegaard owes a great debt to Kant and they both inherit a common Lutheran morality. Kant's ethics are based upon two beliefs: if the rules of morality are rational, they must be the same for all rational beings; and if the rules of morality are binding upon all rational beings, the crucial factor is the will of them to carry them out. In doing so he rejects the bases of morality upon which ▶▶

earlier ethicists had built: the pursuit of happiness and the command of God. This project has failed, says MacIntyre, because neither the teleological argument (what is the result of an action), which finds expression in the utilitarianism of John Stuart Mill, nor the search for a new categorical status to replace God's command, with its discussion of rationality and rights, provide a common basis upon which to argue morally.

When claims invoking rights are matched against claims appealing to utility or when either or both are matched against claims based upon some traditional concept of justice, it is not surprising that there is no rational way of deciding which type of claim is to be given priority or how one is to be weighed against the other.[11]

In rejecting the Enlightenment foundationalism of rationality, MacIntyre also rejects two positions often presented as the inevitable consequence of doing so. First, the relativist challenge so familiar in our postmodern culture, which claims that every set of standards has as much or as little claim upon our allegiance as any other. Secondly, the perspectivist challenge, that puts in question the possibility of making truth claims from within any one tradition.[12]

In contrast, he wants an account of rationality and truth that is genuinely realist but not based upon some form of universal foundation, such as rationality. Thus he develops the notion of traditions, and in particular the notion of virtue which, for Aristotle, amounts to an adequate sense of the traditions to which one belongs.

Those traditions vary, from Homer, whose virtuous man was a warrior, to Aristotle, who decided that men could only be properly human in a community and could only exercise virtues in that community. Aristotle's virtuous man was an Athenian gentleman who lived the good life which was best for the community, while Benjamin Franklin's virtuous man did what was good because it achieved earthly and heavenly success. While the lists of virtues differ from Homer to Aristotle, from the New Testament to Jane Austen, there is a central core to the concept of the virtues which might give it universal appeal. Virtues are exercised by people who live in a particular ▶▶

community, and while the characteristics of those communities differ from place to place and from time to time (Aristotle's Athens differs considerably from Jane Austen's Hampshire), what allows us to decide what is virtuous is an adequate grasp of the values which are embedded in those communities and the practice of life which is in accord with them. Thus the heart of the virtues is practical reason, Aristotle's *phronesis*,[13] or Aquinas' *prudentia*.

In his modernising of Thomist ethics, it might be said that MacIntyre has produced 'something very like the kind of liberal pluralism which is as characteristic a modern error as the various monistic moral theories that he wants us to reject'.[14] This may be so, but there may be better or worse ways of living in the late twentieth century, and the notion of conformity to a tradition and its expression in community is among the better. In fact, it seems to be closest to the theological principles that we argued for earlier, and which will inform our pastoral priorities later: a proper plurality that is the result of the doctrine of creation, and the proper relatedness which is the result of the doctrine of the Trinity. The notion of virtue as the basis of morality in communities which express those theological principles is a very fruitful way forward.

In place of the fragmentation of roles that is so familiar in postmodernity, the tradition of the virtues, particularly as Aristotle expressed it, brings an integration of roles. Drawing on the Homeric era, Aristotle draws no clear distinction between being virtuous, being good at work and being successful. In the single narrative of a human life, virtue is that way of right and successful living. In the seventeenth and eighteenth centuries the tradition of the virtuous man underwent a transformation. So David Hume distinguished between natural virtues, which we find agreeable in ourselves, and artificial virtues, which are socially constructed to restrain passions and desires which would otherwise be socially destructive. With postmodern liberal individualism, the possession of virtues is more often replaced by the will to power, a derision of the virtues in favour of something more superficial or more sinister. It is not the Aristotelian virtuous man we admire, nor even the productive and civil man of the eighteenth century, but the powerful man, the stylish man, the famous or wealthy man.

In this regard, Jane Austen is a late flowering of the older Aristotelian scheme. She identifies that social scene in which the virtues are able to continue, a scene where the purpose of the lives of her heroines is to achieve a certain kind of marriage, without which a spinster is condemned to drudgery. Miss Bates is neither rich nor beautiful, young nor married, and it is therefore uncommon for her to be popular. Her contentment and goodwill, not her outward condition, win her admirers. She is a happy woman, in the Aristotelian sense, because of those virtues.

> It is her uniting of Christian and Aristotelian themes in a determinate social context that makes Jane Austen the last great effective imaginative voice of the tradition of thought about, and practice of, the virtues . . . Her heroines seek the good through seeking their own good in marriage. The restricted households of Highbury and Mansfield Park have to serve as surrogates for the Greek city-state.[15]

The virtues she admires are amiability, a genuine loving regard for others and not just good manners, practical intelligence, constancy and humility. Above all, she dislikes the counterfeit, an appearance of something good which is in fact dissimulation, and places great stress on self-knowledge whereby the person comes to see themselves as they truly are. Akin to this vice is charm, the characteristic modern quality which those who lack virtue can use to achieve social success. Emma is charming, but lacks virtue until self-knowledge comes, while Fanny Price is charmless but virtuous. It is the virtue of constancy which constrains her to disobey her guardian and refuse marriage to Henry Crawford, thus risking the danger of losing the opportunity for social and economic security that marriage represents. It is no coincidence that the expression of those virtues in Austen is in narrative form, telling the story of a life. Any specific account of the virtues presupposes the equally specific story of a human life.

It is curious that in the late 1990s Jane Austen is popular in the media, with films and TV series of her novels, which as spinoffs are now more widely read. Is this just nostalgia for a bygone age? Or is there a hunger for a kind of morality, based upon the virtues, that Austen describes; one which seems unattainable, but attractive? She remains justifiably one of the most popular of novelists, her world a concentration of so much more than polite early nineteenth-century society. It reminds us that pastoral care, which is concerned with ethics, takes place within a specific community and is concerned with specific lives, and that pastoral theology is often practised most profitably in narrative form.

MacIntyre faces the challenge of relativism to his notion of tradition-based virtue by looking for common ground. At stake is the question of the relationship of different traditions. The fatwa against Salman Rushdie, mentioned in Chapter 3, is a case in point. The tradition of free speech, the liberal conscience, tolerance of other value systems, and tolerance of the critique of belief systems, is represented by Rushdie and his Western liberal supporters. Fundamentalist Islam despises those values: they are not virtues, but vices. It values conformity to the will of Allah as revealed in the Koran and views the kind of critique to which Rushdie subjected Islam as blasphemy, which carries the death penalty. Two traditions, two communities. Are both 'right'? Part of the problem is the implicit attempt by Rushdie, with his cultural background in Islam, to subject the Islamic culture to his current liberal, relativistic values. Similarly, the issue of the fatwa concerns the universalising of the tradition of Islam, and the explicit imposition of its values upon another tradition (although one wonders whether the particular ferocity of the response of Iran to the book did not owe a considerable amount to both internal politics and the fact that Rushdie was seen as an apostate). MacIntyre meets this challenge by the attempt to find common ground between the different traditions.

> There must be genuine contact, and there need to be some within each tradition who are able to recognise that the other does offer a vital interpretation of the same realities (and therefore the conceptual incommensurabilities between the traditions must not be too great). There need to be some within each tradition who are able to enter ▶▶

imaginatively into the central beliefs of the other and recognise that problems that appear unresolvable in one tradition might be resolved in the other. This argument for some rational adjudication between the relative merits of rival traditions presupposes that there is no pre-existent rational foundation upon which the claims can be tested, but that that ground must be built as the debate ensues.

Are there limits to the ability of rival traditions to engage? There are some who argue that there are common values still: that all agree that nuclear destruction is wrong, or that the torture of the innocent for the fun of it is abhorrent. But I wonder if the stock of 'universal' moral sensibilities are as universal as they might seem to us in the West, or simply too few to build the kind of bridges required.

The question of what moral judgments are all about remains problematic. Are they the product of our sentiments of approval and disapproval, or are their roots in the eternal relationship of things as God ordained? Are they about increasing happiness and minimising grief, or about attaining the human good within a just society? Different traditions will opt for different answers to that question. However, for a tradition to last and be successful in continuing to attract new subscribers in a pluralist age when the alternatives are more widely perceived, it must be livable, attainable, and must encompass most of social life. It is my conviction that the Judaeo-Christian tradition does precisely that in a way which does build a stable and compassionate society. Even though not many beyond that tradition will agree that its roots are in the eternal fittingness of things because of the will of a good Creator God, on its merits of comprehensiveness, livability and stability it can be promoted in our postmodern age, not least because it answers the problem of how to build a community in a postmodern culture that is more than a collection of competing 'tribes'. Let MacIntyre have the last word.

> What matters at this stage is the construction of local forms of community within which civility and the intellectual and moral life can be sustained through the new dark ages which are already upon us. And if the tradition of the virtues was able to survive the horrors of the last dark ages, we are not entirely without grounds for hope. This time

however the barbarians are not waiting beyond the frontiers; they have already been governing us for some time.[16]

Caring Within the Tradition: The Relationship of Ethics to Pastoral Care

We come to the relationship of this way of doing ethics to pastoral care. What is needed is a community that is both the object of pastoral care and the context in which people make moral sense of their lives, embracing the ethical traditions of that community and aspiring to live according to the virtues which encapsulate how that ethical tradition is expressed in practical living. We turn now to the Church as such a community.

Churches as Moral Communities

Robin Gill argues for the importance of churches as distinct moral communities that can provide a more coherent logical and structural context for the 'doing of' pastoral care than secular society. There are three reasons why this is so. First, in church communities members look beyond themselves to the 'end', the *telos*, of their morality, located in the eternal. Secondly, religious and moral visions are passed on by those communities through a sense of belonging, story, Scripture, rituals and liturgy. These communities have the means to communicate and inculcate their morality. Thirdly, Gill argues that worship – the link between belief and community – changes the way people perceive the world. The first aspect is our concern here. Subsequent chapters will explore the relationship between community and pastoral care, and liturgy and pastoral care.

As we have already seen, more and more pastors are drawing away from a judgmental role and emphasising the love and compassion of God, with a pastoral consequence of an utter acceptance of all, whatever their moral state, and an unconditional positive regard to any given situation. This is not simply a failure of courage (although this is undoubtedly a factor sometimes) but rather the belief that such an attitude gives people the opportunity to gain their full stature and realise their full potential.

The roots of this attitude come from secular humanism rather than traditional Christian theology, and it infiltrates the Christian community via the training in pastoral care and counselling that many now receive. Authoritative advice is no longer part of effective pastoral care in some circles. Pastors are called upon to develop a warm relationship based entirely upon valuing those cared for, understanding them and a refusal to condemn them, says Andrew Jones.[17] Factors behind this shift from the traditional guiding role of pastoral care include a decline in pastoral power and authority in society as a whole, the problem of the plurality of moral opinion and the loss of absoluteness of religious ethics in general. Both the pastor and his or her religion are no longer authoritative in our culture, except in those enclaves of religious affiliation that churches have so easily become.

But when pastoral care ignores ethical considerations it is in danger of promoting a shortcut to the problems that people face, which is every bit as dangerous as the kind of 'quick fix' pastoral prayer that advocates of the importance of pastoral counselling, like myself, deplore. Don Browning, whose concerns for a moral context for pastoral care we shall consider in the next section of this chapter, outlines the psychological aspect of that danger: 'Without a fund of normative, religio-cultural meanings and symbols, the general confusion about the nature of good in living will itself be enough to cause untold personal difficulties, muddled lives, overt illness and emotional conflicts.'[18]

Pastoral counselling and therapy as a means of personal growth and deep change of heart and life need not be effective only when issues of personal morality are 'bracketed out'. John Hoffman has said:

> Without love, acceptance, forgiveness, there is no healing, no regeneration, no restoration of a broken life or of a poisoned relationship. But equally, without a strong moral witness which is willing to affirm goodness and condemn evil, without the courage to risk oneself and one's relationship for a principle, a people perish.[19]

The pastoral dilemma for the pastor is how to care in an accepting way and also 'toe the party line', how to be accepting and also represent the moral position. Take the person wanting to leave a marriage and sue for divorce because they no longer respect or love their partner. How does the pastor continue to help that person to know acceptance in the Christian community, and love and support through the discomfort of the divorce, and also advocate the principle of lifelong commitment, 'for better, for worse', that is the Christian ideal? Where does condemnation of too easy a breaking of covenant, or too loose a commitment to continuing to work at the marriage, come? Many would argue it has no place at all in the personal, one-to-one encounter, even if it is proclaimed publicly in the course of teaching the faith and its lifestyle. But this position has the stench of hypocrisy about it, lacking the courage in the personal encounter to apply what has been so easily proclaimed from the pulpit.

The difficulty lies partly in the understanding, even amongst the Christian community, that marriage is contractual, rather than the covenantal understanding of traditional moral theology. A contractual understanding considers the costs and benefits of remaining married or of divorce, and when the costs of marriage, emotionally and socially, outweigh the benefits, then it is appropriate to end the contract. Alan Storkey links this directly to individualism, and illustrates this by reference to John Locke, the seventeenth-century English philosopher and empiricist, who argued that there was no reason why husband and wife should not dissolve their marriage contract after the children had grown up.[20] However, if marriage is a covenant, then it is not primarily a legal, economic or sexual relationship (although it will be all of those things in some measure), but rather a relationship that takes its norms and structures from the kind of sacrificial love and faithfulness that God has towards his creation, exemplified in Christ's love for the Church.[21]

The call for an ethical dimension to pastoral care has been made most consistently by the American pastoral theologian Don Browning.[22] We now turn to his attempts to call for a revival of the traditional role of the moral community as a community where practical moral reasoning takes place, facilitating a mode of enquiry that will help its members develop a framework of meaning for the whole of life.

Browning and Pastoral Care as Ethical Discourse

In *The Moral Context of Pastoral Care* Browning argues that the practice of pastoral care has become severed from the religio-ethical belief systems that used to provide the undergirding to its community context. He argues that the processes of secularisation and pluralisation are instrumental in bringing about this split, together with the privatisation of faith and ethics that robs ethics of its status as public discourse. (Elaine Graham characterises this understanding of the processes at work in modernity as Weberian in nature.) He also views religious developments in Protestantism as instrumental in detaching ethical guidance from its ecclesial context (unlike the Roman Catholic Church, which continues to root pastoral guidance in a tradition of moral theology). Thus, pastoral counsellors, adopting the 'value-neutral claims of psychotherapy'[23] in non-directive counselling, failed to notice the implicit norms inherent in all practices of care, a point discussed further below. We do need to note at this point, however, the recent growth in interest in the aims of psychoanalysis, in which its values are implicit.[24]

Far from being value-free, psychoanalysis has explicit aims. For Freud,

> our aim will not be to rub off every peculiarity of human character for the sake of schematic 'normality', nor yet to demand that the person who has been 'thoroughly analysed' shall feel no passions and develop no internal conflicts. The business of the analysis is to secure the best possible psychological conditions for the functions of the ego; with that it has discharged its task.[25]

Freud sought in psychoanalysis to explain so much repressed material that not only were the symptoms from the patient's anxieties and inhibitions overcome, but there was no need for the patient to fear a repetition of the pathological processes concerned.

The resistance to moralising emerges early in the writings of Freud's disciples. Ernest Jones describes psychoanalysis as having:

> the single aim of enabling the patient to arrive, on the one hand, at a more complete knowledge of himself, bringing with it ▶▶

> more self-control and greater capacity for adaptation; and on the other hand, at the fullest possible measure of independence. If the physician goes beyond this aim and, assuming the position of a moralist, teacher or guide, proffers a solution of the difficulty based upon his own judgment and necessarily influenced by subjective factors, he thereby oversteps the limits of psychoanalysis, mistakes its mode of operation and stultifies its purpose.[26]

In the years between the two World Wars a number of aims appear: the disappearance of the presenting problem, good appraisal of strengths and weaknesses, more loyal inter-personal relationships with well-chosen objects, free functioning of abilities in productive work and full heterosexual functioning with potency and pleasure. There emerge some implicit values, such as the moral goods of loyalty in human relationships, and effective work, whilst same-sex relationships, or inversions, are disapproved of. The aims are clearly wider than simply the resolution of the transference neurosis, and a residue of the Judeao-Christian moral framework is present in these aims.

With the post-war period, aims become more focused upon self-knowledge and self-fulfilment. Karen Horney adds improvements in relationships and the discovery of the true nature of the personality to symptom cure. 'The aim of the analysis consists in the patient getting to know himself, how he is (current self), to make a new orientation and the finding of the true self possible (real self).'[27] The primary aim is of self-knowledge, derived from the process of elucidation, the leap from dark to light, in order to integrate feelings and events (in other words to make sense). Glueck offers two supplements to this: a more complete self-realisation, the becoming of an individual in his or her own right, liberated from inhibiting fears and anxieties which render difficult or impossible the facing of life's issues honestly and courageously; and a satisfying self-acceptance. He considers these goals of self-understanding, self-acceptance and self-realisation to be indispensable to the achievement of a competence for self-direction. Again, we note the autonomy of the individual holds paramount value in the enterprise.

The pluralist and contingent character of postmodernism is seen in Sandler and Dreher's conclusions that a desirable outcome of ▶▶

analysis will vary from one patient to another, and is not capable of being encompassed by one definition or measured by one single criterion. The cultural influence on psychotherapy is considerable, and throughout its history there has been a reluctance to be clear about the moral values which inform this therapy or that school of counselling.

Browning is not wanting to return to a pre-modern fundamentalist position, a kind of return to some ethical golden age. He remains committed to a pluralist, modern world as the only realistic context in which to engage with pastoral care. But he is convinced that all sorts of pastoral care are ultimately rooted in religious, community beliefs, expressed for instance in myths and narratives.

While pastoral care must be exercised within those ethical norms of the community, it can also be critical of the theological tradition. This is often seen when Christians with fairly closed sets of beliefs, articulated in terms of what is affirmed rather than what remains uncertain, become involved in pastoral care and, particularly, counselling. The actual experience of practice, of people, challenges the basic theological beliefs and frameworks of belief. The conviction that 'in Christ there is a new creation, the old has passed', interpreted to mean that since conversion the pre-conversion past has become powerless to affect the present behaviours and emotions, is challenged by the very obvious ways, in practice, that the old continues to have a major influence upon the present. Upbringing, past trauma or abuse is not eradicated by the conversion experience which was meant to 'answer all of the problems of the past'.

It is often claimed that a choice is needed between continuing to hold firm to those beliefs in an unchanging way, and thus denying the reality of pastoral experience (or implying a very deficient conversion, or poverty of discipleship), or modifying belief in the face of new experience. Those who choose the latter option are in effect subjecting the theological tradition to the critique of human experience. Those who choose the former ring-fence their faith against experience. In their extreme expressions neither of those options allows for the actual presence of the God who is present in all places, but often perceived to be absent. In place of the stark choice is needed a dialectic between faith and experience, knowledge and practice. This epistemological stance has pastorally advantageous consequences, for it does not shipwreck the carer's faith, seek to deny the client's experience, or subject it to a straitjacket. Instead there is a proper dialogue between those two which one could describe as incarnational, the creative tension of belonging to this world and another. It also has the consequence, potentially, of bringing about a wholeness to the carer's faith and experience, rather than the common split between sacred and secular, Church and world, or psychological understanding and religious belief.

Browning is not content that Christian ethical and pastoral discourse should be confined to the Christian community only, with credence and viability limited to that community. He follows David Tracy in wanting to insist that Christian moral discourse should be publicly accessible. This question of the relationship of the normative Christian ethic to the wider public arena is one that we have already encountered in our discussion of MacIntyre. Tracy's means of enabling discourse between traditions and communities is to establish mutually critical ways of engaging the interpretations of the Christian tradition with the contemporary cultural situation; in other words, letting Church and world talk together.[28] Talk about God, about faith, must not become mere private language.

Christian theology, if it is to hold up

> its head in public, must employ criteria and methods which are, so to speak, common property, acknowledged and used by the wider intellectual public of philosophers, historians, natural scientists, sociologists and the rest. The theologian cannot appeal to private authorities or experiences to support what he says.[29]

The roots of this way of relating theology and culture are found in the tradition which begins with Paul Tillich's method of correlation. Tillich has been a potent influence upon pastoral theology in the United States because of his integration of theology and psychodynamic psychology, where 'sin' and 'redemption' are understood as 'estrangement' and 'reconciliation', and it is not surprising that ▶▶

the correlative way of relating theology and culture, rather than a confrontational way, has proved important in the concern to ground theology and practice of pastoral care firmly in the public arena.[30]

Its antithesis is in the method advanced by George Lindbeck,[31] whereby the task of theology is not so much to relate its claims to the public realm, but to concentrate on making clear the faith of a particular community, showing how it is internally coherent and how it illumines human experience. For Lindbeck, doctrines are neither claims to truth (that is, first-order truth claims, mirroring objective reality), as conservatives think, nor expressions of inner human experiences, as the liberal tradition has emphasised from Schleiermacher onwards. They are more like the rules of discourse of the believing community, constituting the communally accepted norms by which the community instructs its members how to live and think about reality. Like Karl Barth, Lindbeck is contending that Christian theology ought to be 'church dogmatics' that help Christian people to articulate and understand their faith. Unlike Barth, however, he is agnostic regarding the correspondence of religious truth claims to a wider reality. We cannot trespass beyond the internal workings of the story that the faith tells.

This relativistic and pluralist position is postmodern, engaging creatively with the scepticism towards absolute truth that we have seen is so pervasive in postmodernity. It invites adherents of, say, Christianity to live as though it were true that Jesus is Lord and rose again from the dead. It confines the task of theology to the internal coherence of a particular community, rather than attempting to make grand claims to public truth. Browning wants to do more than articulate the moral claims of the Christian community and relate them to the task of pastoral care. He wants to make them publicly available and point to a way of living that is true for all: pastoral care as public activity.

In another way Tracy is important for our discussion of the relationship of Christian ethics to the wider world. He is critical of those theologies which are too obsessed with the 'crisis of cognitive claims', the attempt to ground the truth claims of theology in the same soil as other areas of Enlightenment rationality, and which have contributed to the alienating notions of reason as purely technical and notions of practice as mere technique.[32] Pastoral care becomes the application of techniques of counselling or guidance, robbed of personal engagement and commitment, genuine compassion and identification of carer with cared for. A shift from theory to praxis is emancipating; it 'can clarify that the major question in our situation is not the crisis of cognitive claims, but the social–ethical crisis of massive suffering and widespread oppression and alienation in an emerging global culture'. Authentic disclosure of truth in this way will be transformational, involving not only the question 'What do I believe?', but also 'What should I do?' Pastoral care with a moral imperative will therefore not only be concerned with the compassionate support of people in need, but also the transformation of people to more wholesome ways of living, more loving human relationships and greater holiness.

So, in our brief look at Don Browning we have encountered a dilemma. If pastoral care is to embrace a Christian moral perspective, offering guidance as well as healing and sustaining care, in what way does that Christian perspective relate to the wider realm? If pastoral care is to be more than just the care of those who are already 'believers', and is to function, as I believe it must, as the care of the whole Church for the whole world (and thus seize the opportunities for it to embrace the mission potential of caring in a postmodern world), in what way can the Christian ethic be normative for those who do not subscribe to its truth claims? There are those, like George Lindbeck, who say it cannot function in this way, and those who argue for a postmodern understanding of truth claims would agree.

However, the Christian faith does not claim to be just a local expression of one truth amongst many, but actually to describe how things really are. In affirming Jesus Christ as Lord, Christians do not think they are playing a private language game, but affirming his actual existence and deity. This is expressed not as a theoretical statement, but as a means of expressing their commitment to the rule and lordship of Christ: it is a confession of faith. Whether or not the story Christians tell is actually 'true' may be a question that Lindbeck says is unanswerable, and of less importance than the way in which the story enables people to live in community, but it is still of central importance to many believers in the story and to many to whom that story is commended as 'truth'.

Browning wants to be able to commend the morality in pastoral care beyond the confessing community. He also 'reconnects pastoral practice to traditions of moral theology'[33] but takes too little notice of the challenges to his modernistic framework that are made by postmodern critiques of rationalism. Is there another way in which the relationship of the view of reality to which Christians subscribe (theology and ethics) can be related to the wider public realm, so that the moral dimensions of pastoral care are not dismissed as 'only for the Christians' and nothing, particularly or necessarily, to do with anyone else? There is another way, and one which owes much to the community traditions that MacIntyre describes. We turn to this way forward as the next step in our quest for an ethic in pastoral care which is both normative for the Christian community and a search for publicly accountable truth, (one that can be commended to the wider world of competing and often mutually incomprehensible communities or tribes that compose the postmodern world). Because, for Christians, ethics is rooted in their understanding of the faith, it must be a way of 'doing theology' which will give us the tools to also 'do ethics' in pastoral care.

Faith in Search of Understanding

Karl Barth highlighted Anselm's theological method in his *Fides Quaerens Intellectum*,[34] faith in search of understanding. For Anselm, as for Barth, the irreplaceable first step in the search for understanding of God was faith in him. It was from a position of faith that Anselm could proceed to understand the truth about him. In contrast, Barth argued, those who ground faith in some common human attribute of reason, as Protestant liberalism of the nineteenth century had done, were doomed to failure. In the *Proslogion* Anselm puts it thus:

> I desire in some measure to understand thy truth, which my heart believes. For I do not seek to understand in order to believe, but I believe in order to understand. For this too I believe, that unless I believe, I shall not understand.[35]

In this confessional way of doing theology, we would be committed to speech about God being public speech: it does refer to an objective reality beyond the community in which that speech is regulative and normative. In other words, it is ontologically true in every age and every place (contrary to the postmodernist theologians such as Lindbeck).

Is this a return to the old conservatism? I believe not. That was closed, impenetrable (it thought) to the impact of the wider search for knowledge, and actually very defensive in the face of criticism. A confessional way of doing theology is open to a dialogue with the truths that are derived from other areas of public knowledge, such as history or the natural sciences, in a way that believes that, ultimately, all truth is God's truth and reflects upon a reality that is his creation.

Neither is it a return to the older liberal tradition which sought a foundation in the demonstrable facts of reason. That search, the Enlightenment project, has been shown to be faulty, not least by its postmodern critics. The problem with the search for truth in that tradition lay not only in the definition of truth, but more importantly in the manner of the search, the epistemological stance which took an instrumental view of reason.

Polanyi[36] has demonstrated that the Kantian tradition viewed facts as the things which are 'out there' for the mind to grasp. Facts are facts, and it is the task of the scientist, or the detective with whom we opened Chapter 3, to determine them. He is fiercely critical of this stance, and describes a very different way of 'knowing' that is nearer to the actuality. Every act of knowing employs 'tools', concepts, words and so forth, which are taken for granted, their ontological status being pushed to the background. Polanyi is a philosopher of science, and it is in the scientific enterprise that he describes the way that progress is built upon 'theory' or a model, which is accepted in a way which is like faith. The scientist 'believes' certain things about the reality of the world in order to explore the particular problem he is concerned with. Once a theory is accepted by the scientific community it takes on the status that dogma has in religion. It is defended, has prophetic powers, its opponents are ridiculed like apostates. To explore one phenomenon requires a commitment to the truth of ▶▶

the models that describe all the other phenomena related to it. All this sounds very close to the religious way of knowing. In fact, theologians have not been slow to welcome Polanyi as one of their own, and to demonstrate that all of human knowing, including scientific understanding and religious understanding, proceed on similar epistemological lines involving personal commitment, faith and contingency.

Given Polanyi's scientific equivalent of *fides quaerens intellectum*, it is entirely proper that in the search for theological and moral truth we similarly start from a point of personal commitment. The truth for which we begin our search by personal commitment is not absolutely certain, nor beyond the shadow of a doubt, but it will be plausible and public. That personal commitment is to a tradition which has internal coherence and consistency, but also correspondence to reality. It is not enough to say that the Christian story is a consistent world. Works of fantasy are that, yet they are not 'real'. Star Trek is a consistent world, with narrative and understanding, but it is not the 'real' world (although it is interesting how many 'Trekkers' in our post-modern world act as if it is!). Similarly, J. R. R. Tolkien's *Lord of the Rings* is a consistent world, but despite its considerable moral and religious correspondence to the Christian story (which makes it such a 'human' book, and so popular), it is not the real world: it lacks geographical and historical correspondence. Its truthfulness lies in its allegorical relationship to the Christian story.

So, the first aspect of this way of 'doing theology' lies in its prior fiduciary commitment to the proper object of its study, which is not the human religious experience, but the God who gives himself to be known in Jesus Christ. The theologian is committed first, then, to the reality and knowability of his ultimate object of concern, namely the living God who has made and makes himself known. This commitment drives the theologian's quest for knowledge and understanding, undergirds that quest, and gives the quest its focus and concern.[37]

If Polanyi points the way to the starting-point of the quest, MacIntyre gives us the context for that quest. Theological enquiry is not an individualistic enterprise, but takes place in a community of those who are alive and those who are no longer alive on earth, but whose writings and understandings continue to speak to us. This is the tradition, in a MacIntyrean sense, that the Christian theologian is committed to. It is broader than the intellectual community of the theological faculty since it embraces the whole of the Christian community, worshipping, praying, believing and caring. This tradition is, in the theologian's hands at least, open to challenge from outside and must be open to reformulation.

There is always the danger that the community will not seek to be open to criticism, but will only be concerned to preserve, as in aspic, an existing formulation of belief. Such conservatism is sadly all too common, not only in doctrine but also in morals, but need not be the only option. The embracing of a new dynamism in the life of the Church through the charismatic movement and the ordination of women could point to the opposite. This is postmodern in its scepticism concerning the metanarrative of rationality and in its concerns to be found in a tradition, but it is critical of postmodernity in its belief in objective truth and in its ultimate rejection of relativism.

Thomas Oden describes his theology as 'Christian teaching that, having passed through a deep engagement in the assumptions of modernity, has rediscovered the vitality of the ancient ecumenical Christian traditions'.[38] It takes account of critical studies, and scientific and historical knowledge, and through the use of reason, helps us to remain coherent and cogent. Others in this enterprise would include Moltmann and Jungel, as well as Trevor Hart and Colin Gunton. It is a moderate way, one that I believe to be the most productive of living theology and important for effective pastoral care.

How Neutral is Value-free Counselling?

We began by describing how the value-free person-centred counselling has come to influence Christian pastoral care practice. In 1983 Bob Lambourne argued that therapy was a means of ethical persuasion[39] in which the therapist sought to persuade the client to do what was right. We have seen that Christian pastoral care ought to include ethical persuasion, but it has been seduced by the supposedly value-free status of Rogerian practice into abandoning its Christian ethical values. Gordon Lynch[40] argues that instead of substituting a neutral value environment for the manipulative and judgmental Christian one, in fact another more dangerous, because unspoken, set of values is substituted.

While few therapists would see their task as a dialogue in which they seek to persuade their client to adopt their ethical view, the values which the therapist holds are of great significance to the therapeutic encounter. Not only does the client have a notion of the good life which they wish to grow towards, the counsellor also has a notion of the good life which they hope their client will move towards. Rogers is explicit about what the good life consists of.[41] The good life is a process, a direction, not a destination, where there is psychological freedom to move in any direction. That process is characterised by an increased openness to experience and increasingly existential living (to live fully in each moment, unrestricted by preconceived notions of experience). It is also shown by an increasing trust in ourselves as 'doing what "feels right" proves to be a competent and trustworthy guide to behaviour which is truly satisfying', and by functioning more fully, we select 'that behaviour which in this moment of time will be most generally and genuinely satisfying'. The good life is precisely that which emerges from client-centred therapy. It is clear that this is a different conception to the Christian notion of the good life. The characteristics of this include: an increasing trust in God; an ability to select behaviour which is in accordance with the Christian community norms, and is not necessarily personally satisfying nor what feels right; and an ability to follow obligations as well as personal preferences.

Are Therapists Value-free?

In bracketing out their own values, therapists are not value-free. In fact, the very act of doing so implies an important value: the client must direct their own life, be in control of their own decisions. The underlying assumptions are the modernist, liberal autonomous human agent in control of his or her own life. The decisions to suspend values and which values to suspend (for instance, the decision to have the client sectioned under the Mental Health Act when the client is in danger of harming their own life or contemplating suicide) are themselves moral decisions by the therapist according to what they believe will be best for the client. Body language by the therapist and silence in response to ethical questions (such as 'Shall I have an abortion?' or 'Shall I seek a divorce?') all have an impact upon the client, even if a straight answer is not given (and I often avoid those straight answers in my counselling practice).

Lynch does not think that therapy is a hopelessly manipulative venture, however. He argues that certain responsibilities are incumbent upon the Christian pastoral counsellor. It is necessary to establish what vision of the good life is present in the counselling model that they use, and evaluate the adequacy of the good life as an expression of the Christian vision. Together with the wider Christian community, the pastoral counsellor must:

> engage in serious reflection as to whether the form of living that is ultimately inspired by Christian moral vision is healing or harmful . . . Serious moral reflection by Christian pastoral counsellors will therefore involve both a questioning of Christian moral understanding and a being questioned by Christian moral understanding.[42]

Since there is no value-free pastoral care, Christian counsellors and carers would do well to resist the substitution of the Christian moral tradition for a humanistic, and often hedonistic and self-centred, moral vision masquerading under the guise of neutrality. The choice is not between the value-free ethics of Rogerian counselling and the imposition of a restrictive Christian ethic, but between competing ethical visions. Ultimately, the one which builds the better community and gives not only fulfilment, but also courage and virtue, to its members might be the the preferable choice. I would contend that the Christian vision succeeds better by far than the Rogerian alternative.

In common with the theological tradition in which it is grounded, Christian ethics is a community enterprise and must remain open to change and transformation as that tradition is confronted by new evidence for the nature of reality. However, that openness to change is based upon the prior commitment of pastoral practitioners to the ethical norms of the tradition. That in itself is problematical. In the Christian tradition there are a variety of views on some ethical questions: is homosexual genital activity compatible with the Christian tradition; under what circumstances, if any, is abortion acceptable; or is it appropriate for divorcees to remarry? Debate rages within the Christian community over these issues. The conformity to 'the tradition' is difficult to establish in a straightforward way. At the heart of this question is the source of the authorities to which Christians look to establish their ethical norms, and the priority given to certain voices, particular texts, and Scripture in particular.

Suffice it to say here that I want to reject both the biblicist-fundamentalist reading of Scripture, which reduces it to one simple thing, and the historico–critical tradition, which reduces it to one critically established thing, as if the author's original intention could be that easily established. Both these approaches are reductionist and confuse the interpretation of the text with the text itself. When we want a fixed handle upon the Scriptures, so that they are subject to our human abilities, rather than remaining subject to the Spirit who inspired both the writer of the text and the community that supported or confronted him, there have been two traditional means of interpretation: an infallible papal interpretation, and a naive refusal to differentiate between text and meaning by Protestants. In common with our way of doing theology, we must turn to the community of faith to provide the context for the Spirit's work of reinterpreting, of speaking again, through this text. Here is a community of those who share the conviction that this is what this text means, as it is read and unfolded in the place where, distinctively, that community meets: under the Lordship of Christ in worship.

Through these means we can appropriate a normative ethic, and where debate rages still, act in humility towards one another and accept that we do not have all the answers. In fact, we do not even know what some of the questions really are, but we know enough to create a credible description of the tradition which is ours as Christians, and to live out in practical Christian living the consequences for that tradition within the community of faith. Pastoral care will then include not only the healing of the sick of soul and mind, but also the direction and guidance of all members of the community as a vital element of its task, the proclamation of the ethical ways in which reconciliation takes place, and the sustaining of the community in worship, attention to Scripture and compassionate love.

CHAPTER 6

Community

Overview

At the end of January 1997 two pieces of journalism appeared on the same day in the British broadsheet *The Independent*[1]. The first was a piece on the publication of the annual report from the Office for National Statistics, *Social Trends 27*. For the first time this compendium of the changes and trends in everything, from the number of pets we keep to the number of spouses we do not keep, included speculation on how our lives will look in 2020.

Some of this crystal-ball gazing is certain to become reality: an ageing, though not healthier, population, fewer children and a peak in population in 2023, after which deaths will exceed births and the whole trajectory of an increasingly aged population will be set. The fact that in thirty years time, if I am still alive (and statistically I should be), I will be amongst that vast elderly band, is a sobering thought. Take it as a sign of midlife crisis, if you will. I will probably have fled the city, and be living in a rural area, far from the bustle and crime of the inner city. I might, sadly, be amongst the one in three who live alone (though I doubt it: my wife has robust health and I reckon will see me out!) and I believe I will not be amongst the majority of people who will be divorced, despite writing this book. Over the next thirty years the number of divorced people will double, and I guess that more and more of my pastoral ministry will be exercised in the painful business of marriage breakdown, despite my best efforts at marriage preparation and sustenance. The task of marriage preparation will be less common, with only 49 per cent of people getting married, as opposed to 57 per cent in 1992.

The gap between rich and poor will be broader, with the wealthier increasingly employing the poorer in jobs that are personal or protective – nannies, domestics, etc. Maybe I will be someone's 'personal spiritual and pastoral carer' to help supplement the meagre pension that I will enjoy. Service sector jobs, many of them part-time, and the majority held by women (by then 45 per cent of the total workforce), will be increasing, but it remains to be seen if women will have finally succeeded in breaking through the glass ceiling to join, amongst the increasing numbers of managers and administrators, those who lead the professions, business and the media.

Will my children be amongst the minority who are married with children of their own? I like to picture myself spending Christmas with my sons, their wives and my grandchildren, reminiscing about the good old days of the late 1990s when I was a minister in Stevenage and took a three-month sabbatical break to write a book. This endangered species, the so-called traditional family (though actually far from traditional) so beloved of politicians, is already in the minority today, and in thirty years time will have slipped even further towards a small minority social phenomenon. Many questions about the future remain mercifully unanswered: will the Church be stronger or weaker, will we be part of Europe or an offshore irrelevance (you can see where my sympathies lie) and will we be a better community, or an increasingly fragmented society?

The second article was by John Tusa. In it he plays the game of constructing the good society, in best 'if I ruled the world' style. He makes a pungent critique of the postmodern society, which will serve as a backcloth for the discussion of community that will be our theme in this chapter. I am not sure that I would agree with him that:

> a good society would be one where all personal counselling would be banned on the grounds that it does more harm than good, because it is based on bastard and half-digested Freudianism and because it peddles the fantasy that well-meaning chat, deep concern and a readiness to share can solve emotional problems and smooth away the effects of tragedy and shock,

but much else in his essay I would affirm. He argues that a 'good society' is one where rights, privileges and duties are balanced. The modernist emphasis upon rights (we saw from the last chapter that this is an attempt to universalise a replacement for divine law) has been met with a reactive emphasis upon obligations: of absent fathers to their children through the Child Support Agency, for instance. 'A good society would judge measures according to the extent that they conferred rights but answered the calls of duty at the same time.'

He is fiercely critical of the language of the market used in almost every human transaction. It reduces cooperation between individuals, creates administrative and bureaucratic barriers, sets a price on ideas, destroys a sense of corporate community and fragments a sense of corporate belonging. His experience in the BBC World Service certainly informs those perceptions from first-hand experience. Society becomes a collection of marketing categories, whether in their mnemonical form, yuppies, dinkies and the like, or their habitative form, 'Pebble-dash Subtopians', 'Rootless Renters' and 'Stylish Singles'. Real people are reduced to minute selling units for the convenience of the market. 'You no longer inhabit a society in common with other individuals,' but 'we live in a world of niches, where each one is separated from, wholly indifferent to and even hostile to the values, wishes and interests of those in other niches.' Rather than integration, the market thrives by fragmentation and replaces citizens with marketing target groups. The overriding question is not what you believe, who you are or how you live, but what you can be persuaded to buy.

Ivan Ilyich emphasised the importance of 'conviviality' as a crucial social value. Unless social activity, some new urban development or a social project increased human interaction, personal exchange, or conviviality, it was useless, he claimed. As a

Christian I might replace 'conviviality' with fellowship, *koinonia*, or we might simply call it friendship. 'Where is friendship today?' asks Tusa. 'Not in the marketplace. Not in cyberspace. But then fraternity has always been the weak link in the holy Republican triumvirate.' Many of the themes of Tusa's critique of our social ills are encompassed by the socio-political movement called 'communitarianism'. (I am not suggesting that John Tusa is a communitarian. He may be, but I do not know.)

From Nietzsche to Niche: What is Wrong with the Lack of Community?

The breakdown of community has profound consequences for pastoral care, since the good ordering and compassionate functioning of a society is dependent upon there being a community which works. As we have seen, the context for pastoral care is the community, whether the Christian community of the Church, or the wider community of the neighbourhood, city or nation. I am not an advocate of the lone-ranger style of pastoral care, where it is utterly individualistic, but locate one of the most important pastoral tasks where the individual is in relationship to others. If a community is really working well and is stable and healthy, many of the tasks of pastoral care will take care of themselves, will be accomplished though the commerce of family and neighbourhood life, and will not necessarily require the intervention of specialised 'pastoral carers'.

One of the remarkable things about the current trends in Western culture is the way in which care has been both privatised and institutionalised, and also depersonalised. The burden of care of the elderly, the disabled and the mentally handicapped rests either on the privatised family, the attenuated nuclear family of, say, a single daughter caring for an elderly mother, or an older couple caring for an adult handicapped son, or else upon an institution, such as a residential home for the elderly. The caring that formerly took place at community or neighbourhood level, whereby the burden of care is shared amongst a group of acquaintances, family and friends, is generally absent today. For the roots of this change we must turn to the processes of urbanisation and fragmentation.

The postmodernists take some inspiration from Nietzsche, the mid-nineteenth-century German philosopher who reacted to his pietistic Lutheran upbringing by announcing the 'death of God'. He is fêted as the prophet of the postmodern age, anticipating as he does the 'will to power' as the basis of human nature (Foucault's theme), the 'resentment' that arises when that will is frustrated (which is restructured by Freud as repression), and the corruptions of human nature that religions encourage, especially the values of meekness and humanity, so central to Christianity. He sees the world as 'text', denies the existence of essences and celebrates plurality of interpretations and the fragmentation of the self. This is to be replaced by the *Übermensch*, the superman, who rises above passion and gives creative style to his existence, perhaps as the artist, whose 'will to power' is expressed in artistic creativity. Experience has shown, however, that when power is given freedom to be used unfettered, it is more often used as oppression over others and in a form of self-fulfilment that rides roughshod over others.

I would not want to suggest that the responsibility for the collapse of community should be laid at Nietzsche's door, but he does serve as a prophetic figure pointing to many of the changes in values that have contributed to that collapse. Those changes have emphasised rights against obligations, self-fulfilment against self-sacrifice, the meeting of my needs rather than the meeting of others' needs. There is a kind of martyrdom spirit in some expressions of Christianity that views the recognition and meeting of personal needs as entirely sinful: to be holy is to be totally self-denying. I still shudder to remember the charismatic couple who visited my previous church and proceeded to 'discern' a 'spirit of self' in everyone present which called for urgent 'deliverance'! Clearly, such an understanding of the place of the self in the Christian life is pathological.

What is dangerous is the self-centredness that has no room for others, nor any room for God. This self-dependence is expressed in the story of the fall of Adam and Eve, who are promised that they will be like God if they eat the fruit. That kind of self-dependence, so soon expressed in the words of Cain, 'Am I my brother's keeper?', is at the heart of what sin means, for we were created to live with our own self related to God, dependent upon him, and at peace with him. Salvation is the rediscovery that we can remain our true selves, but live not to our selves, but to God as we depend upon his grace for living. We remain our selves, for God made us to be so, but in relationship to him first, and as a consequence, in relationship to others. The kind of *Übermensch* spirit of postmodernism ultimately separates us from others and call us to live simply for ourselves, with little regard for others' needs or rights, so long as our needs and rights are being met.

So, self-reliance can easily absorb the space that is meant to be filled with reliance upon others in a network of shared obligations and rights. In this regard, self-fulfilment can have as bad a press in some Christians' minds as self-reliance. God actually wants us to be fulfilled; after all, did not Jesus' promise life in all its fullness?[2] Nigel Biggar says:

> One reason . . . why it is a mistake to dismiss as sheer self-indulgence our current devotion to the value of self-fulfilment is that, to some extent, it represents a healthy corrective to the more life-denying culture of our recent past. And it is a corrective that Christians who really believe in the goodness of God and of all that he has made, should find easy to applaud.[3]

It is the sheer self-fulfilment of serving others, of being at our most human when we give rather than take, that explains in large part why some give their lives in service of others. If it were not self-fulfilling, I cannot see many people pursuing such living for long. It is not self-fulfilment that is wrong, but its pursuit with little or no concern for the consequences to others. When my self-fulfilment, expressed in the adrenalin buzz of driving at over 100 m.p.h., results in the loss of freedom to be self-fulfilled by the driver with whom I collide and who becomes disabled as a result, that fulfilment should be, and is, condemned by legislation. Our freedoms, our self-fulfilment, are always relative in a just society.

It comes as no surprise, then, that a society dedicated to the pursuit of self-interest with little regard to the impact on the other person, will be a sick and unhappy society. That sickness, expressed in levels of mental and emotional illness, suicide rates, stress levels and relational dysfunction, is precisely what we have in the West today. The overall belonging to a society or nation is being replaced by a fragmented belonging to a plethora of social niches, each with its own subculture. The Christian Church is in danger of becoming one such subculture, with its own music, books, values, beliefs, holidays and so forth. It is now possible to read only Christian books, bought from shops that only sell Christian books and music, go on holiday with Christian travel firms, listen to Christian music, watch Christian TV, exercise to Christian aerobics videos and be educated in Christian schools. Some see this as an advantage. I prefer to view it as a dangerous withdrawal from the wider culture into a Christian ghetto, from which we might occasionally sally forth on an evangelistic campaign to win a few trophies and take a few hostages.

Postmodernism at its bleakest is sceptical about the possibilities of anything but fragmentation, loss of common language of meaning and mutually incomprehensible traditions and cultures. People lose a sense of civic duty and keep themselves to themselves. Who now reprimands the youngster who drops litter in the street? Who, indeed, risks reprimanding any children other than their own, for risk of incurring the wrath of their parents? It is in recognition of such symptoms that the communitarian movement was established in the United States, and has continued to affect domestic politics in Britain in the 1990s.

The Communitarian Agenda

The two-hundred-year-long contest between the ideologies of corporatism and individualism has been decisively settled in favour of individualism (at least for the moment, anyway). In Britain, the influence of the political Left, seen in union power, for instance, has diminished and the decade of the 1980s and, so far, the 1990s has seen the rise of Thatcherism, the destruction of the influence of the old corporate social welfare structures in favour of individual responsibility and, most potent of all, the collapse of the Warsaw Pact and the fall of the Berlin Wall.

In the sociopolitical arena there are signs, however, of a new spirit dubbed 'communitarianism' by its champion, Professor Amitai Etzioni from Washington University. His search for a third way between an ever-expanding welfare state and an unfettered free market has crossed the political divide. Bill Clinton's manifesto was based on communitarian principles, and Etzioni has contacts with Chancellor Kohl, Gordon Brown of the British Centre-Left and David Willets, a key thinker behind John Major's 'Civic Conservatism'.

The starting point for the communitarian diagnosis of the crisis facing the postmodern culture is the liberal emphasis upon the rights that people demand. This encourages people to ask for assistance, but not to offer it. There needs to be a new balance of rights with responsibilities, or as Tony Blair put it, 'we do owe a duty to more than ourselves.'[4] This emphasis upon rights is evident in the family, where Etzioni believes much damage has been done by the 'parenting deficit': the rights of parents to work and enjoyment results in the loss of rights by the less powerful members of families, the children, to care, support, moral guidance and the presence of their parents. He is not advocating a simple return of women to the home from the workplace[5] but a more active involvement in parenting by both parents. Issues for pastoral care will be highlighted in later chapters, but suffice it to say here that the communitarian agenda will reverberate with some of the pastoral priorities we identify, but by no means all.

The communitarian manifesto recognises that there are four levels of responsibility in society:

(i) the person; we do for ourselves what we reasonably can;
(ii) the family; reversing the trend in modern welfare states to strip responsibilities from the family and deposit them with impersonal state-run institutions, such as nursing homes for the elderly;
(iii) the local community, with provision for support of the mentally ill, housebound etc; and
(iv) society at large, which has a responsibility to those who cannot help themselves, to share unexpected calamities and to fund these through treating entitlements as taxable income.

In the past there were other structures in society which carried part of the social load of their own communities, families and individuals. Communitarians say it is time to rediscover them and create a new welfare system in which all can honourably and reliably discharge their part. It is at this neighbourhood level that churches often become involved in social action projects to communicate something of the gospel in action. Child Contact centres, toddler groups, youth work, unemployment projects or homeless havens are attempts by the Church as a voluntary agency to offer pastoral care somewhere between the level of the family or individual and the institutionalised public service.

Politics must rediscover an ethical basis, says Etzioni, and people must find a sense of mutual responsibility through reviving institutions of family, neighbourhood and community. This calls for responsibility in family life, child care, and neighbourliness. This may seem like a very reasonable alternative to the dichotomy of free market and socialism, with much to commend it to Christians. We like talk of responsible family life, community spirit and being good neighbours, for it reminds us of an era when the Church had more influence; a 'back to the blitz' nostalgia. However, communitarianism fails to take sufficient note of one major human characteristic: our innate sinful selfishness. It lacks the power to change the human heart, the power of forgiveness and godly compassion. Etzioni is a firm opponent of authoritarianism and the 'religious Right' in America. He wants a new morality which does not require people to 'consult clergy or a book by Kant'.[6] Indeed, there is little talk in communitarianism of removing rights: 'We hold that the family . . . can be saved, without forcing women to stay at home or otherwise *violating their rights* . . . We hold that our call for increased social responsibilities . . . is *not a call for curbing rights*. On the contrary, strong rights presume strong responsibilities.'[7] (The italics are mine.)

But the source of this new spirit is rather elusive. Etzioni cannot bring himself to relinquish the liberal values of his modernist culture and fails to see that more than a rather sentimental desire for society to be more responsible than it is at present is needed. Roger Scruton, in a review of the book *The Spirit of Community*, argues that:

> It seems not to occur to him that the enormous sacrifice involved in monogamous marriage is possible only in the context of an elaborate social endorsement – an endorsement which frowns on deviant sexual behaviour, on promiscuity, and on the habit of demeaning human love through pornography. He recognises the terrible social cost of illegitimacy, but makes no mention of the principal thing which served to limit it – shame enforced by ridicule.[8]

It is precisely such enforcing social attitudes which are absent, and which Etzioni does not wish to see returning. He takes too modest a view of human selfishness and irresponsibility and too high a view of the capacity of reason to change the human heart. The political theorist Stephen Holmes was quoted by Samuel Brittan recently:

> Communitarian anti-liberals suggest that once people overcome their self-interest, they necessarily act in an admirable and public spirited way . . . but this leaves out of account the prominent place of selfless cruelty in human affairs. It is much easier to be cruel in the course of acting in the cause of others or for the cause than while acting for one's own thing. Those who have homosexuals shot in the name of the Islamic revolution . . . cannot be accused of anti-social individualism or base self-interest.[9]

Exactly. The world Etzioni wants to inhabit is one where all the benefits of community – neighbourliness, care for the needy, sustaining and stable family relationships, and so forth – are won without the high costs of coercion, authoritarian attitudes, shame and humiliation of the deviant and an intolerance of the 'other'. It is a call for the liberal dues to be paid, but only by those who want to do so. He argues that 'the moral voice is the main way communities keep moral order, other than relying on individual consciences,'[10] but locates those moral values in the vague 'what we all share' of the liberal individual disconnected from religious beliefs.

The specific programmes Etzioni calls for are a reduction of the parenting deficit, whereby parents spend more time with their children (and therefore less time at work) and the use of child care facilities for the pre-school child is severely restricted; a curb on the rush to divorce for those whose marriages are in difficulty; the teaching of a 'set of values' to all schoolchildren (recently advocated by the British School Curriculum authority), and a commitment to 'core values' by the great majority. The social and economic benefits may be generally recognised, but the means by which these goals are reached is much less clear. However, it does point towards an opportunity for the Church to seize the spirit of the day, transform it and demonstrate it in reality through prioritised pastoral care.

The Trinity: The Theological Grammar for Community

Unlike the rationalist values of the communitarian movement, Christianity locates the reason for community in something transcendent: in God himself. The Christian vision of community is derived from the vision of God himself, and its manner of existence takes its origins from the doctrine of the Trinity.[11] In the event of God's self-revelation in Jesus Christ as the God who saves mankind, it is not so much simply the saving of individuals as the creating of a new community of persons in relationship that is important.[12] The significance of the individual is never lost, but is relativised by the place of the community of believers. It is this characteristic of persons-in-relationship which is the image of the triune God seen in mankind.

> The *imago Dei* does not lie so much in particular human attributes, such as reason, moral choice or spirit, as in the fundamental characteristic of the God revealed in Christ as Father, Son and Spirit, relationship in unity or Persons in relationship. It is the God who is already a community of Persons and who elects to create a universe crowned, at least on this planet, by humankind, who images himself in man and woman. In the absolute gift of creation, and in the corresponding absolute gift of the creation of the redeemed community, the Church, God expresses his Trinitarian life in making community. That community exists in God's freedom and love as a self-giving expression of himself and thus the redemption of ▶▶

creation is foreshadowed in the free and loving existence of the community of Christ, 'the kingdom of the Son he loves'.[13] The Church has as its end the kingdom of God, brought about not by ecclesiastical act, but by God's act in Christ, and points to that end by being the new community of saved and redeemed men and women. Here, the overriding call is to reject self-interest and love one another, 'looking not only to your own interests, but also to the interests of others'.[14] In this way we point to the Kingdom.

It is the task of the Church to enable persons to become true persons in relationship to God and to the other. True personhood is only possible in relationship to the God who is the ground of being, and that relationship leads to renewed relationship to other human beings. In this way also we point to the Kingdom. Augustine saw the relationship between the two, thought of God and thought of the peaceful community, in his vision of the heavenly city, *The City of God*, where the perfect peace of Heaven could be present, albeit imperfectly, in time and a fallen world.

The Church has often discerned, wrongly, that drawing boundaries around itself is the way to create that pure and peaceful community which echoes the heavenly Kingdom. Excluding the 'sinner' provides the best chance of purifying the remnant, it believes, and thus to promote some practices and to disallow others creates a body approximating on earth what is true in heaven. But the Church has misunderstood its mission if it follows that worldly route, for it only serves to fossilise what should be dynamic, a nomadic city, a pilgrim people at its furthest from the divine community which is its calling when it stands still, becomes stuck and narrow. The way to the heavenly city might be narrow, but those who tread it must have large and generous hearts.

Living in this new community, then, takes a realistic view of human waywardness: the Church is a company of sinners, and will be prone to failing. It also takes a realistic view of the power of God to change the human heart and will therefore always be aspiring to more than it currently experiences of loving care and compassionate living in the community. We experience what it is to love when we first experience what it is to be loved, in families, or perhaps in the Church. 'We can only understand what it means to be accepted by God if we are first accepted by God's people; by God's *community*.'[15] The human experience of friendship is what helps keep community human.

The Church's Understanding of Community

Community is the context for pastoral care, but the attempts to reconstruct community by the communitarian movement are naïve. We do not want to make grand claims for the Church's attempts, nor enter into a triumphalist vision of the Church as the simple answer to the pastoral needs of a whole society. There are, however, distinctive elements to the Church's understanding of community, derived from its Trinitarian roots, that point pastoral care towards its role in building community in a fragmented world.

First, Christian community is personal, built on real and varied expressions of friendship. Of course, there are churches where friendship is minimal, relationships are tense and fragmentary and abusive power play is the basic mode of existence. These are not following in the way of Christ, nor are they a proper example of the kind of community that the Church is called to be. Churches are just as capable of being dysfunctional as families are, and often the kinds of pastoral practice and care in the past history of a church have been instrumental in producing that dysfunctionality. Workaholic pastors who see their existence in terms of meeting everybody's expectations, and performing the pastoral equivalents of wiping snotty noses and cleaning up dirty nappies, inevitably produce infantile communities who react angrily to the first minister who refuses to play the game and expects adult people to take some responsibility for themselves.

In contrast to this caricature is the Church as the community where there is genuine care and love, but also where adult responsibility is expected of and encouraged in people. We can never be absolutely sure that we are unconditionally loved and accepted, but churches should be places where we can be accepted for the true people we are rather than the nice people we want everyone else to believe we are. Sadly this is all too infrequent, and so an urgent pastoral task is to create communities of honesty and integrity. Communities where friendships flourish are pastoral communities, caring for one another because of the bonds of friendship that are forged.

Since the God who reveals himself in Christ is the God who forgives, the second pastoral task for building communities is that of creating forgiveness as a foundational value. This value of forgiveness is rare in contemporary culture. It is the opposite to the scapegoating that projects 'evil' onto certain individuals. The way the tabloid media bayed for the blood of the two boys guilty of murdering Jamie Bulger in 1993 was obscene, but it took its cue from the way society deals with its own inability to forgive, and was aided by the soundbite that Prime Minister John Major offered: 'We must condemn a little more, and understand a little less.' Blake Morrison, in his account of that trial, describes the young men who gathered at the court 'wanting to kill the kids who killed the kid, because there's nothing worse than killing a kid'.[16] The scapegoating and demonising of 'evil killers' is an extreme, but symbolic, pointer to a culture that no longer believes in redemption, in the possibility of change. Such a culture loses faith in humanity because it does not know what to make of forgiveness: it confuses it with forgetting, with condoning, with weakness.

Forgiveness is also to be distinguished from the other response of indifference, of saying it does not matter. Forgiveness takes the seriousness of sin and the reality of evil, and allows hope to triumph over revenge. It says 'that we believe in the potential for change, that we choose life over death, that . . . we endeavour in whatever way we can to remain human'.[17] Communities that know the reality of forgiveness, that do not keep accounts, that offer new beginnings because God offers new beginnings, are urgently needed. However, an understanding of God's forgiveness is vital in the building process, and those communities which know that best will be able to demonstrate that best. Sadly, churches are often very unforgiving places, more concerned for their purity of life than their openness to sinners. Pastoral care, and especially counselling, offers the possibility of a way forward by allowing people to face their fears, their disappointments and their own failings in a constructive way. As Jesus says, 'he who has been forgiven little loves little.'[18]

Christianity claims that the life of Jesus of Nazareth, enshrined in the narratives of the Gospels, shows what that forgiving love looks like. These narratives tell of a man shaping the lives of his disciples, coping with their ambition, vanity, faithlessness and even betrayal in such a way that, after his resurrection, the community impetus is almost irresistible. The continuing existence of that community of faith is witness to the power of those stories and of the presence of the Spirit of Christ and is the sign of hope that genuine human life, always in community, can be reappropriated.

> Christianity is primarily about this hope for community. It remembers perfect community as once instantiated by the shores of Lake Galilee. It is not that we have a few fragments *in lieu* of the real presence of the resurrected Christ, but that these fragments are the real saving presence; they provide us – within the whole network of tradition within which they belong – with a new language of community.[19]

Pastoral care is exercised within communities, and its greatest challenge is to enable those communities to become shaped by the gospel as a sign of hope to all creation.

PART TWO

Priorities in Pastoral Care

Introduction

In this second part we are going to explore the priorities and methods for pastoral care in the postmodern world. There will necessarily be much continuity with the practice of the past few decades as well as some continuity with the experience of the past two thousand years of church history, but there will also need to be readjustments to those priorities in order to face the new cultural challenges, the new mission possibilities and the new theological nuances that arise from those challenges.

Ernst Troeltsch said something like the gospel is always being forwarded on to a new address because the culture to which it is addressed is constantly moving. The same is true of pastoral care. People's needs, traumas, joys and sorrows are remarkably similar to those of Shakespeare's day, or Isaiah's, come to that. Joy attends the keenly anticipated birth of a much-loved child, sorrow the death of a beloved friend or parent. Lovers continue to become fixated with one another in that intoxicating experience of falling in love, and that love deepens into the gentler experience of commitment in marriage or its modern surrogate, co-habitation. The pain of betrayal is no less keenly felt today, even if perhaps more commonly experienced, while forgiveness continues to be a hard-won virtue, more commonly experienced in its absence than in its presence. The journey of faith is still discovered and followed by many, though with greater variety and fewer travelling companions in the Western world. Pastoral care will continue to pay attention to the great unchangeables of human existence: birth, death, love, companionship and faith.

Yet even here even a cursory glance shows how subtly the landscape has changed, and the issues faced in pastoral care are reshaped. Alongside the support and shared joy of those who become parents, and the heartache of those who remain unwillingly childless (both conditions witnessed to in the Scriptures) are the new pressures of those who look for assisted pregnancy (and choosing medical assistance rather than Abraham's solution of surrogacy) and the pastoral consequences of a couple choosing to remain childless through concerns over age or work. In previous generations, the childless couple wanting children might find a resolution through adoption, and the social stigma of childbirth out of wedlock ensured, rightly or wrongly, a steady supply of children 'up for adoption'. Today the pressures are different: more widely available abortions and the much more common experience of single-parenthood by the unmarried (as opposed to the experience of the widowed parent, more common in the generations closer to death through war or disease) reshape the pastoral priorities that circle around birth and parenthood.

Similarly, the pain of grief and loss are familiar to every age and every culture, particularly when that loss seems untimely. As I write this, a young member of my own congregation died last night, from a rare medical condition, and the shock of that upon her contemporaries in the church is profound, especially after the suicide of another member, a young man, only a few months ago. Yet here too pastoral care wrestles with the consequences of changing technologies and values. So issues of medical ethics arise which were unthought of fifty years ago. The ability to prolong bodily existence contrasts with the quality of life so prolonged. Voluntary euthanasia raises issues of a person's right to death as well as to life, particularly in the agonising terminal stages of some diseases, whereas the hospice movement has pursued another path to dignity in death's shadow. Then, of course, there is the abortion issue, which continues to ignite passions on both sides of that particular argument.

Cultural changes point to a widespread belief in the efficacy of medical treatment, denial, even, of the reality of death, and shock when the limits of medical science are reached. This is accompanied by the much more restricted belief in the afterlife, and together makes death harder for our culture to accept. The denial of the reality of death, especially where the relationship with the dead person was highly ambivalent, makes the work of grieving all the harder, and thus increases the amount of psychological harm associated with loss. Pastoral care needs to come to terms with the increasing need of skilled help in bereavement counselling, at the forefront of which is the sterling work of Cruse.

The changing nature of family and marriage point towards another evolving landscape in pastoral care. In Britain in the 1990s, divorce is running at a rate of two out of every five marriages, the percentage of people getting married for the first time is at its lowest since records began, and the incidence of cohabitation is at its highest. These changes call for sensitive pastoral care and determined guidance if the trends in family breakdown are to be reversed.

Some would put these changes in family structures at the heart of the causes of the near epidemic in depression and anxiety disorders assailing Western societies. Relationship breakdown and depression would be among the most common causes of suicide, and the most familiar reasons why people seek therapeutic help in a counselling context. Most pastoral carers and counsellors will be only too familiar with the scale of this epidemic. Was it ever thus? There have been depressives in every age, and those suffering from melancholia in previous generations were by no means rare. It could well have been Elijah's condition, under the broom tree running for his life from Jezebel,[1] while otherwise successful and dynamic individuals can be afflicted with this condition in every age, from the great nineteenth-century preacher Spurgeon to Winston Churchill's 'black dog'. However, it does seem that its incidence is increasing, and not just because more are willing to seek help for their condition. This is another reshaping of the landscape of pastoral care that significantly affects the Christian carer.

I do not think that I am alone in detecting growing levels of relational and psychological ill-health in contemporary Britain. While the therapeutic aspect to the pastoral task is not the only dimension to pastoral care, its urgency often obliterates the others, so that preventative work and developmental work become downgraded. The image of the cliff over which the unsuspecting fall highlights the two responses. Pastoral care has perhaps become too involved in providing the first-aid station at the base of the cliff to pay sufficient attention to the need for a fence and warning signs at the top. In the long run it is surely better to prevent the casualties in the first place, however effective the patching-up that takes place below.

In this review of the tasks of pastoral care, therefore, we shall attempt a balance between its varied characteristics of not only healing, but also sustaining, guiding, reconciling and forming personal and societal strengths. Neither can we ignore the spiritual dimensions of those tasks.

CHAPTER 7

Metaphors for Pastoral Care

Overview

Theological language is metaphorical language through and through,[1] using images drawn from the world of experience to image divine realities: fatherhood, wind, light and so forth. The very word pastoral is metaphorical, referring to the shepherdlike care for people described, perhaps somewhat unflatteringly, as sheep. 'The Lord is my shepherd', says the shepherd King, David,[2] and the human attribute of waywardness is likened to sheep by Isaiah: 'We all, like sheep, have gone astray, each of us has turned to his own way.'[3] Jesus calls himself the good shepherd,[4] while Peter encourages the elders among the scattered Christian communities to 'be shepherds of God's flock that is under your care'.[5]

Metaphor is the conjunction of two horizons of speech or language in such a way as to be a gain to understanding. The original meaning of a word is suspended so that a new, related meaning can take its place, and this new combination of words initiates a new relation of meaning. The nature of metaphorical language about God is problematical, and does not concern us here, but there are parallels to those problems in pastoral care. If speech about God is only possible if God has already spoken in certain language events, and, as Jungel argues, the particular character of the Christian faith is the word of the cross (that is, talk about God's unity with the man Jesus who was killed on the cross),[6] then we must start our talk about pastoral care from the cross, if it is to be seen as an expression of God's care in the world, and not just an incidence of human caring.

Returning to our basic metaphor of pastoral as descriptive of care, the shepherd who tends, guides, feeds and protects his sheep is the human picture of caring that the Scriptures apply to God. He is the shepherd and we are the sheep. The two horizons of worldly care and divine care are brought together in the picture of the shepherd. However, we have already seen that the cross is the event that is the proper starting-point for Christian talk about God, not only in describing who he is, but also how he acts in saving compassion towards the world. Pastoral care must then take its parameters and characteristics not from the world of professional care, but from the cross of Christ. Indeed, it is his death that is uppermost in the mind of Jesus when he talks analogically about the shepherd: 'I am the good shepherd; I know my sheep and my sheep know me – just as the Father knows me and I know the Father – and I lay down my life for the sheep.'[7]

In our reflections upon the metaphors for pastoral care (gift, proclamation, service and sacrament), we will turn to the One who died on the cross as the divine horizon that we will bring close to the human experience of caring. What does Christ as God's gift to humankind mean for the character of pastoral care? In what way does the proclamation of the Kingdom of God in the preaching of Jesus help us to see the missionary character of pastoral care in the postmodern world? How can he who came not to be served, but to serve and give his life as a ransom for many become the pattern for human pastoral care? What does the incarnation, the sacrament of the life of Jesus as John sees it in the prologue to the Fourth Gospel, mean for the significance of pastoral care? The use of metaphors will bring new meaning to light, inform and creatively energise our practice.

Pastoral Care as Gift

The Christian faith resonates with gift. It begins with the gift of Christ to the world in the incarnation: 'He came to that which was his own, but his own did not receive him,' but to all who did receive him 'he gave the right to become children of God'.[8] At Pentecost, the Church is constituted by the gift of the Spirit, and in his proclamation, Peter invites his hearers to 'Repent and be baptised, every one of you, in the name of Jesus Christ so that your sins will be forgiven. And you will receive the gift of the Holy Spirit.'[9] The response of the believer is to give worship and allegiance to Christ, to give thanks to God,[10] and to give to the needs of others: 'If a man's gift is . . . contributing to the needs of others, let him give generously.'[11]

The giving of God to humankind could be seen as the basic movement that he makes towards us. In describing the gift of eternal life, Jesus, praying that he might give eternal life to all those the Father had given to him, equates this *aeonios zoe*, the life of the age to come, as personal knowledge of God and the gift of God himself in relationship: 'Now this is eternal life; that they may know you, the only true God, and Jesus Christ whom you have sent.'[12] God is both gift and giver.

What constitutes a gift?

When is a gift not a gift, but a contractual obligation? John Milbank approves Pierre Bourdieu's two distinguishing features.[13] First, for a gift to be authentic, there must be a delay in return. To return a gift straight away implies a lack of gratitude, a desire to discharge an obligation as soon as possible because the original gift was not really welcomed. Thus, to be invited to dinner is to receive the gift of hospitality. To return the invitation next day, to have those people back to dinner tomorrow, is insulting: it implies that the gift imposed a debt which must be discharged immediately because continuing relationship is, at best, of no significance, and at worst positively unwelcome.

The second feature of an authentic gift, as opposed to a binding contract, is that the gift given back must be different, and not obviously equivalent. To return the gift of a record of a certain artist with the self-same recording seems strange, or to respond to a gift of flowers with the giving of a similar bouquet implies that the first gift was not, perhaps, welcome.

God's relationship to us as gift

These principles apply to our relationship to God. The original gift is from God (we love because he first loved us),[14] and our response is different in kind and necessarily delayed.

> To be a Christian is *not*, as piety supposes, spontaneously and freely to love, of one's own originality and without necessarily seeking any communion. On the contrary, it is to *repeat differently*, in order to repeat, exactly, the content of Christ's life, and to wait, by a necessary *delay*, the answering repetition of the other that will fold temporal linearity back into the eternal circle of the triune life.[15]

The character of that dissimilar and delayed response is seen in the pastoral care with which we express not only our compassion towards others, but also our love towards God.

> This is how we know what love is: Jesus Christ laid down his life for us. And we ought to lay down our lives for our brothers. If anyone has material possessions and sees his brother in need but has no pity on him, how can the love of God be in him?[16]

So, the first implication of pastoral care as gift is its necessary response to God's love towards us. It is the way that we properly return God's gift of himself to us, seen with greatest clarity in the cross, by giving ourselves to others. Christ laid down his life for us, so we lay down our lives for others in pastoral care, which is costly and gracious.

We should not overemphasise the characteristic of difference between the gift of God and the responsive gift of human pastoral care. Paul, in 2 Corinthians, is at pains to demonstrate the *similarity* of response:

> Praise be to . . . the Father of compassion and the God of all comfort, who comforts us in our troubles, so that we can comfort those in any trouble with the comfort we ourselves have received from God. For just

> as the sufferings of Christ flow over into our lives, so also through Christ, our comfort overflows.[17]

The movement, however, is the same: God first encourages us[18] and we respond in the comfort and encouragement of others. Pastoral care therefore becomes an instance of the incarnation, the enfleshing, of God's compassionate care for humankind. Indeed, it is the only way that certain aspects of God's care for us can be received: for the person who is gripped by the severity of depression in all of its despair, the physical embrace of another human being can be the only experience of God's comfort that is capable of being received.

A second feature of the giftedness of pastoral care concerns the nature of the gift. Milbank explores the origins of the phrase 'giffe-gaffe' in early modern English. It means the equivalent to 'give and take', and we continue to speak of a gaffe as a loss or mistake. He makes the perceptive comment that the difference between giving and taking is a single vowel. The word giffe, or gift, can also mean poison (as in the Latin *dosis*, meaning the dose of something which can be healing, as in medicine, or harmful, as in a dose of the flu). In a similar vein, the word 'present' has a complex meaning: it is both the 'present time' and another word for gift, as in a Christmas present. The gift of time, for instance, combines these two meanings.

> The present moment, especially, can only be held as a gift, since it lies entirely *in* the gift of the passage of time and cannot be owned by a subject after it has been given to him (thereby obliterating its gratuitous origin). The moment never *stays* as present even for a fleeting instance.[19]

This knot of meanings has a fascinating implication for pastoral care. The utterly unconditional giving of pastoral care can be poisonous. For instance, in families, giving to children would be folly if it were too unilateral. Parents who shower gifts on their children without any expectation of gratitude as a response, nor any regard for the wisdom of their use, give a poisoned gift, a gift of spoilation. An unlimited allowance made available to the child who spends it on self-destructive drug abuse would be an act of folly, not freedom. In families, giving is good to the degree that it induces gratitude and appropriate usage by its recipients.

It is popular to speak of the unconditional nature of pastoral care. It should be available, or rather, the pastoral carer should be available, without reserve. It is an unconditional gift. Yet some forms of limitless pastoral care can become poisonous, toxic to the recipient's dignity, personal responsibility and self-esteem. The ability to seek a solution to life's problems with one's own resources of character and intelligence withers and is replaced by an unhealthy dependency on another. The pastoral carer needs to remain alert to the dangers of dependency, while also accepting that awareness of those dangers can be an inappropriate excuse for inactivity and a cloak for that lack of proper compassion that is rightly judged as sin.

A further aspect to the metaphor of gift lies in the area of fulfilment. Pastoral counsellors are rightly taught to be aware of the dangers of co-dependency where, in order to be self-fulfilled, the counsellor needs the client as much as, or more so, than the client needs the counsellor for their growth and healing. In such cases, there is a danger that the therapy will continue beyond the point of helpfulness into a web of self-deception and destructive dependency. However, the issue of the counsellor's sense of fulfilment needs to be addressed. Where the counsellor, or pastoral carer, finds no fulfilment in the task, then the quality of care is likely to be low, the level of resentment high and the whole endeavour blighted by misery. However, if we conceive pastoral care as gift, there is a measure of return,

> if not the gratitude of another and delight in her pleasure, plus the sense that we have benefited her, then at least the self-awareness that we sought to do so, such that the thwarting of the gift is outside our control, and need not deprive us of our 'present' status of generosity of heart.[20]

There is a proper sense of fulfilment in the offering of pastoral care as a gift that derives from the generous heart. Seeing pastoral care as gift legitimises those very human responses of wanting to find some sense of worth and value in the tasks to which we commit ourselves and puts gratitude in a safe context for the carer.

The final way in which 'gift' illumines pastoral care returns us to the Scriptures, for pastoral care is seen by Paul as one of the gifts of the risen Christ to the Church. In Ephesians 4 it is he of whom the Psalmist says he 'gave gifts to men',[21] including pastors and teachers, 'to prepare God's people for works of service, so that the body of Christ may be built up'.[22] In Ephesians 1:22–23 Christ is appointed head over the whole universal realm of creation for the privileged place that now belongs to the Church.[23] He is given to the Church, and the Church becomes his chosen instrument in carrying out his rule. The Christ gives gifts of ministry to the Church to equip it for the role which that rule implies. The exalted Christ gives gifts of particular people to the whole of God's people, and amongst them are the pastors, the shepherds of the flock.

The relationship of the gift of pastor to that of teacher has been much debated. For each of the categories of gift, including pastors, the definite article is employed, e.g. δε ποιμενας, *de poimenas*, the pastors, but is omitted before 'teachers'. Some have claimed that this implies that pastors and teachers are the same gift, the local leadership of a church by a pastor-teacher (Barth is of this view), but this is scant evidence to conflate the two functions. The one definite article is best interpreted as identifying a close relationship between the two functions, but not their identity. This close relationship points to the way in which teaching and training, guiding and discipling are all aspects of the pastoral care of people, and evidence of the role that guidance plays in the pastoral care of people, (as we have seen in pages 96–99, in contrast to the prevailing ethos of person-centred counselling so influential in some pastoral care circles).

The word 'shepherd' or 'pastor', *poimen*, is used of Christ three times in the New Testament.[24] It is only used for church leaders in Ephesians, although its cognate verb is used by Luke[25] and Peter.[26] It is closely allied to the role of leader, called *episcopos*, bishop or overseer[27] or *presbuteros*, elder.[28] Such leaders are to serve the flock, not lording it over the people of God like pagan rulers, but imitating Christ himself. Thus pastoral care is a gift of servant leadership to the Church and world, a way of representing Christ to others and of serving them in leadership and care. The symbols of the pastoral office are rightly the shepherd's crook and the Scriptures, pointing to care and teaching, but could helpfully be supplemented by the bowl and towel, the symbols of Christ's condescension and service, for pastoral care is rarely glamorous, often mundane and sometimes messy.

The Gift and Postmodern Notions of Health Care

The concept of the gift is also important in post-structuralist and feminist readings of the relationship between carer and cared for.[29] Cixous suggests that there is an opposition between the male, possessive desire called the 'Proper' and a feminine desire which is based on generosity, the 'Gift'. Derived particularly from a psychoanalytical background based on the work of the French psychoanalyist, Jacques Lacan, what is entailed in a Gift relationship is contrasted with that of a Proper relationship. Proper, property and appropriation are all dimensions of an arrogant domination and self-aggrandizement. The resultant relationship between carer and the patient/client empowers the carer to control the patient, who becomes increasingly dependent. Thus care becomes a subtle means of gaining power. In opposition to this is the Gift relationship, which can be described by generosity, trust, love, benevolence, commitment, esteem, and so forth.

While many caring relationships are Proper ones, the value of the distinction between the Gift and the Proper rests on the observation that things could be different. A 'Gift is not given with any expectation of reciprocity; in the realm of the Gift, those who care do not expect gratefulness or even an acknowledgement of their effort.'[30]

Furthermore, the rigid dichotomy between healer and patient, the powerful and the vulnerable, is transcended by the concept of the wounded healer. This involves carers recognising their own vulnerability, their potential to be wounded, or the actuality of their woundedness. This perspective imbues caring with elements of Gift and helps caring to avoid becoming power and dominance.

Pastoral Care as Proclamation

The second metaphor for pastoral care that helps to illumine its character and manner is proclamation, the declaring in word and deed the good news of the gospel, the *evangel*. Pastoral care and mission are often seen as conflicting priorities among the tasks of the Church, competitors for time and resources which are scarce. The pastoral carer sees new converts as potential pastoral problems, increasing its load, while the evangelist understands the essential task of the Church to be mission and cannot abide the reluctance of the overworked pastoral carer to embrace the newly converted with unalloyed joy.

Ways of Being Church

Robert Warren contrasts two styles of 'being Church': the pastoral style and the missionary style. When most people are baptised, and believers at least nominally know the basics of the Christian faith and share a world view which is coherent with the Christian faith, then the pastoral style of being Church is appropriate. The focus of the mission of the Church is to develop and sustain its flock. When the Church is in a minority, however, its priority needs to be a missionary style where telling and living the Christian faith becomes paramount.[31] This might seem to support the tension that I outlined above, between pastoral care and mission, but in the postmodern world, where claims to truth are hard to hear when simply announced, it might just be that pastoral care is the most potent way of telling the gospel, of being Church in missionary mode. The key elements to pastoral care as proclamation are:

(i) the generosity of spirit, which sees all people as recipients of pastoral care, not just the members of the Church;
(ii) the way in which that care is exercised in a community; and
(iii) the way in which the truth claims of the gospel are witnessed to in the exercising of pastoral care.

(i) Generosity of Spirit

An exercise in narrative theology of a particularly personal kind might help us here. My first appointment to the staff of a church was at the tender age of twenty-six, when I left four happy years of teaching and became a pastoral elder at Lewin Road Baptist Church in Streatham, South London. I was already a member and lay elder in the church, but responded to a call to ministry that the church recognised and supported, following the departure of the Associate Pastor to his new congregation in Devon and the subsequent move by the Senior Minister, Douglas McBain, to an itinerant ministry of preaching, teaching and church-planting called 'Manna Ministries'.

The church was strongly evangelical and had been quite famous in the 1950s and 1960s as an evangelical 'preaching shop' under its previous minister, Angus MacMillan, a doughty Scot and defender of the evangelical faith. In 1968 Douglas McBain became his successor, continuing 'Lewin's' strong reputation for able preaching of an evangelical character, but also gradually and sensitively (and for a few, therefore, far too slowly) opening the church to charismatic experience following his own experience of renewal in Wishaw, Scotland. Douglas had been a founding member of the Fountain Trust which pioneered charismatic renewal among the denominational churches of every tradition, and also of the mainstream, which encouraged renewal and mission among Baptist churches. The church became well known in South London for its charismatic churchmanship and, being a large congregation, drew many visitors to its Sunday services. However, it lacked involvement in its local community – an ethnically mixed, socio-economically varied and increasingly disadvantaged community halfway between Brixton to the north and Croydon to the south. Streatham's larger houses were still in private ownership and attracted professionals who could not afford Fulham or Wandsworth Common, but many of its streets were full of bedsits. There was a growing drugs problem and it hosted South London's biggest red light district, with over a hundred prostitutes regularly working its patch. There was little in the life of the church which addressed those kinds of problems, despite an emphasis upon evangelism under Angus MacMillan.

In response to this lack, in the late 1970s the church established a project to reach out in service to the local community. The vision was for a bookshop, coffee shop and counselling centre, initially called the Open Door Project. By 1980 a shop on the High Road had been leased and Manna Christian Centre was born, opening first as a bookshop, then with the taking of the lease on the shop next door, a coffee shop with counselling work above. This latter was established in 1987 as the Manna Counselling Service and has been a major resource for Christian counselling provision and training in South London for a decade. Half a mile away, at Tooting Bec, was a major psychiatric hospital (now closed), and many of the regular customers at the coffee shop were residential inmates there. Counselling support was occasionally appropriate from Manna, but more often it was simply a welcome not available elsewhere on the busy High Road, and friendship that kept them coming to Manna Christian Centre. It was pastoral care in the community!

I joined the staff in 1982 and nine months later Mike Wood was called to be Minister there. We were both evangelical, although Mike had been in earlier days something of a radical theologically, and I was moving towards the liberal end of the evangelical spectrum (or was that the evangelical end of the liberal spectrum?). We were also both committed charismatics, and continued the charismatic evangelical churchmanship that had developed under Douglas McBain. However, we were also concerned to see the love of Christ put into action in the community, and the 1980s saw the church embrace a number of community projects that were essentially pastoral care exercised in the community.

The Job Club that opened in 1986 was successful, not just in helping individuals to find work, but also in providing support and care for the whole person, especially when undertaken by George Giles, one of the elders who was retired and worked almost full time in the Club, and its Leader, Peter Moore. The needs of the elderly residents of Streatham were identified and another of the full-time elders, Brian Moughton (an administrator by profession, but a pastor by inclination if ever there was one), oversaw the establishment of a club for the elderly and a residential home in co-operation with Abbeyfield Homes. The youngsters were served by a full-time youth worker and young mothers by the long-established playgroup. The presence of the Asian community in the area was recognised and the Asian project was established under the leadership of a former missionary to Bangladesh, Jean Westlake, later joined by a missionary from South Korea, Sung Hee Kwon. More recently, and since my departure for Stevenage, links with the Oasis Trust have seen the development of a hostel for the homeless in North Streatham.

Friendship, pastoral care and welcome characterised all these attempts to provide a Christian presence in the community. On reflection, they were all, essentially, ways of doing pastoral care in missionary mode, caring in the name of Christ in the wider community from the base of a strong Christian community church. The pastoral care was indistinguishable from the church's mission, and the continuing flourishing of that church through a major redevelopment of its premises in the mid-1990s in order to be more effective in that kind of socially responsible pastoral care is witness to its integration and health. The temptation is always to withdraw from that kind of mission, perhaps to more overt evangelistic enterprise, or to less costly care for its own only, 'a form of chaplaincy to the religiously committed,'[32] but thankfully accountants do not govern churches as they do professional health care provision . . . at least not there, and not yet!

In a postmodern culture, the Church as a sign of hope through its care for the whole community might very well be the key to the renewal of its sense of mission.

(ii) The Exercise of Pastoral Care in Community

The second feature of pastoral care as proclamation concerns the way in which that care is exercised. Too often social action in evangelical churches is barely concealed evangelism, or at best the sugar that sweetens the evangelistic pill. It is the decoy to attract sinners onto our patch so that we might 'bag' them and convert them. Such a policy lacks integrity and those 'sinners' who get close enough to smell it get put off by the stench of hypocrisy that surrounds it. Pastoral care in the community should not be seen as a useful supplement to the real task, that of saving souls, but as an essential response to the call of Christ to care for 'the least of these' his brethren, amongst whom are included all who religion would want to exclude.

The gathered Church model is particularly prone to the dichotomy of member/non-member, saint/sinner, believer/unconverted. Whenever the Church draws such hard lines around itself it ceases to be Church in the same way as Jesus was human, but becomes a religious institution standing under the judgment of God. Instead, the Church which views itself and those around it as fellow members on a journey of faith enables it to care for whoever that should be without calling upon the condition of an acceptable level of faith beforehand. This is not to be confused with universalism, which views all as recipients of saving grace and heavenbound whether or not they want to believe. I still believe that there are some who will not be saved in that sense of eternal fellowship with God, although I am not so sure as I used to be just who they will be. However, I am convinced that God is at work in every human life, and those whom the Church is often quick to dismiss might be further on the road to genuine faith than some within the Churches who make those judgments.

Richard Holloway and Brice Avery, in their book *Churches and How to Survive Them*,[33] identify the need to be in control of the threatening chaos as lying at the root of fundamentalism, the need to have an answer to everything and a paralysing fear of uncertainty. Such people dump their unacceptable feelings onto others – the enemy, the worldly or the liberal 'other' – and need the strict boundaries to keep in control of that chaos. Perhaps that is one of the reasons why fundamentalists who become involved in pastoral counselling tend to either gravitate towards the 'biblical' counselling wing, live with a split between faith and pastoral experience or move away from their previously held certainties into a place where there are more doubts than questions.

Pastoral care as proclamation calls for a low level of conditionality on the part of its providers: certainly the condition of faith as a requirement should be abandoned if the exercising of pastoral care is to be a part of the overall mission of the

Church. Conversely, if mission to those beyond the Church is to be an element of the pastoral care of the Church (in other words, pastoral care to the whole community) and a sign of the gracious presence of God in the midst of all of human life, then the role of chaplaincies to hospitals and industry, colleges and professions will need to become more integrated with the life of the whole Church. At present they have something of a Cinderella status, with the (unfounded) suspicion that they attract those who do not make the grade for the real pastoral work of the Church, local parish or church leadership.

(iii) The Exercise of Pastoral Care as Witness to the Truths of the Gospel

In the postmodern world, where intolerance is not accepted and where there is still a reluctance to admit faith claims to the public arena, especially in the social sciences, for pastoral care to be proclamation a third condition must be met. There needs to be a new-found confidence in the explanation of the truth claims of the Christian faith to accompany the quality of caring to the whole community. We have already seen that any pastoral care or social action which is a thinly veiled form of evangelism is to be avoided. However, there is a suspicion (widely held among the evangelical tradition) that those within the Christian community who have continued to promote social action as the Church's priority have little confidence in the explicit call to belief in Christ. This suspicion must be shown to be unfounded, as pastoral care in the community is accompanied by sensitive and culturally appropriate ways of helping people to faith in Christ and membership of the Church. There are elements of the *modus operandi* of the Alpha courses, for instance, which do resonate with the hunger for belonging, for community within the wider culture. Similarly, the content of the Emmaus courses, which adopt the 'road to faith' approach advocated above, allow people to start where they are and take every stage of that journey seriously, from the beginnings to the end.

It is no longer possible to simply care for people and see them come to faith in Christ by some magical non-cognitive process. Ignorance about the claims of Christianity, about its world-view, and, indeed, ignorance of its story as witnessed in Scripture, is too great for the Church to rely upon the general knowledge of the community to supply the understanding of what faith in Christ might be. Remember, we are in a missionary mode, with only ten percent of the adults in England attending Church on any normal Sunday. The Christian story needs to be retold and the Christian life relived in the community.

Mission in postmodern Britain needs to counter the ephemerality of the culture by a new rootedness in the great traditions of the Church, and it needs to offer hope in place of despair. Mission to the fragmented culture needs to show that enduring, costly and deep relationships are possible, both to other humans and to God. That mission begins as we listen to our culture and to the Scriptures and traditions of the Church, and engage them in creative dialogue, but it continues in pastoral care. That is not an optional extra for those who manage to integrate all aspects of Church life particularly skilfully, but an indispensable way of being Church if there is to still be a Church that proclaims the love of Christ in word and deed in the twenty-second century.

Pastoral Care as Service

If the metaphor of proclamation orientates pastoral care towards those beyond the Church, then that of service orientates it towards God. 'Service' has an ambiguous set of meanings. It refers to the work that is voluntarily done to help the life of the Church or community: thus, 'his sphere of service is running the soup kitchen'. It refers also to the worship events that happen regularly at Church: thus, 'the evening service begins at 6.30'.

The ambiguity is rooted in the New Testament word for service λατρεια, *latreia*, which is translated in Romans 12 as variously 'your spiritual worship' (NIV, RSV, Revised English Bible) or 'reasonable service' (AV). Paul is using terms that he has appropriated from the world of Hellenistic Judaism, itself echoing Philo, the Jewish philosopher who derived his thought from both Plato and Stoicism. Paul has devotion in mind, which is not simply the offering of the mind (rationality, *logikos*, translated 'reasonable') but in contrast to the Hermetic worship, is rooted in the bodily reality of everyday living, 'offer your bodies as living sacrifices'. James Dunn[34] also sees a contrast with the worship, the cultus, of traditional Judaism, as Paul sets out the markers which will distinguish the new community of Christians from their Jewish antecedents, the Greek culture and the influences of 'this age' with its potent mix of cultural norms, social groups and institutions.

Thus, worship is not to be simply a cultic experience, liturgy alone, but as the rest of Romans 12 explains, it involves serving the wider community in a variety of ways: prophesying (inspired speech, which is both spontaneous and rational), ministry (*diakonia*), teaching, exhortation or contributing to the needs of others. We should not seek to separate the worship of God in the liturgy of the Church from the expression of that worship in service of others. (Amos and Isaiah, among other prophets in Israel, make plain God's abhorrence of the hypocrisy of worship without love for others.) Therein lies the relationship of pastoral care to worship.

However, neither should worship of God collapse into mere social action, such that any form of help expressed towards one's neighbour becomes explicit worship of God. That is far too poorly focused a relationship towards God. Pastoral care needs the energising power of the Holy Spirit if it is to be kept fresh and lively, and that power is appropriated through living relationship with God, expressed in prayer, devotion and worship. The gracious love of God becomes not only the reason for pastoral care that is costly and demanding, but also the resource for that quality of caring, the energy to sustain it and the defining limits to it.

We dare not separate pastoral care from the worship life of the Church. Similarly, pastoral care without the resources of an appropriate spirituality soon becomes the path to burn-out or neglect, and these issues will be considered in Chapter 12. Pastoral care of others must be one of the ways we express our love for God, and should rightly be part of the discipleship of every Christian, not just 'professional carers', but pastoral care without divine resources of grace soon becomes poverty stricken, dutiful and destructive. Pastoral care is Christian service of others and of God; it is our reasonable worship.

Pastoral Care as Sacrament

A controlling metaphor for the Church, particularly among post-Vatican II Roman Catholic theologians, is the sacrament. Schillebeeckx says:

> Churches are of the order of 'the sign': a sacrament of salvation. They are the explicit identification of that salvation. Churches are the places where salvation from God is thematized or put into words, confessed explicitly, proclaimed prophetically and celebrated liturgically.[35]

Peter Hodgson and Robert Williams, for whom the Church is 'a transfigured mode of human community', describe the Church as:

> an anticipatory sign and sacrament of the coming kingdom of God, which is a 'Kingdom of freedom,' a liberated communion of free subjects created and empowered by the indwelling Spirit of the God of freedom.[36]

The documents of the Second Vatican Council describe the Church as the universal sacrament of salvation,[37] although in the post-conciliar phase the term 'people of God' attained preeminence. The Constitution of the Church, which begins *Lumen gentium cum sit Christus* – since Christ is the light of humanity – embeds the sacramental nature of the Church in Christ. He is the primal sacrament, the *mysterion*, and the Church is a provisional and anticipatory sign of his kingdom, its seed and beginning on earth.[38]

This is not to say that the Church is an eighth sacrament, as that term has been understood since its development in the twelfth century. The term is used in an analogous sense, and the Council returned to the older patristic use of the term as the translation of the biblical term *mysterion*, that is, the salvific, transcendent divine reality which is revealed in a visible way.[39] Jesus Christ as the 'primal sacrament' is the final revelation of God himself and also fulfils to an all-surpassing degree the character of all human beings as made in the image of God. He, as the new Adam, 'in the very revelation of the mystery of the Father and of his love, fully reveals man to himself and brings to light his most high calling'.[40] The Church is the sacrament of the saving kingdom of God in this sense: as a means not only ▶▶

of revealing divine realities, but also of conveying the reality of them to the believer. 'It is simultaneously the fruit of salvation and the means of salvation.'[41]

One of the principal architects of the Second Vatican Council, Karl Rahner, wanted to avoid the misconception that the Church was somehow a 'point-like' divine intervention from outside the world, or that sacrament meant something other-worldly. He sees the whole of normal 'secular' life as held fast in the grip of grace, sustained by God's communication of himself. What happens in the sacraments is not something that does not happen in other ways in the world, but becomes a visible sign of God's saving act in the world and the liberation of humankind.[42]

The Church is the sign and agent of the saving power of God to liberate, nourish, sustain and guide humankind into the peaceable kingdom of Christ. Is this not the task of pastoral care? The metaphor of pastoral care as a sacrament of the loving care of the Father for his world invites us to see the care by the Church for all humankind as a vehicle of that divine love, as a visible sign of its reality and presence in the world. Following Rahner, this is not something somehow absent elsewhere in the world, as if Christian pastoral care was the only caring taking place in the world, but is rather a particular and preeminent expression of that caring which takes place generally in human existence, albeit misshapen and thwarted by human sinfulness and selfishness.

Gunton reminds us of the dangers of what he sees as monophysite tendencies in the christology underlying the Dogmatic Constitution of the Church,[43] and argues that the humanity of Christ determines the kind of ecclesiology we construct, as much as his divine nature, lest we become triumphalist in our claims for the Church.[44] If our christology should take on board the implications of the full humanity of Christ, then a corresponding ecclesiology will equally emphasise the role of the Spirit. Rather than make claims for too confident a doing of God's will, the Church would depend more upon the prayed-for presence of the Spirit.

In the role of pastoral care, therefore, a certain humility will need to be exercised, rather than a dogmatic or paternalistic provision of what the Church claims to be right for the individual or person. It must proceed, like all good counselling, by listening, taking in full seriousness the humanity and responsibility of the other, and by wise dependency upon the presence of the Spirit in all human exchange that seeks to follow in the way of Christ (and not just on those occasions when he is invited to be present, like the guest of honour at some party!).

By way of these metaphors for pastoral care we have gone some way to constructing a theology of pastoral care. We must now proceed by looking at the tasks that must shape pastoral care in a postmodern culture, tasks that not only reflect the central concerns of that culture, but also reflect the heart of what Christianity claims it means to be human and to know God in that humanity.

CHAPTER 8

The Urgent Tasks of Pastoral Care: Building Christian Community

Overview

The postmodern condition of fragmentation and short-term commitments, of life imitating art, especially the pervasive art of the television, and the resulting personal and social disintegration call for some searching questions to be asked about the pastoral priorities that the Church should adopt. Pastoral priorities in our age of instability cannot be the same as in an age of stability, any more than the pastoral priorities in a time of war can be the same as in a time of peace. There will be common themes, but different nuances and emphases must be given to those themes. I want to argue for four pastoral priorities: building Christian community; creating relational health, especially in marriage; healing the wounded soul; and nurturing and sustaining faith. I believe that these both reflect the central concerns of the Christian faith and respond to the postmodern condition.

We have already argued that the community is the context for pastoral care, compared to the predominantly individualistic approach of much secular therapy and counselling. For Christianity, its roots are in the Trinitarian nature of God himself, the circle of relationships that opens out to include the world in its embrace. Sadly, the Church does not always portray those divine relationships in its own human relationships. As we saw, churches can be tense, fragmented places riven by discord and subject to power-play and abuse. Forgiveness and grace are sometimes in short supply, even within the Church, let alone in the wider world. The first pastoral task is to build a community that is true to the realities of human experience and genuinely reflective of the love of Christ. A naive expectation that a perfect community could be built on earth can be as destructive of hope as a cynical shrug of the shoulders that says there can be no growth in loving human relationships. Pastoral care needs to be as grounded in the realities of human failure as in the promise of restoration and transformation if it is to be credible.

Biblical Realism

(i) Old Testament

That combination of gritty realism about the human condition and expectation of its hopeful transformation characterise the biblical traditions. The Old Testament expected the people of God to act in covenant love towards each other because they were the object of God's gracious love. The blessings of being in the land of promise were to be received thankfully, but also responsibly, with concern for the alien, the fatherless and the widow,[1] and violation of this concern for the weakest in the community is met with the gravest of condemnation by the prophets. Thus the religiously active people of Isaiah's day, celebrating the feasts and apparently faithful in prayer, are condemned because of their breaking of those covenant commitments to one another.

> Your New Moon Festivals and your appointed feasts my soul hates.
> They have become a burden to me;
> I am weary of bearing them.
> When you spread your hands in prayers, I will not listen.
> Your hands are full of blood;
> wash and make yourselves clean.
> Take your evil deeds out of my sight!
> Stop doing wrong, learn to do right!

> Seek justice, encourage the oppressed.
> Defend the cause of the fatherless, plead the cause of the widow.[2]

Amos echoes those concerns in his condemnation of Israel.[3]

The character of covenant love is expressed in the Torah, the law. It proscribes certain actions which break relationship and destroy trust within the community: false accusation, theft, adultery and incest and other violations of marriage, murder and oppression. A man should not be deprived of his livelihood[4] nor of his due wages,[5] and trade should be fair, with reliable weights.[6] The Torah is designed to ensure just and merciful social living, although we may find disturbing the severity of the punishments for the violation of those laws. Sustained by worship of God and obedience to the Torah, the community was meant to become a sign of God's presence to the nations, a kind of missionary presence in the world through the quality of its life. The reality was a narrow nationalism that avoided contact with what would be known as the gentile world and a pride in its status as the chosen people which survived the exile.

(ii) Jesus of Nazareth

Jesus of Nazareth builds upon the demands of the Torah and the interpretation of those laws, *halakah*. In the Sermon on the Mount, it is not just conformity to the letter of the law that God looks for, but obedience to its spirit as well. Certain aspects of the law are overturned in favour of a more demanding righteousness that flows from the heart. Thus, the precept 'an eye for an eye, and a tooth for a tooth'[7] – the principle of proportionate retribution which prevented the excesses of blood feud by stating that the legal punishment must not exceed the crime – is replaced by a freedom not to insist upon one's own rights. Love for neighbour is to be supplemented by love for enemy. Outward fulfilment of the law is only the beginning of ethical rectitude: it must be met by an inward disposition. Jürgen Moltmann calls this ethical stance 'the ethics of community'.[8] If it is the ethics of the community of Christ it is bound to be in contrast to the ethics of the surrounding society. The messianic community 'breaks through the fateful compulsion of violence which lies heavy on mankind' and responds with love. This is what makes it visible and identifiable, for 'it acts alternatively not conformistically'.

The meaning and intention of Jesus' messianic interpretation of the Torah can be put like this: taking the Sermon on the Mount seriously and following Christ go together. Moltmann dismisses the various easier options that sometimes serve as interpretations of the Sermon on the Mount. Those who consider it impossible to fulfil in principle, mock God. Anyone who considers that it can be fulfilled only in the sentiments of the heart, but not in public action, says that Jesus is wrong, for he preached the sermon precisely in order for it to be put into practice. Those who consider that it can be fulfilled only for themselves personally, but not in the context of their responsibility towards other people, do not know God the Creator. Anyone who believes that only Christ was able to fulfil the Sermon on the Mount, and all others are doomed to failure, is stifling the truth of the community of Christ, about which Paul says: 'Bear one another's burdens and so fulfil the law of Christ.'[9] This community exists in the hearing of Jesus' word and in the doing of it.

Several of Jesus' parables also deal with the quality of relationship for the disciple within the kingdom of God. In the parable of the unmerciful servant,[10] the principle of unbounded forgiveness towards others is rooted in God's unconditional forgiveness of the disciple. The parable of the Good Samaritan[11] points to the limitless demands of responsibility towards others, irrespective of race or religious ties. Concern for others in need transcends the usual divisions between social groups. The obedience to the letter of the law is always subordinate to the demands of love towards those in need.

The problem with any religion which interprets its regulations in a fiercely literal sense is twofold. First, while one knows exactly where one stands in regard to correct behaviour, situations outside those strict limits defined in the law are undefined, risky and out of bounds. The religious professionals, the priest and the Levite, do not know whether the body they see is a corpse or a non-Jew. Contact with either would result in ritual impurity and a necessary return to Jerusalem to become cleansed. The situation is risky and to be avoided. Secondly, fulfilment to the letter of the law implies that the person has met all of God's demands, and the parable points to the way in which the demands upon the obedient disciple will continually take him beyond the limits of what is required in law. There are prophetic anticipations of this new emphasis upon inward motivation in the hope for a new law written on the human heart.[12]

(iii) St Paul

This inward response to the demands of the law that goes beyond the mere letter is probably what the Apostle Paul meant by love being the fulfilment of the law.[13] In his teaching on the manner of community life there is great emphasis upon the centrality of love: 'Love must be sincere. . . . Be devoted to one another in brotherly love;'[14] 'Let no debt remain outstanding, except the continuing debt to love one another, for he who loves his fellow man has fulfilled the law.'[15] Fulfilment of the letter of the law for gentile Christians is replaced by 'faith expressing itself in love.'[16] There is to be a practical concern for others that arises from the confession that Jesus Christ is Lord,[17] and that concern is summed up in love, put on like the garment appropriate to the status of one seated with Christ.[18] The character of that love is described in 1 Corinthians 13 and also in Colossians:

> Therefore as God's chosen people, holy and dearly loved, cloth yourselves with compassion, kindness, humility, gentleness and patience. Bear with each other and forgive whatever grievances you may have against one another. Forgive as the Lord forgave you.[19]

As in the parable of the Good Samaritan, the old racial limits are transcended by a new unity in Christ,[20] and it is no longer the keeping of the letter of the law that counts, but the fulfilment of the demands of the Spirit of Jesus who both calls for those demands and enables the disciple to fulfil them.

The building of this new community of love, based upon mutual love rather than enlightened self-interest, and with forgiveness as a way of life rather than a strict holding to account of those who wrong us, takes place in real human communities with real human failures. At Corinth, the material wealth of some disciples leads them to disregard the needs of others and eat at the Lord's Table when others go hungry,[21] while the sexual impropriety that the Torah goes so far to outlaw is easily present in the Church which is as yet barely indistinguishable from the prevailing culture.[22] At Philippi there is disagreement and argument between members,[23] while at Thessalonica there are those who take advantage of the generosity of others and refuse to work for a living.[24] The vision and promise of the way of life in the new community is met by ordinary human failure, yet Paul continued to work, teach, encourage and pray to the end that the life of the Church might be a true reflection of the faith that it professes in Jesus Christ, who loved her and 'gave himself up for her'.[25] Pastoral carers must do likewise if they are to be faithful to their calling.

Fellowship

The characteristic description of the relationship between people in this community is fellowship, *koinonia*. In classical Greek this means the community, or common property, and when applied to people, it means a partner, impartial. In the New Testament, the word *koinonia* is absent from the Synoptic Gospels and from John, but is typically Pauline and used by Luke, possibly under Paul's influence. In Acts 2:42 it describes the unified life that the Spirit brings: 'they devoted themselves to . . . fellowship,' and Acts 4:32ff gives a picture of the communal sharing of goods that was a spontaneous reaction to the needs of others by the enthusiastic love that was inspired by new-found faith in Christ.

Paul never uses the word meaning church, *ekklesia*, in the way that some today, in speaking of their local church, refer to 'the fellowship'. It is not a group of individuals united by a common idea or interest, but rather united by faith in Christ and constituted by the Spirit. He speaks of 'the fellowship of his Son',[26] 'the fellowship of the Holy Spirit',[27] 'fellowship in the gospel'[28] and 'fellowship of faith'.[29] In the Eucharist there is fellowship in the body and blood of Christ, meaning participation in Christ. That union, fellowship, is the work of the Spirit and prior to the experience of fellowship between disciples. The Church may look like any other human society, but it is actually constituted on a very different basis. Indeed, when the Church is merely another form of human society, it ceases to be the Church of Jesus Christ. The task of pastoral care is to respond to the already existent nature of the Christian community as a group based upon the forgiveness of sins and relationship to Christ, a group that transcends all normal human divisions of race, age, sex, background and politics. That means it is not the task of pastoral care to constitute the Church, to establish it, but to help the Church become in the actuality of concrete human relationships what it already aspires to be in Christ.

In the words of 'the grace' we invoke 'the fellowship of the Holy Spirit', which is both the presence of the Spirit and fellowship with others in the Spirit. Because the Spirit is the Spirit of the Age to come, the *eschaton*, fellowship in the Spirit which the Church seeks is part of the anticipation of the coming Kingdom, a 'placing itself in the cosmic context of the restoration of all things'.[30] The Church as a community of forgiven and redeemed people is filled by the Spirit of Christ, not in just the narrower sense of 'charismatic', and pastoral care in its task of realising the character of fellowship amongst the Church is fundamentally resourced by the Spirit, for 'where the Church is, there is the Holy Spirit too.'[31] The Spirit is not confined to the Church by any means, but where the Church invokes the Spirit in the continual *epiklesis* of openness to God, then the Spirit confers fellowship. The church which is open to the Word will be enlivened to live in that fellowship as a true community of free individuals, since the Spirit and Word must not be divided, as some traditions have tended to do, both charismatics who have undervalued the Scriptures, and evangelicals who have demeaned the Spirit.

> Where the Word is, there the Spirit is too – otherwise the Word is not the Word of God; and where the Spirit is, the Spirit shines from the Word and illumines the understanding of faith – otherwise it is not God's Spirit.[32]

Let us not suppose that the development of community in the Church is a merely human endeavour to which the skills of conflict management, listening and communication can be applied as if it were a business enterprise. Let us neither suppose that restoring a sense of community in the wider world can be undertaken as if God does not exist, for the work of the Spirit is to create human community wherever it may be found. Nor has the Church an exclusively pedagogic role in this endeavour: to make it simply the model for all of human communality is to put too high a strain on its sometimes fragile humanity. The Church not only must be an example of how true community exists, but can also learn from other ways of being community beyond itself.

The great impetus towards the recognition of the equality of men and women came not from the Church, which has been amongst the most conservative institutions in its reluctance to give to women the status, opportunities and responsibilities they deserve as fellow bearers of the Spirit in Christ through baptism, but from the world of secular feminism. There is still great ignorance in the Church about the proper relationship of stewardship towards the physical environment that sits in contrast to the exploitative relationship of Western materialism. A sense of 'fellowship' with God's world, involving proper respect and care, comes mostly from the environmental movement, not from the Church.

There is plenty for the Church to learn from others beyond itself, but also plenty for it to teach also, not least in the great variety of people from all races and backgrounds that are the Church, and which is increasingly given visible expression in the rich diversity of backgrounds of the members of churches in our more cosmopolitan areas. Far from embracing the divisive 'homogeneity principle' of the Church Growth movement, these Churches, often in our inner cities, are a glorious mix of black and white, Asian, African and European Christians, young and old, single and married. In their very diversity these Churches express something of the eschatological hope for unity and harmony among the whole human race.

Pastoral Tasks that Enable Communion

The pastoral task of enabling the Church to become in concrete human relationships what it is in Christ, and thus to be a sign of hope to a fragmenting and disintegrating culture, could be summed up under four themes:

(i) the enabling of trust so that the basic attitude to others is one of trust and trustworthiness;
(ii) the expression of relationship in friendship is vital;
(iii) the realisation that fellowship, or community, is embodied will mean there needs to be a confidence and competence in human physicality and sexuality; and
(iv) the results of the rich diversity that is the Church will require abilities in relationship restoration and reconciliation, since conflicts and difference will arise which must be resolved.

Trust as a Basic Attitude

Trust is in short supply in our culture. The old figures of authority are no longer trusted, partly due to the way in which, at a very basic level, we no longer believe in the metanarratives they represent. Politicians are among the most mistrusted figures in public life, while those who report on the events in the world, the journalists, are near them in public disregard. That figure of quasi-divine status in the immediate post-war period, the scientist, who could have been relied upon to bring about greater human happiness and progress, is now also generally mistrusted after Three Mile Island and Chernobyl, global warming, BSE – the list is extensive. We do not trust the clergy either. Not many trust their neighbours as they once did, while the climate of fear resulting from the perception of increased dangers to the elderly and the young from crime, and the possibility that child abuse is widespread, results in a climate of mistrust that is endemic. Communities cannot be built upon mistrust.

The Christian community must therefore be built upon a different foundation: one of trust. It is actually oriented towards trust in its very genesis. Christ's attitude towards his Father is quite simply one of trust: 'Not my will, but yours be done. . . . Father, into your hands I commit my spirit.' That experience of the trusting relationship between Father and Son which is the springboard of the doctrine of the Trinity points towards the trust that there is within the Godhead. Not only can God be trusted, but he continually goes out to others in trust, and makes them trustworthy. Faith is the experience of trusting Christ, and the

Scriptures hold the Word of promise which awakens trust within us. The Eucharist points to that promise, and as we hold bread and wine in our hands, God entrusts himself to us, and as we share that bread with one another, so we trust our neighbour. Those who share in this communion and are attentive to this Word are capable of community that is built on mutual trust. Pastoral care helps to build that trust and to identify what prevents that trust from being realised in individuals.

Trust is damaged easily by untrustworthiness in those we expect to trust, especially leaders and pastors. Churches are unsettled when a fellow member breaks trust, cheats on the finances, or has an affair with another church member, for instance. But how much more a church is damaged when that member is the minister or the pastor? It is right that exemplary standards be expected from those the Church calls to leadership, and therefore it is also right that particular resources of pastoral care be available to them in order to assist them in maintaining those standards of fidelity in family, public and private life. A recent extension of pastoral counselling resources to all ministers within the British Free Churches,[33] in order to provide a confidential place to seek help apart from the Church hierarchies (themselves mistrusted since the role of pastoral supporter becomes confused with that of career promoter), is to be welcomed.

Churches need to find ways of restitution for those who break trust (since Churches are communities of forgiveness), but more importantly they need to find ways of enabling trustworthiness through adequate supervision of those who hold responsibility. The courage to confront those who break trust is one of the most costly virtues of the pastoral carer, but indispensable to the creation and maintenance of a community built upon trust in God and in one another.

For some the inability to trust lies not in the adult experience of disappointment at the untrustworthiness of others, but in the early experiences of parental inadequacies that result in a basic approach to life which finds trusting others difficult or impossible. The psychotherapist Erikson points to 'good enough' mothering being vital for the development of basic trust in the infant in the first eighteen months of life.[34] When this is present and when the mother, or her substitute, responds to the needs of the infant with food, warmth, comfort and company, and when distress is not allowed to become acute, then the result is one of trust and optimism on the part of the infant. Trust in the environment provided by the parents will result in trust in themselves and the development of skills and abilities.[35] The parent, through eye contact, smiles and welcome, says to the infant 'you're wonderful!' and through reliability says 'you can trust me', and hence the infant learns to trust the world.

Where that environment is not good enough, the infant does not resolve the early task and believes that they are not okay. 'I am bad'; people cannot be trusted. This is seen in, for instance, problems with food, withdrawal from parents, slowed development, and in later life, an inability to make and sustain relationships of depth and trust and a belief that they are guilty or worthless. These early inadequacies in parenting resulting in psychological disease need not be determinative of the whole of life if there is suitable support and healing in adult years. The trustworthiness of a counsellor, their presence and reliability, their reflecting back the beliefs and perceptions of the client, can all help in resolving the issue of trust versus mistrust in adult years.

The pastoral care of those who are mistrustful of life could include that kind of therapy which enables the person to change to trusting, but should also include its setting within a trustworthy community, like a genuine Church, where there are opportunities to experiment in trusting others without rejection when the experiments are hard won, or fail. A person who has failed to negotiate and resolve this most basic approach to life will often make indiscriminate choices over whom to trust, because they lack the intuition to make wise choices. Adult experience will therefore only serve to reinforce the original damage, and its subsequent replay will be strenuously avoided. A caring environment will need to allow for the steep learning curve from mistrust to trust that will result if the person is to become a trust-filled person.

If trust is only relearnt through the experiencing of trust in another, often the pastor, counsellor or therapist, the client is vulnerable to the abuse of the dependency that inevitably develops. Many pastors and counsellors are wary of the charge of dependency and thus avoid the very work which is necessary to create the trusting community. The essence of the therapeutic encounter is that both the treatment and the cure are found in the struggle to form a real trusting relationship.

The difficulty for the therapeutic relation is that it is based upon reexamining the fundamental difficulties of making meaningful relationships and then examining the self-destructive responses. For this to happen, the business of dependency, trust, control and fear of being taken over or devoured is inner-world material that must be faced by pastor and client. Ironically, this can only be examined properly where there is trust between the two people involved and dependency of the client on the pastor. It is for this reason that, in relational therapy, 'the journey itself is the destination. . . . A good enough relational therapist is one who has inquired of their inner-world to a degree that makes them available to the client for emotional use. . . . This process goes on over and over again in relational therapy, if the pastor is found dependable and trustworthy.'[36]

The dependability of the pastor extends to such matters as the time and place of the counselling session, and greeting and departure rituals. The very familiarity of these elements mimics the repetitiveness of the adequate dependability of the early mother–infant encounters. It also extends to elements in Church life. Where there is no routine, no familiarity, those who find it hard to trust will not be helped. In this regard, a fixed liturgy is an aid to the building of the therapeutic community. The liturgy becomes transparent and other work can be done in relation to God, others and the self. Where the energy is consumed in understanding or experiencing the liturgy (especially the non-liturgical kinds of liturgy, where 'anything might happen') then there is little left to actually experience *koinonia*.

Friendship as the Experience of Community

Jesus begins his relationship with the disciples by seeing them as learners at the feet of a rabbi, as servants even. But by the time of the Passion, the relationship has changed. 'I no longer call you servants, because a servant does not know his master's business.

Instead, I have called you friends.'[37] Friendship is a personal relationship between people who like one another. It combines affection with respect, liking someone for who they are, not for what they bring by way of business or social networking. It has to do with the being of a person. Moltmann calls it a 'vulnerable atmosphere of life',[38] while Alistair Ross calls them 'an endangered species'.[39]

Friendship grows out of free encounter; it cannot be insisted upon, nor is it an official role. When my wife, Gill, and I arrived at our present church, we were aware that a number of people wanted to be our 'special friends', mainly because we were aware of a dearth of friendship in an otherwise happy and successful church. It is difficult to be friends when you are the minister and feel that it is the role people want to relate to. I do not believe that friendship with the minister is forbidden, as I was unhelpfully told at Theological College, but it is difficult. In fact the closest friends we have, as a couple, all predate my entry into ministry and I am profoundly grateful to them and to God for the friendship that we have as people, not roles.

However, the pastoral carer has difficult choices to make, since it is important that we are at least friendly with others in our local Christian community – if there is no friendship in the Church, what do we have to say of any reality to the wider world – but it is hard to maintain the necessary distance that pastoral care may imply if everyone is our friend. In friendship we are aware that there is space to be ourselves, in the same way that in creation, we are aware that God gives us space to be. There is no desire to possess the other, nor to be beholden or indebted to the one who is our friend, or if there is, the friendship withers. Friendship is not a temporary condition, but is characterised by faithfulness: we can rely upon friends, even in misfortune. Nor is it a manipulative state, for we do not constantly feel the need to change the other who is our friend and make them into someone different. They and we can just 'be' without calculating the benefit.

> Friends throw open the free spaces of life to one another, and accompany one another in sympathy and immense interest. . . . (They) help one another without reward, but without helper syndrome either.[40]

Aristotle says the foundation of a shared life is *philia*, which presupposes a community of interest, the exclusive friendship of those who are the same.[41] In the New Testament, we find friendship between people who are different and an acceptance of one another in our differences for the sake of Christ. He was the friend of those who were different to him, the friend of sinners and tax-collectors, publicans and prostitutes. Among his friends were the outcasts, the disowned, who in his acceptance found the kingdom of God come among them. The more we pastorally help people to know themselves to be the accepted friends of God, the more they are enabled to accept one another in all of their rich diversity as friends together. I am convinced that those churches which know least about friendship also know least in experience about grace (although they may know a great deal about grace in its scriptural theory).

Pastoral care will help people to overcome the barriers to true friendship: suspicion of others, narcissism which stops us seeing the world through the other's eyes and becomes instead egocentric, a martyr-spirit which can only give but never receives from others, and the distorting of all companionable relationships into sexual ones. This is not easy in a culture which is riven by the destructive effects of competition in every sphere, where boundaries for appropriate sexual relationships are imprecise and individualism so easily spawns a self-reliance and self-absorption that is toxic to friendship. But where it can be encouraged and the environment in which it flourishes is maintained, there is a community that is a sign of God's friendship to his whole world: a sign of hope to our world.

Embodiment as a Way of Being Community

One wit has penned the rhyme:

> To fellowship with those above
> why that's all grace and glory.
> To live below with those we know
> is quite another story.

Community in theory is beautiful. Community in practice is messy. Fellowship is not just 'in the spirit', in the sense of an ethereal kind of disembodied affection; it is also in the flesh. We are called to love others who have not only a soul, but also a body, and the Church does not have a very good record at coping with embodied relationships, because human beings are sexual beings through and through. Somehow, we have to come to terms with our sexuality within the proper bounds of holiness and friendship. Here pastoral care must step sensitively, but boldly, in the sustenance of lively community that is as at ease with the bodies of its members as their souls.

Certainly, since Augustine, the Church has viewed sexuality at best ambiguously, at worst as something to be eradicated and hated. This is strange, since the language of worship is so often the language of love, the experience of faith is so close to the experience of true human love, and Jesus seemed particularly at home in his sexuality, without it ever becoming demanding. The woman who anointed him at the Pharisee's house was a 'sinner', – which probably refers to her dubious sexual reputation. Was she an adulterer or a prostitute? Most commentators conclude she was the latter. Entry to the feast held in honour of the visiting preacher was open to the whole village, the less important members of which would stand at the edge, in the shadows. The senior synagogue official, a Pharisee, is obliged to offer the hospitality, but by a calculated snub of failing to offer water to wash Jesus' feet and by offering no kiss of greeting he demonstrates his disapproval of this 'friend of sinners'.

If the woman's presence at the feast is no cause for shock, but almost expected, her actions are quite the reverse. She was fine as a spectator, but when she becomes a player, everyone becomes upset. Her actions spring from overwhelming emotions: love for the one who has already, we presume, offered her some acceptance; shame, anger and bewilderment that he should be humiliated by the lack of greeting and common decency of foot-washing; and sorrow at her own condition. She takes her most cherished belonging, perfume that was probably both expensive and precious, and anoints his feet. She lets down her hair to wipe those feet, wet with her tears, and kisses them. The letting down of her hair is culturally shocking, the kissing of his feet outrageously intimate, and everything about her actions was both offensive to the self-righteous guests and erotic in interpretation: it is as if she had turned the dinner party into a brothel!

The Pharisee is first to react. The construction of the Greek reveals that the Pharisee is thinking that he is not a prophet (hence the offensive snub upon Jesus' arrival), and the failure of Jesus to respond with condemnation of her actions merely confirms the fact. Jesus tells the parable of the two debtors and grudgingly the Pharisee agrees that the greater the debt, the greater the love for the one who cancels it. Jesus demonstrates his 'raw authority'[42] in forgiving her sin (not even prophets can do this, only God alone), and the religious guests quickly pick up on its significance: 'Who is this, who even forgives sin?'

The significance for us, in our context of being at ease with our sexuality, is in the extraordinary acceptance of these intimate and erotic gestures, because Jesus knows that they flow from a depth of gratitude the Pharisee knows nothing of, and that he is not about to abuse the trust of this woman, because he is in control of his sexuality. Even in our much more liberated day, these actions of a woman toward a man in public would be embarrassing. We can only guess at the courage of the woman and the inner ease of Jesus.

Moltmann likens the experience of God to the lover's experience:

> First of all there are the beginnings of the experience of love, in which something stirs us without any act of our own: the look – the lightning flash – the kindling touch, the loving embrace, the heart-warming closeness. A spark, a flame, springs from the one to the other, sometimes of almost mystical immediacy . . . Erotic relational fields come into being, with their personal resonances and shared harmonies.
>
> Experiences of God are often described in a corresponding way: the electrifying touch of the Holy Spirit, the experience of faith which warms the heart, the thrust of energy which is called 'rebirth' to a new life, life's charismatic blossoming, and not least, the shining face of God which is invoked in every benediction and from which the Spirit comes to give life peace.[43]

Not surprisingly, the expression of that love within the Christian congregation takes physical, though not sexual, form. Touch is a way that we experience the world, and a way that we can express the companionship and love of the Christian community. At the peace in the Eucharist, fellowship is expressed through the joining of hands, or the more intimate embrace. An expression of mutuality, it is an egalitarian gesture, unlike the bowing of head and knee towards the bishop in the Catholic tradition. The most intimate of signs was the 'holy kiss', taken as a matter of course by Paul.[44] The kiss on the cheek as a greeting is as common in France (currently four kisses is *de rigueur* in fashionable society) as in the Middle East, but generally reserved for family and very close friends in Britain. It again, like the embrace, is a sign of the exchange of love. Originally used at baptism and at the consecration of a bishop in the Early Church, by the fourth century it was forbidden between the sexes, and gradually waned.

The Protestant Churches emphasised the hearing of the word and eschewed the other senses, and it has only been in the recent history of the Church, under the influence of the ecumenical movement, that the more expressive ways of greeting have been rediscovered. There is always the danger of the abuse and misunderstanding of the more intimate greetings, but it seems a pity to exclude gestures which most express love from the community which is called to 'love one another'.

There is a twofold pastoral dimension to this awareness of the embodied nature of community. First, careful discipline and openness is essential if these greetings are not to be used as a pretence for a more sexual motivation, or to be misunderstood by their recipients. Personally, when greeting women, I reserve these gestures for family, close friends outside of the local church and a few elderly members, towards whom a more affectionate greeting seems to be in accord with their status as 'mothers in Israel' (the psychotherapists will have their own interpretation of my behaviour, I guess!).

Second, some in distress, both acute and chronic conditions, are helped by the gentle touch or embrace of someone of their own sex. Counselling boundaries are important here, and it should not be the role of their counsellor, nor a pastoral carer of the opposite sex, to reach out in this way, but how healing such a gesture can be in the right context and from the right person. Because we are aware of the all-pervasive misuse of sex in our culture, and perhaps because British culture is reserved in its physical expression of affection, the Church has generally shunned such expressions, to its impoverishment. We are physical beings and the two sacraments of baptism and the Lord's supper remind us of the dangers of a too cerebral setting of the faith: in them we get very wet, if full immersion is practised, and eat and drink real food. They are signs of the physicality of the resurrection hope that is the eschatological end to death.

Coping with Disagreement

The final theme in building community concerns the difficulties that arise when members disagree, fall out with one another and the unity of the community is threatened. These are often the results of the rich diversity that characterises the Church, will require abilities in relationship restoration and reconciliation on the part of the pastoral carer and leader.

The communities in the New Testament, and Jesus' disciples particularly, seem to have been familiar with conflict,[45] and the Christian community will not be able to avoid the disagreements that arise whenever any group of people become close. It is not my intention to explore in depth the reasons for conflict and the means of resolving them: that would take a book in its own right. These issues have been ably explored by others[46] and I want simply to point to some of the roots of conflict that pastoral care must uncover.

Conflicts in churches often seem to be over either minor issues (who should do the flowers on Easter day), issues of doctrine and belief (Arminian versus Calvinist, Millennial disagreements, or the place of charismatic gifts in the Church today), or over traditions and values (should we allow the baptism/dedication of children of unmarried parents or accept into full membership those in same-sex relationships). These are real areas of disagreement, and some stances are held in very non-negotiable ways based upon strongly held convictions. It is the task of leadership to find a way through those disagreements, but it is the task of pastoral care to uncover and transform attitudinal problems that arise from underlying unresolved personal issues.

The unwillingness to confront the inner hurts in a person will not see them healed, but they will only continue to fester below the surface and be a cause of irritation to themselves and others. A fear of vulnerability, a fear of losing control which leads to a 'win at all costs' response to conflict, the minimal self-image which leads to an avoidance of conflict at all costs and a sullen resentment towards the 'winners', or the fear of unacknowledged rage which spill out in murderous power, all have their impact upon conflicts and disagreements. Justin Dennison likens these to the roots of the dandelion which infests the lawn. The pastoral carer can either spend their time mowing up the leaves, or take the weed out by the roots. That means getting close, on your hands and knees, and being apparently more invasive than simply dealing with the symptoms, the unsightly leaves. Pastoral counselling is more invasive in this regard than simple resolution of the disagreement, but ultimately more healing and wholesome if the underlying causes are resolved in one or more of the protagonists.

Small Groups and Building Community

One of the most significant changes to have affected the churches in the English-speaking world over the past thirty years, and throughout the developing world for a longer period, has been the growth in importance of small groups in the Church. From the base communities of Latin American Catholicism to the charismatic house groups of the New Church movement, new contexts for worship, learning, prayer, fellowship and pastoral care have sprung up everywhere.

One expression of the growth in small groups is the base communities of South America, described by the liberation theologian, Leonardo Boff.[47] With over eighty thousand of these small groups in South America, they are lay-led groups of people at the base of society, at the bottom of the social heap. Poor and marginalised people support one another in the name of Christ, and exercise pastoral care together as they build community.

Given the poverty of their members, they work at the level of practical and physical survival the most basic level of pastoral care, and, structured around the laity, they relate to the parish (with its emphasis upon priest and sacrament) as cells within a body. In the very different social and economic conditions in the

West, direct copying of base communities has met with limited success, and an imaginative and appropriate response to their vitality awaits the Church in Britain.

Cell churches and house groups are the Western expression of the small-group movement, where the emphasis is upon prayer or Bible study and fellowship. The potential of small groups for pastoral care is enormous, and helps the move away from an individualised form of pastoral care, and, in their lay leadership, from an over-clericalising or professionalising of pastoral care. They allow people to offer pastoral care to one another within appropriate limits of competency and challenge.

The creation of small pastoral care communities within the larger life of the local church is both an imaginative response to the postmodern social challenges, and an opportunity to offer the base level of pastoral care more effectively than would otherwise be possible if pastoral care were to remain the exclusive province of the professional minister or counsellor.

The relationship of these small groups to the larger congregation could be maintained by lay leaders who have easy access to more specialised areas of pastoral care. Once the emphasis of the group has shifted from Bible study to care and friendship (which is not to say that these groups will not meet to read and study the Scriptures), then the focus moves from the meeting on, say, a Tuesday evening at 8.00 p.m. to the whole of life. The group's purpose is not so much about its meeting as about the strengthening of relationships and the building of community amongst its members.

These themes have concerned the establishment of the community, its sustenance and direction by pastoral care. It concerns human relationships in particular, and the next chapter turns to a specific relationship, that of marriage, which is in urgent need of pastoral assistance in our culture.

CHAPTER 9

The Urgent Tasks of Pastoral Care: Creating Relational Health

Overview

The second major task of pastoral care is the maintenance and nurturing of good quality relationships, particularly in marriage and family life. Many of the attributes of good relationships are generally crystallised in marriage, and so we shall look at this most intimate, but also most pressurised of relationships.

Marriage, the Problem Child of Liberal Social Contracts

Are marriages less successful than in earlier generations which had a lower rate of marriage breakdown, currently running at four out of ten marriages? It is fashionable to point to the divorce rate and cry alarm. I do not wish to appear complacent, for any marriage breakdown is a painful and potentially destructive process which, like ripples on the pond, spreads out from the couple involved to touch their children, if they have any, with particularly acute hurt, their other family members and friends. Finally, it affects the wider community in many ways, from the resulting increase in housing units required (the current growth in housing need projected to the early years of the next century is significantly fuelled by the growth in single-person households, some of which will be divorcees) to the levels of social security budget.

However, the divorce rate is a very crude indicator of the health of marriage in contemporary Britain. How much the rise in divorce rates indicates a greater ease of formally and legally ending a marriage, and a lessening of the social stigma of doing so, rather than a rise in marriage breakdown, is debatable. It may be that in earlier generations, a failed marriage was invisible to the scrutiny of statistics since the couple simply continued to be legally married and to live under the same roof, but with the relationship in terms of intimacy, companionship and love in tatters.

The willingness to tolerate the long-term consequences of a chronic marriage breakdown is declining while the expectation that a marriage relationship should be intensely affectionate and intimate (that is, meeting many of a person's needs for close and intimate human relationship) is higher than ever. At the same time, the social and cultural resources required to meet those expectations are reducing. The higher the divorce rate, the fewer the people of the succeeding generation whose experience of marriage in their parental home is one of permanence and commitment, and for most of us, the only real prior experience of marriage upon which we build our own is that of our parents.

As we have seen, the model of marriage adopted by the general mass of people is increasingly contractual as opposed to covenantal, and the general cultural milieu of postmodernism is not conducive to long-term committed relationships either. However, successful marriages are still contracted (albeit in decreasing numbers[1]) and the majority of marriages do not end in divorce, though for how much longer that will be true is anyone's guess.

In preparing for marriage those couples who wish to have their wedding in my church, I have over a number of years included some consideration of what causes marriages to fail as well as those attributes which help them to last. Among those failure-inducing factors are poor communication, sexual and emotional infidelity, chronic power struggles and the inability to successfully negotiate the stormy waters of disagreement. Some partners need to subjugate the other by a continual attack upon their needs, a continual robbing of resources from their partner in order to stay in control. Such marriages generally fail. Where trust has so broken down in the marriage that one of the partners cannot believe the truthfulness of anything their partner says, that marriage has failed. Once physical proximity to a partner has reached the flesh-crawling stage, such that being in the same room with them is unbearable, the relationship is probably beyond repair. Surprisingly, marriages can survive infidelity and the development of strongly divergent values, providing there are other factors to sustain the relationship, so that affairs and arguments are not necessarily the marriage-killers they are sometimes said to be. However, where the affair or the chronic arguments are symptomatic of a deeper malaise, they often signal the end of a relationship and cover up the other, deeper rooted condition.

Modelling Successful Marriages

The pastoral task of sustaining marriage relationships begins earlier than the first marriage preparation interview. The modelling of rich, supportive, faithful and intimate relationships within the Christian community is a necessary counterbalance to the more negative views so often experienced through the media. The kind of dysfunctional families and marriages that make great cinema do not always tell the positive side of marriage. It is too easy to portray the happy family in a schmaltzy way that implies that real life families are angry, violent places. Few films manage the balance competently: Robert Redford's directorial debut, *Ordinary People*, perhaps gets the balance better than most, with its portrayal of the family not coming to terms with the death of the elder son. Donald Sutherland plays the open-hearted father and his emotionally shrivelled wife, who is unable to give or receive love, is played with devastating coolness by Mary Tyler Moore. The final breakdown in their relationship is the counterfoil to the renewed relationship between father and younger son, who is recovering from the mental breakdown resulting from the trauma and guilt of being the survivor of the boating accident that killed his brother.

Marriage Preparation

If sustaining a climate of lasting and fruitful marriages is the first pastoral impact that can be made in the nurturing of relationships, creating a sense of realistic hope that the Christian ideal of life-long fidelity and growth is no pipe dream, the second means of developing those relationships is in marriage preparation. Far more than organising the details of the wedding ceremony, marriage preparation seeks to help couples think through the issues that will enable them to lay a strong foundation for the years that hopefully lie ahead for them. A recent course written by Paul Beasley-Murray[2] covers the quality of the present relationship, the decision to marry, communication, fighting, finances, sex, and the Christian dimension, as well as material for use with those who have already been married and are widowed or divorced. The practicalities of the wedding service are not forgotten. Its interactive style, posing questions to the couple as they work through the material, perhaps with a minister, means that the material must be discussed.

The pastoral task of preparing couples for marriage is largely limited to those married in Church, with the minister's role in preparation increasingly shared with others in the local church and aided by the availability of audio-visual courses such as the one produced by the Church Pastoral Aid Society.[3] Even so, the quality is variable, and for some, marriage preparation is little more than planning the ceremony and an act of collusion on the part of the clergy with the misguided belief that marriage is all about the wedding.

Good quality marriage preparation will avoid a didactic approach that brings in the experts on finances, health (and therefore sex) and the law to lecture the couples. This approach lacks personal engagement with the real issues and avoids working with the current difficulties in the relationship. Rather, marriage preparation should 'help the couple to understand and engage with current areas of conflict and help them understand and work through unresolved conflicts from the past',[4] aware that 'we all have to repeat compulsively the old patterns from the past in all our new relationships'.

Those married in a registry office fare less well, with no preparation offered other than that the couple choose to use from published materials, which varies from self-help books, Christian or otherwise,[5] to the shallower articles in magazines. A spokeswoman for Relate (the former Marriage Guidance Council) recently observed that more effective marriage preparation was possibly the single most effective means of cutting the rising divorce rate. The experiments being currently conducted in taking Relate counsellors into schools where they offer some teaching on relationships and marriage might go a little way to developing that, but it lacks the specifics of marriage preparation with your own partner.

Support in the Early Years of a Marriage

Support in the early years of marriage is the third pastoral task, followed by help through the typical transitions from stage to stage of a marriage: from being single to coupledom, the arrival of the first child, the departure of the last child from the parental home, and retirement. At each of these stages in the life cycle of a marriage there are particular pressures and risks, and help may be needed to negotiate troubled waters. Sue Walrond-Skinner remarks:

> A great deal of research suggests that families experience the greatest stress at points of major transition in their life cycle. It is at these points that families are most likely to seek help from friends, clergy or specialised professional workers and where we are most likely to be given the privilege of being able to respond.[6]

However, 'routine maintenance' might be more effective than crisis management, and the use of marriage enrichment teaching and experience could go some way to enabling that. Some Christian counselling organisations now provide such 'preventative' care in an attempt to supplement the first aid station at the foot of the cliff with warning notices and fences at the top.

The Qualities of Those Preparing Others for Marriage

Marriage preparation and therapy both require particular abilities and qualities in their practitioners. Bruce Reddrop, an Australian Anglican priest and former director of the Anglican Marriage Guidance Council in Melbourne, and his wife Mary, also a counsellor, describe four qualities that are essential in those pastoral carers committed to this task:[7]

- optimism about the ability of most people to change their behaviour, at least to some extent;
- optimism about marriage, even if they themselves have experienced a divorce or separation;
- the ability to learn and change by reflecting on their own experiences; and
- sturdiness and consistency in facing the difficulties that arise in their own relationships.

These qualities are undergirded by those common to all kinds of counsellors: a clarity of thinking about what the counsellor does, an ease with their own emotions and those of others, firm boundaries, and availability to others.

Clearly, simply 'having a successful marriage' is no qualification for the task on its own, and so that older couple in the congregation with a happy marriage may serve as an example to others, but may not have the other qualities necessary to be of help to couples in difficulty or to prepare other couples for marriage. Such couples may all too easily expect others to follow the aids to success that they have found work, without really listening to the pain and confusion of the couple considering separation and responding to the particularity of their woundedness. These are pastoral tasks that require skill and training that the 'successfully married' may consider unnecessary. However, experience tells me that working with couples whose marriages are in turmoil calls for the most delicate of tightrope walks between supporting both partners equally, and the need to handle jealousy, shame, anger, fear and misunderstanding, together with disappointment. The counsellor's attempts at even-handedness will be interpreted as bias differently by both partners, and always one wishes for the wisdom of Solomon in handling tricky disputes!

The Pastoral Tasks of Divorce

Where, despite the good efforts of the marriage counsellor, the relationship ends in divorce, a different set of pastoral tasks are needed. A historical perspective is helpful here, as we attempt to put the current rising divorce rate into context. Just as those who have lived through the balmy warmth of the exceptionally mild climate in Western Europe during the latter decades of this century find it hard to imagine that just three hundred years ago we were in the grip of a 'little ice age', and could be so again without much warning, the rising divorce rate is set against the context of a historically lower rate of marriage.

Walrond-Skinner quotes D. J. Dormer,[8] who poses three questions: Will marriage become obsolete? Will serial monogamy become the norm? And will Europe become a matrilineal society in the next millennium? In each generation of the first half of the twentieth century, a greater proportion of people married and at a younger age until what has been called the 'Golden Age' of marriage was reached during the 1960s and 1970s when the popularity of marriage was at its height. 'Rarely have marriage, sex and child bearing been so tightly bound together,' says Dormer, and levels of premarital sexual activity, extramarital child-bearing and cohabitation fell to very low levels. It forms a central part of the fantasy of a golden age of stability. This was echoed by John Major's evocation of England: 'long shadows on county grounds, warm beer, invincible green suburbs, dog lovers and old maids bicycling to holy communion through the morning mist', a land of Agatha Christie nostalgia and John Betjeman quaintness.

But this golden age was the exception rather than the norm, and after 1975 marriage rates fell dramatically, matched by a steep rise in the level of cohabitation and incidence of divorce. That rise in the numbers of divorce is not uniform across the social spectrum. Those who profess a religious faith and those who are in the Registrar General's social class 1 are less likely to be divorced, while those whose jobs entail long periods away from home, such as those in the armed forces, or those in social class 5, are more likely to divorce.

The period of high marriage rates in the 1960s and 1970s has been replaced by a period of falling marriage rates and rising divorce rates. This is clearly not a simple return to the characteristics of the early twentieth century, when cohabitation and divorce rates were low, but a new phenomenon of serial committed relationships as the norm. Many who divorce start new relationships, either cohabiting with their new partner or marrying them. This has a range of pastoral implications, from the care of those traumatised by the divorce process (both family members and partners who are unwilling participants in the divorce), to the new shapes that children from previous marriages bring to the family. These implications extend to the help that previously married couples need to avoid repeating the relational mistakes that contributed to the breakdown of previous marriages, and the way in which the Church affirms the life-long commitment of marriage and at the same time accepts those whose experience is of a severing of that commitment.

The pastoral carer has to walk a very ambiguous path, accepting all who warrant his or her care, irrespective of their family or marital status (because Jesus was no respecter of persons, but a friend of sinners), and at the same time guiding and preparing people to expect marriage to be life-long and strengthen the resolve of couples so that it should be so. In the postmodern experience of fragmenting relationships, short-term commitment and weak community bonds, the sustaining of marriage and the care of the divorced will, I believe, become among the most demanding and yet most valuable tasks of pastoral care.

Pastoral Care of Gay Men and Lesbians

This chapter has focused upon the sustaining of marriage in the face of the postmodern collapse of the traditional family. There are couples, however, who were never part of the traditional concept of family, but upon whom the spotlight falls in the latter years of the twentieth century: gay and lesbian partnerships.

It is almost an understatement to say that the Church is divided over the appropriate response to homosexuality, for it might well prove to be the most contentious social and ethical dilemma that the Church faces as we approach the new millennium.[9] The diverse opinions within the Church reflect a continuing diversity in society as a whole, with some arguing for the acceptance of such relationships as entirely normal, while others continue to argue for the outlawing of such relationships on the basis of perversion.

The variety of responses towards gay couples within the Christian community is rooted in the changing character of tradition and authority within the Church. Those who want a maintenance of the traditional rejection of homosexual genital sexual activity as sinful point to the 'plain reading' of Scripture[10] and the 'unnatural' nature of the relationship (on the basis that procreation requires both male and female in sexual intercourse). Others, who want a more liberal approach, argue that the Scriptures are not at all plain on the matter, with the texts supposedly prohibiting homosexual sex actually prohibiting either pagan cult prostitution or a promiscuous pursuit of sexual gratification without the commitment of a loving relationship.

In the New Testament, the key texts are all found in the epistles of Paul.[11] Paul uses the word *arsenokoitai* (did he coin it, or was it extant in Hellenistic Judaism as a result of the rendering of Leviticus 18:22?), which is best translated as 'men who sleep with other men', to describe those, amongst others, whose behaviour will exclude them from the eschatological kingdom. On the basis of these scriptural grounds, I would argue that same-sex genital relations are sinful. However, much else is sinful. It is not 'going soft' on sexual sin to point out that gossips, liars, the greedy and the swindlers also come under Paul's condemnation. Do we reject these people outright? No, we allow for grace and 'time to amend life'. The same process should be afforded to gay and lesbian couples.

The dilemma over the morality of homosexuality reflects the characteristics of the modern ethical debate that MacIntyre identified, discussed in Chapter 5. The debate is interminable because there is no longer any common ground upon which the logical claims of the competing positions can be weighed, and the plurality of historical roots means that the language we use no longer has any shared sense. The Church is and will continue to be divided over the issue, and that shows no sign of being replaced by a new consensus.

No doubt the biblical scholars will continue to debate, the theologians to theologise and ethicists to pronounce upon the rightness and wrongness of gay and lesbian couples. Meanwhile the pastoral needs of the gay and lesbian communities cannot be put indefinitely 'on hold' while the Church decides whether to sanctify them or demonise them.

For my own part, I am sufficiently a traditionalist (and, yes, I know, a heterosexual) to argue that gay and lesbian sex falls short of God's best, and does not reflect a 'normal' sexual relationship to which must be afforded all the privileges of other committed sexual relationships. However, I am sufficiently a liberal to want the Church to be a place where gay men and lesbians can find a welcome, a place to belong and a place of pastoral care, whether or not they subscribe to my own view on the morality of their sexual relationships.

Promiscuity in all of its forms, homosexual and heterosexual, is destructive and the Church rightly condemns it, but the acute pastoral question is how we should respond to the gay or lesbian couple who are in a committed, lifelong relationship of trust and love. Certainly, I believe that the Church should have a place for such couples who forego genital sexual activity and remain celibate, for it seems wrong to condemn all such people to a life of isolation and living alone. I am not so sure that the Church can condone the sexual dimension of such relationships, however, and far less celebrate it. The homosexual community will condemn me as homophobic and the traditional Christian community (including some in my own congregation and church) will condemn me as being soft on sin!

I am always struck by the fact that the friends of Jesus were the outcasts of his day: the tax collector, the publican, the prostitute, the 'sinners'. The Church must beware when its voice seems closer to that of the Pharisees than to that of its Lord.

Equally, Jesus condemns sin in the strongest of terms, while accepting the sinner in the warmest of terms.

I wonder if the Church ought not to be enabling committed gay couples, who clearly intend to live celibate lives out of respect for a 'plain reading' of Scripture, to grow in the same qualities of trust, communication and faithfulness as heterosexual couples. While I do not think that this constitutes a marriage, it seems preferable to the demonising of such people. Equally, those who want to leave behind a gay lifestyle because their conscience dictates so should not be prevented on the grounds of 'political correctness', but enabled through the agency of groups such as Courage or True Freedom Trust to receive the assistance, counselling and companionship they need.[12]

We must be clear in our distinction between temptation and sin, in order to help those who are consumed by guilt merely because of their sexual orientation. There is also a case for the rehabilitation of same-sex friendships so that companionship between members of the same sex is not regarded as 'queer', but is normal and to be encouraged. We should not be forced to read every relationship in overtly sexual terms. Furthermore, Christians should be vocal in their condemnation of discrimination against homosexuals in the work place or public life and reject the kind of vituperative and simplistic statements that owes more to homophobia than to an authentic Christian pastoral practice.

However, the Church will remain in a place of tension and ambiguity in its pastoral practice, and perhaps rightly so, for simple answers in this, as in other areas of life, are rarely helpful and generally misleading. Bonnington and Fyall put it thus:

> Pastoral struggles that focus on the exclusion and silencing of those who engage in homosexual behaviour risk driving people underground, into resistant subcultures or sectarian 'churches'. The impression of transformed community may be easier to maintain, but the tough task of demonstrating the transforming power of Jesus Christ in hard cases can too easily be avoided. Pastoral strategies that focus on inclusion and acceptance may provide an easier 'ramp' into the Church but they risk compromising its ethical integrity.[13]

Too often the gay and lesbian community hears only condemnation from the Church, as if every other dimension of life is secondary to this one area of sexuality. It is time for the Church to be truer to the heart of Jesus and reach out to these communities and help them as people first, homosexuals second.

Relational Skills in General

The relational skills needed in marriage are similar to those needed in relationships generally: effective communication and active listening, faithfulness, trust and risk-taking in deepening the relationship, forgiveness and acceptance of the other, taking personal responsibility for mistakes and a willingness to change. How many relationships break down for lack of understanding, because one partner resorts to clichés like 'I never understand women' or constantly fails to keep promises and lacks personal integrity. And how many relationships flourish, friendships as well as marriages, because small acts of thoughtfulness and concern – the letter written in times of difficulty, or trouble taken in selecting a gift that the other person will appreciate – although seemingly insignificant in themselves, express a real concern for the other person that goes deeper than words.

In a postmodern culture dominated by the market principle and competition, it takes insight and courage to show such unconditional love to another person. Relationships can so easily be conducted on the same basis as the competitive business market: 'to survive I need to get as much from this relationship as I can at the least personal cost.' This very reversal of the way of Christ, who gave all he could at utmost personal cost in order to achieve his purposes ('Who for the joy set before him, endured the cross, despising its shame'[14]), destroys healthy relationships. It seems so obvious that relationships flourish on giving, trust and forgiveness, yet time and again that proves so hard to achieve. Stephen Covey puts it thus:

> When we truly love others without condition, without strings, we help them to feel secure and safe and validated and affirmed in their essential worth, identity and integrity. Their natural growth process is encouraged. We make it easier for them to live the laws of life – cooperation, contribution, self-discipline, integrity – and to discover and live true to

> the highest and best within them. We give them the freedom to act on their own inner imperatives rather than react to our conditions and limitations. This does not mean that we become permissive or soft. That itself is a massive withdrawal. We counsel, we plead, we set limits and consequences. But we love, regardless.[15]

Relational Health at Work

The pastoral task of helping people to build and sustain healthy relationships that are close and full of integrity not only makes an impact upon family life, but is also of great significance in the one area of life most neglected by the average church: the occupation of those who worship there. The gulf between Church and work has probably never been greater. Church life generally assumes the greatest importance, followed by family life and the community in general, but the working life of Christians, unless they are in an 'acceptable vocation' like health care or teaching, is rarely considered. Yet, with the current trends of people in employment working longer and harder, while the unemployed struggle to find work, the importance of work for the average person is growing.

Equipping people for the specific tasks that they face in their work – a knowledge of the law for the lawyer, or an ability with a lathe for the machine tool maker – may not be one of the tasks of pastoral care, but enabling people to build and sustain good working relationships with colleagues and clients probably is. Through guidance (including for some that much maligned vehicle, the sermon) and by example, and with a concern for underlying emotional and psychological issues as well as current difficulties, the pastoral carer seeks to enable the individual to develop the life-skills that will sustain good quality relationships in marriage, friendships, family and work, as well as in church life. We dare not assume that such skills come naturally to people. In fact quite the reverse is true, not least because of the corrosive effects of postmodern values upon community and family.

CHAPTER 10

The Urgent Tasks of Pastoral Care: Healing the Wounded Soul

Overview

We noted at the beginning of this second part of the book that depression is at near epidemic levels in the West and that the reasons for this have been variously located in the demise of the traditional family, in the general climate of uncertainty over work, truth and family, in the loss of religious faith or in hitherto hidden levels of childhood abuse, amongst a host of possibilities. Depression is not alone in being a disease of the soul. Clients with anxiety states and episodes of panic, low self-esteem, unresolved grief or sexual incapacity are all likely to be familiar to the counsellor or pastor. While we build community and enable relationships we cannot ignore these wounded people, any more than the community building a new hospital can ask all its ill people to kindly wait for two years until it is completed and then they can be sick. The tasks of prevention and cure go hand in hand. However, where the single focus of pastoral care is in responding to the wounded the vision for prevention is considerably narrowed. The demands made upon some pastors by the individuals who are severely wounded in soul can occlude that broader vision, and, as we shall see in Chapter 13, the development of a pastoral team can help ease the load on the individual carer or pastor and enable them to keep all the urgent tasks in focus. The opposite is also sadly familiar: the pastor who is so concerned with the group and the community building processes that they have no time left for the individual who simply cannot cope with the pain of living any longer. I take it as axiomatic that the two poles of the individual in need and the community relationships that need building and sustaining are both of concern to those engaged in the pastoral task. In the previous two chapters we have considered the latter. Here we shall consider the former.

Of the five traditional tasks of pastoral care listed by Clebsch and Jaekle (see Chapter 1), the task of healing is most in focus here, while sustaining and reconciling were most in evidence in the previous chapters on building community and building relational health. Of all those tasks, the one concerned with healing has been most influenced by Freud's 'talking cure', as we saw in Chapter 2. Whether the pastor is professionally trained in psychotherapy or counselling, or simply influenced by the insights of therapy and counselling, few remain untouched by the therapeutic revolution of the twentieth century. 'The gospel of counselling is gradually leavening pastoral practice even at the level of general and subconscious assumptions.'[1] So it seems fitting to make some observations at this point on the relationship of pastoral care to the practice of counselling.

The Revolution in Pastoral Care: Christian Responses

The historical processes described in Chapter 2 have resulted in nothing less than a revolution in the way that pastoral care has approached the individual in need. As Atkinson and Bridger note:

> The modern notion of a one-to-one privatised counselling relationship in which the troubled client comes for help to the professional expert representative of nobody but himself is in historical terms anachronistic.[2]

Historically, pastoral care was a ministry of the whole community of faith, represented by the pastor, who acted on behalf of God and his people. A theological understanding of people and their needs, their createdness, sinfulness and redemption, was central. The practice of pastoral care was never morally neutral, but always embraced the values of the Christian community, and personal growth was grounded in Christian spirituality: the Bible, fellowship, worship, the sacraments and prayer.

The revolution consists in the shifts of emphasis in the psychotherapeutic model. Here, a one-to-one model is the locus of pastoral care, with the therapist or counsellor trained in therapeutic skills and theory as its practitioner. A generally humanistic understanding of people and their needs replaces a Christian one, with the translation of traditional theological concepts into psychoanalytical ones: failure replaces sin, resolution and self-acceptance replace atonement and redemption, and self-awareness replaces guilt. Given such a transformation in the mode of pastoral care, it is not surprising that there have been a range of responses to the revolution by the Christian community, as we saw in Chapter 1.

Psychological and Theological Interfaces

The relationship of the theological model to the psychological categories will determine the nature of the integration of therapeutic practice and theological concepts. The analysis of this relationship has been thoroughly explored by Roger Hurding and Kirk Farnsworth, among others. Roger Hurding identifies five different responses to the challenge of psychology[3]

(i) Its insights are excluded and its value rejected, ranging from outright rejection to more particularising views that point out alien methodologies and concepts. Among those adopting this position are Jay Adams and Paul Vitz.

(ii) There is a compartmentalising response which values both psychological and theological perspectives, but sees little area of overlap between them, either from a theoretical point of view, or for more pragmatic reasons of personal compartmentalising of the working world and the worshipping faith.

(iii) There is an assimilative response, whereby the Christian practitioner or theoretician adopts uncritically the concepts derived from psychotherapy, seeing them as usurping traditional Christian understandings. The rise of pastoral counselling in the United States owes much to this response, as does the work of Leslie Weatherhead and William Kyle in Britain. The latter founded the influential Westminster Pastoral Foundation, currently a significant training organisation in psychodynamic counselling.

(iv) If the trade in the assimilative approach just described is essentially one way, the eclectic approach sees ideas and methodologies adopted from a variety of sources, including Christian concepts, for essentially pragmatic reasons – if it seems to work, then use it. Others adopt an eclectic approach for more thoughtful reasons, and numbered in this category are Paul Tournier and Frank Lake.

(v) There is finally an integrational approach. This is an attempt to bring together psychological and theological insights into a specifically Christian methodology. Either there is an attempt to find common ground, or psychological approaches are subsumed within a controlling theological framework, often of a more conservative than liberal nature. Larry Crabb and Gary Collins in the United States follow the latter route, as do Atkinson and Bridger.

Another exploration of this territory has been undertaken by Kirk Farnsworth in the United States.[4] He is concerned with those who attempt the integration of psychology and theology (that is, those who adopt the latter four of Hurding's five categories).

(i) In the credibility model, psychological insights are only admitted if they pass through a theological filter, usually a conservative reading of Scripture. If the insight conflicts with Scripture, it is rejected. Farnsworth cites Crabb as his example of this approach.

(ii) He describes the converse as the convertibility model, where theology is revised by a controlling psychology.

(iii) In the conformability model, the psychological findings are revised by a broader 'Christian worldview' rather than a narrower scriptural perspective. The question posed to a psychological insight is not 'is this idea commensurate with scriptural passages or ideas?' but rather 'does it conform to the whole Christian worldview?'

(iv) The attempts to equate theological ideas with psychological categories is dubbed the compatibility model. Here, psychological notions like resolution and self-acceptance are placed alongside theological categories like reconciliation or redemption, and points of similarity are used to show that they are describing the same phenomena.

(v) Farnsworth's own position is the complementarity model. Phenomena are described from different perspectives according to the disciplines asking questions of it. Since the psychologist and the theologian are asking different questions it is not surprising that different descriptors are forthcoming, but the insights complement each other at different levels.

Both Farnsworth and Hurding, as well as Atkinson and Bridger, reject the extreme positions of exclusion and outright assimilation. These positions reduce either psychology or theology and 'run the risk of imposing either a theological or psychological imperialism'.[5] The problem of compatibility arises when psychotherapy interprets a phenomenon like guilt in a quite different way to theology. Christians at that point can too easily recall that theology is paramount, and reject all the insights from psychology. Thus, while psychotherapy cannot account for the objective guilt of sin before a holy God, it does accurately equate the 'false guilt', which is so much more difficult to handle, with the super-ego of the Freudian model.

Atkinson and Bridger argue for 'a kind of critical perspectivalism in which no discipline is allowed hegemony or totality of explanation but in which all disciplines subject themselves to mutual criticism'.[6] Thus, psychotherapy can account for false guilt, but not an exhaustive account of all guilt, whereas theology, focusing on moral guilt, gives a better account of some forms of guilt, but not as sophisticated an account of false guilt. The disciplines need one another. This approach is a more developed version of the approach that Hurding also takes, and is one I am happy to adopt. It is predicated on the belief that all truth is God's truth, and that theology is as ill-equipped to answer questions of a scientific character as science is to answer questions of a religious character. The common enemy to both is the cultural hegemonist. This means that Christianity should not fear to cry 'wrong' when psychology makes claims that seem to differ from the world-view and moral values of orthodox Christian faith.

The Client–Counsellor Relationship

A well-known piece of research by two therapists in the 1960s describes three personal qualities for effective counselling. Charles Truax, a colleague of Carl Rogers, and Robert Carkhuff analysed the available literature and concluded that, irrespective of the theoretical background, the effective counsellor possesses genuineness, non-possessive warmth and accurate empathy.[7]

Genuineness describes consistency in the counsellor, or 'authenticity', which comes from sufficient self-awareness to see his or her weaknesses and a degree of transparency in relationships. Together these enable the counsellor to have sufficient security as a person to weather the storms of helping another person in distress, without being over-concerned about status or success. This sets the client free to be unconcerned about the therapist's well-being and enables the counsellor to be available to the client. Genuineness cannot be manufactured: it must be really present, but can be learnt by self-awareness.

Non-possessive warmth is the quality of really being concerned for the client's welfare. Rogers described it as 'unconditional positive regard', the communication of respect and concern. This comes from the counsellor being 'safe' in the realm of emotions and feelings, and not being flustered by painful or hostile material. We have already commented upon the non-judgmental qualities in our discussion of value-free therapy, but here it means the avoidance of dismissing clients with a summary comment, such as 'He's just neurotic' or 'She is simply irresponsible'. An open mind must be kept, and careful listening to all that is said and left unsaid. Non-possessive also means non-manipulative, in the sense that the counsellor does not leave the client feeling beholden to or owned by the counsellor. Here again, self-awareness and honesty on the part of the counsellor should be sufficient to avoid the traps of voyeurism, dependency or power over others. Also, supervision is necessary to help keep those destructive demons at bay. The result of this uncontaminated caring is self-responsibility and independence by the client.

Accurate empathy is the act of metaphorically stepping into another's shoes, seeing the world through their eyes and following their story. A couple of years ago, on holiday in Scotland, I saw a skua attacking terns to force them to drop their catch. The skua followed every twist and turn of the unfortunate tern, itself a nimble flier, until it dropped its fish and the skua swooped and caught it. That skilled following of another was a powerful picture of the accurate empathy the counsellor needs to journey with her client through all the twists and turns of his journey. There are skills to be learnt in active listening to the client that help this accurate empathy, but there needs to be a basic understanding of others that cannot be learnt if its seeds are not present.

The importance of the presence of these qualities for the counsellor and pastor cannot be over-emphasised. Irrespective of the theoretical perspectives we hold, these very human qualities, which are also very divine qualities (akin to faithfulness, *agape* love and the incarnational presence of Emmanuel, God-with-us) point to the quality of the helping relationship as the key factor in the effectiveness of the therapy. Let us not suspect that it is true only for the pastoral counsellor, for all ministry ultimately depends on the qualities of the divine relationship and human relationships: that is, the spiritual and relational characteristics of the pastor. Tom Oden points to the near equivalence of the concepts of therapy and ministry:

> A *therapon* (from which . . . 'therapist' comes) is one who helps, serves and heals. The Latin translation . . . is *ministerium*, from which . . . 'minister' comes. Thus the roots of therapy and ministry are closely intertwined . . . the pastoral office has from the beginnings been thought of literally as a therapeutic relationship.[8]

In the pastoral task of healing the wounded soul we dare not embrace the philosophy of the technical society, where the skill with techniques is all that matters. That might be just about acceptable for learning the techniques of cooking, but even here, I guess, it is the recipes that one learns from one's mother that count, because of the relational quality, hence the approbation 'Umm, just like Mother made.' This emphasis upon the relational quality of the counselling exchange is not surprising, given Christianity's understanding of human existence following the patterns of the divine life: we are made in the image of God, and he is Being-in-relationship, the triune God. The healing of human psychological woundedness will come from relationships of trust, responsibility and empathy: precisely the kind of relationship that pastoral counsellors aspire to.

The Therapeutic Relationship

Petrüska Clarkson, in her profoundly humane book *The Therapeutic Relationship*,[9] explores the nature of this relationship in great depth. The approach is postmodern in its distrust of one kind of therapeutic relationship. In its place is a matrix of five kinds of relationship between therapist and client 'by which to make sense of all the many competing, contrasting or even contradictory views on the human condition and what to do about it'. Her agreement with the findings of Carkhuff and Truax of some thirty years ago is fundamental: 'Now the bulk of research points to the fact that the most important factor in effective psychotherapeutic work is the relationship between the client and the psychologist.'[10] Indeed, the relationship between therapist and client is not so much the medium in which the work is done, but is actually the work itself. This leads to a flexibility with the boundaries, 'the rules of the game' that, when adhered to, help novices to be safe. It is a well-kept secret that more-experienced therapists resemble each other in what they do more than their differing ideological systems would suggest. Rules are broken, for the sake of the healing process, just as they are, sadly, sometimes broken because the therapist loses self-control and enters into abusive activity with the client.

Clarkson identifies types of psychotherapeutic relationships that are potentially present in any psychotherapeutic encounter. A current definition of psychotherapy emphasises this relational priority: psychotherapy is 'the . . . systematic use of a relationship between therapist and patient – as opposed to pharmacological or social methods – to produce changes in cognition, feelings and behaviour'.[11] The five relationships are:

(i) The working alliance. This is the cooperation between client and therapist that enables the long and painful work of psychotherapy to be undertaken. It includes the agreement of goals to be aimed for, the nature of the tasks to reach that goal and the personal bond, or therapeutic relationship, between client and therapist. Fundamental to the establishment of this working alliance are those familiar qualities found in the effective therapist: accurate empathy, unconditional positive regard and genuineness.

(ii) The transferential/countertransferential relationship. In the Freudian and psychodynamic schools of psychotherapy the key process is transference. It is a process whereby infantile prototypes re-emerge and are experienced with a strong sense of immediacy in the context of the analytical relationship with the client mistaking the therapist for a significant other person, such as their mother or grandfather. Thus feelings towards the therapist of hate or envy may indicate, actually, hatred of the step-parent, and feelings of love or protection towards the therapist may resonate with a grandparent who was a source of comfort in an abusive home environment.

(iii) The reparative/developmentally-needed relationship. Here, the therapist intentionally provides a corrective/reparative or replenishing parental relationship where the original parenting was deficient, abusive or over-protective. The therapeutic relationship goes some way to repair earlier damage, for instance where the client was overburdened with parental intimacies or caring responsibilities for an ill parent. Here, what is communicated by the therapist is 'Do not worry about me, I am here to take care of you and I am ready to do that.' This kind of relationship is closer to that of parent and child than any other kind of psychotherapeutic relationship, and calls for great demands upon the therapist or counsellor.

(iv) The person-to-person relationship is the focus of the humanistic and existential traditions within psychotherapy, for instance in person-centred therapy. Here, the therapist is not representative of a parent, or a significant other, but is only representative of herself. It is a real relationship between therapist and client, and not an object relationship. Emotional involvement between therapist and client is between person and person, and has potential for profound healing. It is difficult, demanding and potentially abusive work by the therapist, which is why orthodox analysands viewed it with suspicion. 'It probably requires the most skill, the most self-knowledge and the greatest care because of its potential for careless or destructive use is so great. Its influence is, however, unavoidable.'[12] It is important for the therapist to want to help and cure the patient, and there must be some emotional commitment to the patient: prolonged dislike or disinterest, as well as too strong a love, interfere with the therapy. The skilled use of immediacy and self-disclosure, whereby the therapist 'lets down the professional mask' are key to establishing this person-to-person relationship.

(v) The transpersonal relationship refers to the spiritual or inexplicable dimensions of relationship in psychotherapy. This is the least explored aspect of the therapeutic relationship, possibly because many therapists are embarrassed by the notion of a spiritual dimension (psychotherapy, after all, has pretensions to be a science), or by the admission that:

> after all the years of training and personal analysis and supervision, ultimately we still don't know precisely what it is that we are doing or whether it makes any difference at all. This is the kind of statement one can only be sure of being understood by experienced psychotherapists who have been faced repeatedly with incomprehensible and unpredictable outcomes – the person of whom you despaired, suddenly and sometimes apparently inexplicably, gets well, thrives and actualises beyond all expectation.[13]

It is as if the real work is numinous and goes on in the space between the therapist and client by some unseen power. As a Christian, I would recognise that numinous presence as the Spirit of God, present in all healing processes, as Eric Berne recognises when he quotes 'Je le pensay et Dieu le guarit' – 'We treat them, but it is God who cures them.'[14]

At heart, there needs to be a real human love for the client by the therapist, or to use a phrase that seems less threatening to the perceived boundaries, 'empathic warmth'. Brian Thorne, a person-centred therapist who is also a Christian, writes of the recognition of this love through reading Carl Rogers.

> I had reached a point, I believe, where I was painfully confused about what it might mean to love another human being; furthermore when I tried to do so I often felt naïve or sensed that I had illicitly moved across sacrosanct boundaries, As I devoured Carl's words in *On Becoming a Counsellor* (1961) and *Client-centred Therapy* (1951) my confusion evaporated. I recognised instantly that to offer clients the kind of relationship characterised by the presence of the core conditions was, in practice, to love them.[15]

In the multiplicity of therapeutic relationship modes in pastoral counselling and pastoral care we assume different roles: we will be perceived as friend, parent, sibling, fairy godmother and wicked witch. All sorts of expectations of salvation, liberation, rescue and seduction will be projected onto us. In recoiling from those projections which we find distasteful and threatening we must not lose sight of the continuing need to love. Self-awareness and self-discipline are indispensable requirements for the effective, but safe, pastor. As Clarkson puts it:

> We are required to act constantly in the arena of love, yet renounce all personal gratification; we work in one of the most potent cauldrons of intimacy yet we are prohibited to drink from it; we give solace or wisdom perhaps to those who suffer, knowing full well that we ourselves are wounded healers, scarred by similar terrors, griefs and excesses as those who consult us . . . Of course there is joy, satisfaction, awe and wonder as well, but is it any wonder that there is such a high incidence of breakdown, loneliness, burnout and cynicism in this profession?[16]

Exactly so, not only for psychotherapists, but for pastors also. In a subsequent chapter we shall investigate the resources needed for the pastoral counsellor and carer to sustain the self-awareness and self-discipline that I believe are indispensable.

For an existentialist and humanistic psychotherapist like Petrüska Clarkson, as also for the Christian transpersonal counsellor, relationships are the medium and the work of therapy. For the Christian, that is derived from an understanding of what it is to be human rooted in Trinitarian theology and a belief that Jesus Christ is the defining human being as well as the perfect revelation of who God is. God's grace is at work in the sustaining of human relationship and the particular relationship of therapist to client, whatever the philosophical or theological beliefs of that therapist. However, I do believe that the specifically Christian understanding of forgiveness and grace, sin and guilt, places therapy in a broader context with more appropriate resources to resolve guilt than any secular therapy that ignores the relationship we have with a creator and redeemer God. It is to the knotty issue of forgiveness and shame that we now turn to illustrate the distinctive shape that Christian pastoral care gives to the healing of the wounded soul.

Forgiveness and Guilt: A Spiritual Dimension in Pastoral Counselling

One of the most common conditions encountered in the therapy or counselling room is an overwhelming, constricting sense of guilt. That guilt may be rooted in an objective experience of breaking God's law, of transgressing an objective moral order and of being indebted thereby to God. The experience of it might be a pervasive sense of shame, a distance from God and others, and even physical ill-health. The Psalmist puts it thus in Psalm 51:2–4:

> Wash away all my iniquity and cleanse me from my sin.
> For I know my transgressions, and my sin is always before me.
> Against you, you only have I sinned and done what is evil in your sight,
> so that you are proved right when you speak and justified when you judge.

Here is a sense of failure to meet God's standards, an uncleanness of the soul that is responsive to only one cure, forgiveness. David's experience of guilt is described as feeling filthy (wash away all my iniquity), an inner self-deception (surely you desire truth in the inner parts), an exposure to judgment (hide your face from my sins), a lack of inner integrity, peace and joy (create in me a pure heart; restore to me the joy of your salvation), and results in a broken heart. No amount of psychological help can restore that broken relationship between the psalmist and his God, any more than it can restore ours. It is not a psychological problem but a spiritual one, and the promise of Scripture and the experience of every generation of Christian is that God does have mercy on us, he does forgive sin, and he does restore our broken relationship with him when we turn to him in repentance and faith.

Part of the pastoral task is the hearing of confession, the affirming of God's forgiveness in the expression of absolution and the encouraging of the faint-hearted to believe that: 'If we say that we have no sin, we deceive ourselves, and the truth is not in us: But if we confess our sins, He is faithful and just to forgive us our sins, and to cleanse us from all unrighteousness.'[17] The nouthetic (from the Greek *noutheteo*, to warn) counselling approach of Jay Adams at least has value at this point. This approach has little to offer in other areas, I believe, but here it points to a central concern of the Christian gospel: sinful men and women need to receive God's forgiveness and new life, and the reception of that has a therapeutic result. We are moral persons with responsibility for our actions, capable of great evil and of great good also. Forgiveness points to our state betwixt the angel and the animal, created yet fallen, neither all bad nor wholly good. We are not irredeemable, nor are we perfect, and forgiveness recognises both aspects. The good news that Jesus speaks to the sinful woman we considered in an earlier section was: 'Your sins are forgiven, go in peace.' There is the invigorating breath of grace to blow away the dust of a guilty conscience, not by ignoring it, but by confessing it and receiving God's forgiveness. This distinctive Christian viewpoint must not be ignored.

Chronic Shame

However, there is another kind of guilt, a chronic sense of shame, that can be a 'life-long affair with chronic not-goodenoughness'.[18] This is not the result of some proper sinning (lacking the courage to sin bravely and the imagination to sin in style!), but of a chronic sense of failure, inadequacy, self-loathing and despair. It is a heaviness of spirit like wading through heavy snow: every step is an effort, and confession only makes us feel worse. Smedes differentiates it from feeling embarrassed, like when you drop the glass of red wine on your host's new white rug, feeling discouraged when you fail that exam yet again, being depressed, which is a clinical condition, and feeling frustrated at our limits. None of these are shame or false guilt. Rather, there are types of people for whom chronic shame is a living reality. Those with over-scrupulous consciences, for whom one slip makes them the worst of all sinners, those who carry the responsibility for the whole world on their shoulders, those who are in constant need of the approval of others or who never feel they deserve any good. Those who cannot live up to the successes and standards of their parents are candidates for this unhealthy shame: everything they do falls short of Mother's brilliance, of Father's diligence.

Even successful people can be dogged by a sense of shameful failure. John Quincy Adams, the US Ambassador to Holland, Great Britain and Russia, Secretary of State, Senator and sixth President, 1824–28, wrote: 'My life has been spent in vain and idle aspirations, and in ceaseless rejected prayers that something beneficial should be the result of my existence.' That is unhealthy shame. It was probably derived from his father, the second President of the United States, who taught his children that they were to strive to be moral examples to the masses. Each of his children was haunted by a sense of shame, and some silenced that voice in suicide or alcohol. John Quincy tried to silence his in great distinction, to little avail. False shame comes from parents who demand too much or from religion which is devoid of grace but heavy with condemnation. It can also come from the false values of secular culture which declare, for instance, to the young woman that to feel good about herself she must look good, dress in designer clothes and be a size 8, and to the young man that he must succeed at work, be wealthy and drive a smart sports car.

Such chronic shame is a sickness of the soul. The ungracious and narrow-minded pastor will identify a point of leverage and amplify the sense of shame by demanding repentance and talking in simplistic terms of the need for forgiveness. What is actually needed is a gracious acceptance by another as the catalyst to an accepting of ourselves, the shadowy self as well as the public self, and an enjoyment of who we are. The antidote to shame is grace. The skilful pastoral counsellor or pastor has a significant part to play in the discovery of graced existence for shame-filled people, and the more gracious we are the greater the significance of our role in healing this sickness of the human soul.

The means for healing this sickness, as for others that we shall not explore in depth – depression, grief, or anxiety – lie in the quality of relationship we forge with the person in need and the meaning we create with them for living, since people are always persons on the way to becoming, and in the sense of meaning that is discovered. This means, with Paul Ricoeur[19] and Jurgen Habermas,[20] that counselling is a search for meaning, a form of hermeneutics of a person's life, with the therapist as midwife to the client's discovery of meaning. As the client tells his story, the counsellor provides interpretive clues to the meaning of the events and responses. The client moves into the world of language and out of the private world in telling their story to the therapist, and analogy is a key stage in that interpretation. 'It's like I'm . . .' and 'It's as if I . . .' are stages on the interpretive journey towards meaning and healing. Finally, though, after the relationship is forged, the story understood and meaning found, there is still a step towards healing that is mysterious. We need to ask next, if God is the one who cures, where is he in the counselling room or the pastor's study?

God in the Counselling Room

We saw already that transpersonal counselling has room for Another in the relationship between client and counsellor, although traditionally psychotherapy had little room for 'God stuff'. Secular and Christian counsellors alike, however, speak of the spiritual dimension, the transcendent, the numinous, the sacred or the unknown, the language used reflecting their religious perspectives. It has to do with the grace that attends therapeutic work.

Responses to this perception of graced therapeutic encounter range from rejection of its validity because of the compartmentalising of psychology and faith that some Christians indulge in (how can God possibly be in something as unspiritual as psychotherapy?) to the converse rejection by others derisive of New Age influences on the rational science of psychotherapy. Christians of a charismatic persuasion often want to make the whole enterprise transcendent (although they would not want to use that phrase) by drowning the real hard work of the person-to-person and transferential exchanges in a sea of spiritual interpretation and direct divine intervention. Neither of these responses is helpful. Rather, there needs to be a proper place for both the human and the divine work in the counselling room.

Before becoming too explicit in our placing of the Christian God in the therapeutic exchange, we need to note that there is widespread admission that there is more to the process than the human elements. Such admissions are often clouded by the ambivalent attitude towards the spiritual in the therapeutic community, as if it is not a legitimate part of the work (we have already seen the roots of this in the public/private dichotomy in modernism). There is also difficulty in employing language to describe the ultimate experiences, language which spirituality forged but which a secular culture is profoundly uncomfortable with, as well as a fear that to describe such experience is somehow to lose it. Despite such ambivalence, Maslow can speak of the transpersonal dimension as 'resacralising . . . being willing, once again, to see a person "under the aspect of eternity", as Spinoza says, or to see him in the medieval Christian unitive perception, that is, being able to see the sacred, the eternal, the symbolic.'[21] Roberto Assagioli is another psychotherapist working expressly with transpersonal material, and Carl Jung hardly needs mentioning, so well-known is his inclusion of a spiritual dimension.

The Christian might ask, just because it's spiritual, does it necessarily mean it's good and it's God? Of course it does not, and the Christian pastoral counsellor needs to be aware of spiritual forces present that are malignant and evil. The Freudian analyst and Director of Psychological Services at the Lister Hospital where I serve as Free Church Chaplain, Phil Mollon, writes of the work with patients suffering from multiple personality disorder and the apparent perverse evil that sometimes seems to lie behind it. He says that while the source of evil is obscure, its presence 'suggests the possibility of a state of mind which is dedicated to evil and to a perversion of normal values. Evil appears to be an active component of mental life and not merely an absence of good.'[22]

On the whole, I believe that the transpersonal experience has its source in God, whether explicitly Christian or not, when found in the course of therapy which has the healing and welfare of the client in mind. The Christian would want, perhaps, to be open to that presence in a more conscious way through prayer *for* the client, and sometimes (used with great discretion) prayer *with* the client. The pastoral counsellor becomes aware that they are both truly themselves, that is, not taken over by some divine force in a trance-like state, and yet at the same time they are a vessel for God's use, even though that vessel might be a clay pot.[23] In the substance and hard work of the counselling relationship there is a presence, an empowering, that is grace, God himself. He is the unseen listener, healer, insight-giver, and grace-provider in the space between counsellor and client. His presence is not limited to those occasions when it is specifically sought through prayer or epiclesis, but is preveniently present at all times, holding the process within the embrace of his grace.

This is also the place to observe some of the opportunities and dangers of prayer in the counselling room. For some clients, and also for a few counsellors, prayer is the way that God is brought into the therapy. If there is no prayer, the suspicion is that he has not turned up, and the counselling feels desacralised and unsafe. I am sure that much of this is infantile, prayer becoming a sort of transitional object, yet some Christian clients need that object to make the journey safe enough to do the work. Prayer can, of course, be abused in this way and used, on the part of client and counsellor alike, as a way of avoiding the uncomfortable work that needs to be done. Similarly, it can be a way of saying something that is too uncomfortable to say face-to-face. Worse is the use of prayer by the counsellor as a way of giving advice, moralising or manipulating the client. Also reprehensible is the use of prayer to short circuit the therapeutic process, to somehow speed it up and save time. This rarely has long-term effectiveness, although it often seems to the inexperienced to have short-term benefits.

Prayer is not a therapeutic technique but the expression of the relationship between us and God, and more often listening than speaking. While the counselling room is not generally the place for such prayer, there is often great comfort found by the client in knowing that there are those praying for them. It is a sign of thoughtfulness and fellowship, of concern by the wider circle of close friends. Heaven forbid that the pastoral counsellor's or pastor's appointment list should be open to general scrutiny for 'the purposes of prayer' but the client might want to take responsibility for asking two or three trusted and close friends to be praying for them before, during and after the therapy sessions. Similarly, knowing that the pastoral counsellor is not just there for that session only, but prays for the client at other times, can be reassuring and part of the person-to-person relationship that includes a shared faith.

Healing the Postmodern Wounded Soul

We have been concerned with the healing of the troubled soul. This is not a 'how to' guide to Christian counselling, but a suggested programme for the priorities of pastoral care, and the details of the means and wherefores of counselling are amply covered in many textbooks. However, there are some ways of engaging in the therapeutic relationship that are congruent with the postmodern condition which is our cultural and social context. I have suggested that the key factors in the process are the therapeutic relationship and an openness to the transcendental dimension which I interpret as the gracious presence of God. Skills levels are not to be ignored, but in this technical society, faith can be put in the use of skills apart from the human relationships that contextualise and humanise them. The acquisition of skills and an adequate theoretical grounding in the Egan model, transactional analysis or psychodynamic counselling cannot be a substitute for the core quality in the counsellor:

a willingness to love the other, the client, within therapeutic boundaries and a desire to see them healed, whole and growing, both in their humanity and in grace, which are, of course, one and the same thing.

CHAPTER 11

The Urgent Tasks of Pastoral Care: Nurturing and Sustaining Faith

Overview

There are distinctions about pastoral care because of its religious, particularly Christian, world-view and practice. To be sustained, pastoral care needs to be the practice of credible and effective care, but also it needs to nourish the faith of the community that makes it *pastoral* care, and not just good social work. The priority of nurturing faith, then, is not just a rather quaint aspect of pastoral care to keep it sufficiently religious, it is the nurturing of the very community of faith that gives pastoral care its distinctive character.

Half a century ago there would have been no necessity to argue for a place for the nurturing and sustaining of faith within the tasks of pastoral care. The heart of what many pastors would have considered to be their calling was the preaching and teaching of the faith and the discipling of men and women in the Christian faith. Such an understanding of the main task of the pastor is still to be found in many places. But there has been a subtle shift, generally, away from that priority to a much greater emphasis upon the therapeutic roles we outlined in the previous three chapters. The changes were outlined in the opening chapter, and I do not want to labour the point, but change has been profound. Whether you bewail it as a sign that pastors have sold their spiritual birthright for a mess of humanistic pottage, or welcome the change as an indicator that pastoral ministry has rediscovered its true focus, the perception remains that pastoral care has become overwhelmingly therapeutic in style and content and does not always feel comfortable with an overtly didactic role in teaching the faith or nourishing spiritual values.

There is, however, another trend which seems to contradict the move to therapeutise pastoral care. I refer to the growth in interest in spirituality, in spiritual direction in the Church, and in the 'spiritual' generally within the wider community. The impact of postmodernism upon the religious world has been most evident in the growth of New Age spirituality, with its potent mix of Eastern Hindu spirituality, late nineteenth-century theosophy and spiritualism, the occult and self-help philosophy. Mainstream Christianity in the West has also been impacted in various ways by postmodernism.

The influence of the postmodern culture on the Church comes first from the way in which society as a whole is affected, because like it or not we are part of that society. Firstly, postmodern culture is acutely aware of its multicultural composition. Before Elizabeth David, the English writer on cookery who introduced the post-rationing generation to Mediterranean and French cuisines a generation ago, how many British families ate foreign food? Even on holiday they looked for their Sunday roast or fish and chips. Now we eat pizzas, pasta, Indian and Chinese dishes with little thought. In the cities you can eat Mexican, Thai, Japanese and endless variations on the Chinese theme with ease. However, postmodern culture levels the significance of these cultures, so that Western culture should not be imperialist. At the same time it exaggerates the differences between them so that society breaks up into contending interest groups and mutually unintelligible tribal groupings.

This fragmentation is encouraged by the plethora of TV channels now available on cable and satellite. We are beginning to see tribal narrowings of the appeal of these. So we have the Asian channels and Premier Radio, a Christian Radio channel. Indeed, in this postmodern culture Christianity has become a distinct subculture already: it has its own bookshops, music, radio station, satellite TV channel, schools and festivals. Postmodern society allows room for Christianity, but only in its cultural space. This may result in a more faithful Church, a closer Christian community, but the cost might be too high if we cease to be salt and light to the whole.

The Shape of Postmodern Religion

The battle lines with modernism were drawn in the closing years of the last century. Traditional Christianity, taking the Bible as its foundation, accepting the truth of the supernatural and the reality of God and the eternal, found itself fighting a modernist, liberal Christian faith which sought to make the faith palatable to modern, scientific man. There was scepticism about the supernatural, the historic truth of the Bible and the traditional Christian doctrines. Now the battle lines have moved on. The postmodern era holds promise for orthodox Christians, but it also holds new and different perils. Modernists may not believe the Bible is true, but as we have seen, postmodernists have thrown out the category of universal truth altogether. In its place emerges the chaos of New Age religions and moral diversity. The danger is that, far from clearly countering this new enemy, the churches actually absorb it, and this time round the evangelical churches are affected as much as the liberals.

Remember that it is said of postmodernists that they do not believe what is true, they believe what they like. 'I like Church,' people may say; 'Christians are nice folk, good to be around, helpful when you are in a fix. But I do not like what the Church preaches about judgment or holiness.' Postmodernists pick and choose what they believe on the basis of choice. We now have the supermarket of religion where you choose what takes your fancy and leave the rest.

The trends in postmodern Christianity are varied. Among them I would identify the following.

Postmodern Christianity values experience over belief. We have a generation which wants to experience God but lacks the will to think about their faith. The charismatics are most vulnerable to this. Experience becomes the criterion for evaluating doctrine. They must be right (whatever they teach) because 'God' was experienced there. In this regard the Toronto Blessing might be the first international postmodern Christian phenomenon, as well as, perhaps, being a genuine move of God's Spirit.

It is becoming a subculture, less interested in addressing the society as a whole and settling for a kind of tribal ghetto providing its own music, literature, entertainment and education.

Postmodern thought is impatient with transcendent spiritual beliefs; the focus shifts to the here and now. People have little interest in heaven; they want health and wealth now. Since postmodernists are oriented to power, they will be drawn to churches that promise to solve every problem. Luther describes this as a theology of glory, in contrast to the theology of the cross, based on the suffering of Jesus Christ. If the Church allows this culture to dance like Salome before it and to seduce its affections for short-term gratification, the Church ought not to be surprised if it then demands its head on a platter.

It is fascinated by spirituality which draws upon a great variety of traditions. For the average evangelical or Broad Church believer up until the 1970s 'spirituality' was the preserve of the Catholics. It concerned retreats, ritual, direction and devotion to Mary, none of which was to the taste of the non-Catholic. I can identify a sea change within the tradition that I grew up in, the evangelicals, which began around the mid-1970s. Elements of Catholic spirituality, previously shunned as dangerous or irrelevant, became fashionable. It was acceptable to go on retreat, to read the writings of the spiritual giants such as St John of the Cross or to explore contemplative prayer. The reasons behind this change include the impact of the Ecumenical movement, particularly in combination with the discovery that charismatics could be both Baptist and Roman Catholic, High and Low Anglican,' and the impact of two popular authors upon the Evangelical scene, Richard Foster[1] and Joyce Huggett.[2] Perhaps more significant is the growth in interest in all things spiritual in the postmodern reaction to the scientific and materialist metanarrative.

Richard Foster, an American Quaker, drew upon the resources

of the New Testament, the Early Church and the spiritual writers of the Catholic tradition especially. His book was helped by a foreword written by David Watson, whose endorsement in the early 1980s really counted, and the book was widely read. For many evangelicals it opened up vistas on discipleship that they hardly knew existed, such as meditation, simplicity, and solitude.

Joyce Huggett had written books before *Listening to God*, particularly around the theme of courtship, marriage, relationships for teenagers and so forth. She espoused standard Evangelical positions on morality in these areas and was not perceived as in any way threatening to the Evangelical *status quo*. In this new book she wrote about prayer, and included an account of her own spiritual journey. Here was a well-known charismatic evangelical describing her discovery of contemplative prayer, spiritual direction, retreats and the resources of the Catholic tradition. It made a profound impact on many, myself included.

Similarly, writers such as Brother Ramon,[3] a former Baptist minister and now a Franciscan hermit; Anne Townsend,[4] whose journey from being a doyen of the Evangelical missionary world to a High Church psychotherapist and priest was both creative and painful; and Sister Margaret Magdalen CSMV,[5] an Anglican nun from Wantage, demonstrated that the Catholic tradition could be compatible with the Evangelical tradition.

The link with pastoral care is also significant. Joyce Huggett followed up *Listening to God* with *Listening to Others*,[6] which, again in a semi-autobiographical way, introduced basic counselling skills to a general audience. Her sources included not only the inner healing movement, reflecting her charismatic evangelicalism, but also Henri Nouwen and an eclectic mix of Scott Peck, Michael Jacobs, Frank Lake and the Americans Gary Collins and H. Norman Wright. Anne Townsend now practises as a psychotherapist and her more recent writing has reflected that.

The exposure to the Catholic traditions in spirituality is paralleled by movement towards counselling and therapy. It seems as if these two trends go hand in hand, and those who have been most resistant within the evangelical world to the new interest in spirituality have also been most critical of the growth in counselling and therapy within the world of pastoral care. There have been all manner of other influences upon Evangelicalism, of course, over the past twenty years, all with pastoral consequences. These include the fascination with deliverance ministry and exorcism, the discovery of inner healing as a charismatic alternative or complement to counselling, and the growth of small groups in the Church (house groups, encounter groups and now Alpha evangelism groups), with their emphasis often upon deeper relationships and fellowship. However, the growth in counselling and spirituality is perhaps the most significant.

Priorities for Nurturing Faith: Teaching the Faith

Where does this leave pastoral care and its task of nurturing faith? In the face of the growth in interest in spirituality and its postmodern counterpart, the New Age movement, there is clearly a need to teach the orthodox and biblical faith. Where postmodernism argues for the failure of all metanarratives, we must not lose the courage to proclaim what is, after all, a metanarrative, the gospel of Christ, if we believe that it is the truth, and that the truth liberates. This needs to be undertaken in pastorally sensitive ways, however, and with greater humility than has traditionally characterised evangelism. The use of community-based and small groups resonates with the prevailing *zeitgeist*, and goes some way to explaining the success that Alpha groups have enjoyed and the success that the similar (though not as partisan) Emmaus project deserves to have.

We also need to rediscover the place of spiritual direction throughout the whole Church as a valid and urgent part of pastoral care. This will occupy the remainder of this chapter, being more central to the tasks of pastoral care than perhaps evangelism is.

Rediscovery of Spiritual Direction

In his critique of the North American pastoral scene, Eugene Peterson has argued that pastoral counselling has assumed far too great a priority in the everyday ministry of the pastor, as well as the pursuit of success and statistical growth.[7] In Britain, the cult of success is not likely to be adopted with such zeal: we are too much enamoured with the cult of failure! But Kenneth Leech, writing from a British perspective, identifies a similar trend away from the traditional tasks of ministry to the professional, the managerial and organisational roles of parish administration, with its emphasis upon a kind of chaplaincy role.[8]

For Peterson, there are three indispensable pastoral acts, which are also the most easily neglected: praying, reading Scripture and spiritual direction.

> Besides being basic, these three acts are quiet. They do not call attention to themselves and so are often not attended to. In the clamorous world of pastoral work nobody yells at us to engage in these acts. It is possible to do pastoral work to the satisfaction of the people who judge our competence and pay our salaries without being either diligent or skilled in them. Since almost never does anyone notice whether we do these things or not, and only occasionally does someone ask that we do them, these three acts of ministry suffer widespread neglect.[9]

Peterson defines the three acts as: giving attention to God in prayer; giving attention to God in his speech in Scripture; and giving attention to what God is doing in the person who is before me in spiritual direction. We shall look at prayer and Scripture, among other things, when we look at the resources for pastoral care. Here we shall examine spiritual direction as an urgent task of pastoral care if it is to be genuinely *pastoral.*

He describes this as 'teaching people to pray, helping parishioners discern the presence of grace in events and feelings, affirming the presence of God in the very heart of life, sharing a search for light through a dark passage in the pilgrimage . . .'[10] It is a giving of attention to those things that we generally do not want to attend to, sin and the Spirit, the mundane journey and not the crisis moment. The time available to the pastor is limited, and the urgency of the sick of heart (and body) can seem more pressing, and there is always that magazine article to write, that committee to attend, those sermons to write. Spiritual direction, the travelling with another human on their journey, not necessarily in crisis, hits the bottom of the 'to do' list, and so rarely is attended to. Peterson concludes:

> By its very nature – obscure, everyday, low profile, non-crisis – this is

> the work for which we need the most encouragement if we are to keep it at the centre of our awareness and practice. It is in fact the work for which we get the least encouragement, for it is always being pushed to the sidelines by the hustling, career-development mentality of our peers and by the hurrying, stimulus-hunger demands of our parishioners.[11]

Paul, writing to the Corinthians, deplored their lack of 'fathers' in the faith,[12] although they had many guides. There are countless Christian books on every subject to help guide the Christian, but pastoral care involves a personal attention to the individual, a 'father' (or 'mother') in Christ.

Part of the problem is the lack of training, or even the expectation that training in this might be necessary. In the course of my ministerial and theological training for the pastorate I was equipped in the areas of homiletics, biblical studies, pastoral counselling, church administration, taking weddings and funerals, holding evangelistic events, leading a team and understanding a little theology. I was never taught spiritual direction, and there was scant attention paid to prayer. Perhaps I was expected, having reached the exalted status of a 'Baptist ministerial student', to have already learnt those, or perhaps in my college's tradition most of the direction took place from the pulpit. However, one of the most important things I do is helping people to make sense of where God is in their lives, discerning with them what God might be saying, and I confess I do far too little of it.

Kenneth Leech describes spiritual direction as 'a relationship of friendship in Christ between two people by which one is enabled, through the personal encounter, to discern more clearly the will of God for one's life, and to grow in discipleship and in the life of grace'.[13] It is freely chosen, not imposed; not authoritarian, but a mutual sharing; concerned with the whole of life, and not just the dysfunctional parts; and involves help, support and teaching. Spiritual direction is dependent upon inner holiness and cannot be learnt simply by the acquisition of techniques. Completion of a course in the techniques of spiritual direction does not make one a spiritual director. Just as we saw with pastoral counselling, the relational qualities are paramount, and in the case of spiritual direction, it is not only the quality of the relationship between director and directee, but also the quality of the relationship between the director and their God (not something easily ascertained) that is vital.

The Functions of Spiritual Direction

Writing in the early 1980s, Leech could observe that:

> Today's spiritual explosion is confused and diverse. Much of it bears a close resemblance to early gnosticism. Many of the new spiritual movements are syncretistic, lacking roots in any authentic tradition, and they often rely on a view of humanity and of 'spirit' which is alien to biblical theology.[14]

In the late 1990s the situation is no better, with the use in retreats of all manner of New Age practices and the uncritical baptism into Christian dress of some of the weirder flowerings of transpersonal counselling. It is as if anything which smacks of 'spirit' is better than materialism, and in a panic response to connect with our culture, all manner of strange and potentially harmful practices have been harnessed to authentic spiritual disciplines. The work of the spiritual director. then, is in part one of gate-keeping and discernment.

Some would interpret the burgeoning of interest in spiritual direction as a symptom of a wider drift towards pietism in the Church and an avoidance of the prophetic and political dimension that challenges the individualism of the postmodern culture. Certainly, Leech, with his roots in radical and committed political action as the expression of authentic Christianity (he has been involved in drug rehabilitation and works for better race relations, alongside parish work in Soho and Bethnal Green, London) is concerned that spiritual direction should serve the prophetic witness of the Church rather than siphon of resources into a narrow pursuit of spiritual growth. 'The popular division between prophetic and pastoral ministry does not seem . . . to be biblically based, nor to have good historical support. Frequently movements of spiritual renewal combine the renewal of the inner life with a call to the pursuit of social justice.'[15]

The task of spiritual direction is akin to that of the prophet, the one who speaks out God's word to a society and culture. It is concerned with the attainment of spiritual discernment, a clear vision of the distinctions between the paths that lead to maturity and wholeness and those that lead to destruction. It seeks to perceive reality correctly and clearly, not just the reality of the soul, but also the reality of the world's structures. 'Radical action begins with radical contemplation.' The spiritual director is concerned, like the prophet, to interpret the world aright, to see the significance of events both within them and without. They are 'entrusted with the theological task of seeing the events of the day *sub specie aeternitatis*, in the context of eternity'.[16] And the director is concerned, like the prophet, with humanity and resists religion that diminishes humanity but builds religion, that narrows vision instead of enlarging it and which keeps people in spiritual immaturity and dependency.

Thus, another, associated, function of spiritual direction is to challenge faith which consists of a quest for inner peace and comfort. Here there is a direct challenge to some forms of pastoral counselling, which have as their goal the avoidance of inner conflict and the pursuit of inner peace.

> Non-prophetic spirituality, spirituality without struggle, spirituality without justice, is notoriously popular in times of turmoil and upheaval. Ruysbroeck had much to say of it in the fourteenth century, and our own era is full of its manifestations. Spirituality can so quickly and so easily lose its contemplative, visionary dimension, and become a quest for salvation by technique, a matter of finding the right mantra or formula for instant enlightenment . . . [It] can become a drug, a form of illusion, of clouding of consciousness, 'another resource of the culture instead of a resource against the culture' . . . privatised spirituality.[17]

The task of spiritual direction is one of sowing holy dis-ease, a refusal to acquiesce to the prevailing ungodly status quo.

Spiritual direction also has the function of helping to bring to maturity both the individual, with whom it works, and the whole community of faith with which it is concerned. This has been the traditional focus of spiritual direction, and the image that this task often creates is of the aged and holy Director from the Catholic or Anglo-Catholic tradition who guides the prayer life of a spiritual elite – monks or nuns, perhaps even parish clergy – with an authoritarian hand and great wisdom. Indeed, it has traditionally been a rare calling: St Francis de Sales said that not one in ten thousand is capable of such work. The whiff of elitism is compounded by the view held by the eminent writer Thomas Merton that it is not necessary for the ordinary Christian.

However, spiritual direction today seems much closer to the everyday, humdrum ministry practised by many pastors. It starts, like counselling, with where people actually are and seeks to help them move to where God is calling them to be. It is neither narrowly spiritual, nor very directive. Indeed, the influence of the non-directive counselling world seems very strong, with almost an embargo on telling people where they ought to be. As in counselling, the most important qualities are open listening to the directee, and close attention to one's own journey as a director. A working knowledge of a particular tradition in direction is preferable, and Ignatian-style direction is common, but openness to a wide range of traditions is encouraged, and resources are used from almost anywhere within the Christian tradition and beyond. So, the traditional resources of Scripture or the Jesus Prayer might be supplemented by the use of Myers-Briggs workshops;[18] pictures and icons, natural or found objects such as stones, fossils or shells, used as aids and stimuli to imaginative and attentive prayer; groups, such as contemplative prayer groups; and music.

It is fairly widely acknowledged that the frequency of meeting with the director is much less than with a counsellor – perhaps four times a year, instead of once a week, and the focus is growth, rather than healing. In other ways counselling and direction have become much closer, with some counselling being more about growth than therapy, and some direction being for a while more frequent than normal and having a distinctly therapeutic edge. Gordon Jeffs writes:

> Where there is a purely psychological problem getting in the way of spiritual growth, it will be worth while stopping to look at it. The important thing is for the director to be aware that the session is no longer looking immediately at the God-relationship, and to ensure that the sessions do not get permanently 'stuck' in a counselling mode. I quite often suggest to directees that we have come up against something that may need a bit of extra work done on it, and that we might change

> from, say, a quarterly meeting to monthly or weekly until we have sorted out this problem, and then revert to our longer time scale.[19]

Similarly, for a member of the clergy, direction may at times draw close to work supervision, with the directee talking about some problem in the Church that is difficult to discuss elsewhere.

Thus, the spiritual director needs to see his or her ministry integrated into the wider work of pastoral care, sometimes overlapping with other aspects. There is also the need to draw upon the broader traditions of the Church, particularly the Protestant traditions, to help this task become one which is perceived as central to ministry, and not peripheral to the 'real work' of pastoral counselling. Thus, awareness is needed of the Puritan traditions in spiritual direction, exemplified by Thomas Cartwright (1535–1603), William Perkins, and especially Richard Baxter, whose *The Reformed Pastor* (1656) we encountered in Chapter 1.

Kenneth Leech argues that there are five marks of a spiritual director:[20] they are possessed by the Spirit (holiness of life and closeness to God), a person of experience who has struggled with the realities of prayer and life and encountered their own darkness within. They will have discernment, from whom we receive *diakrisis*, perception and insight, and will be able to give way to the Holy Spirit, for the end of direction is not direction itself, but God himself. These may well be the kind of qualities that one would look for in a pastoral carer, but we need to conclude with an articulation of the proper distance between pastoral counselling and spiritual direction, so that we avoid either collapsing into the other (that is, all direction being seen as an aspect of counselling, or all counselling becoming implicitly spiritual direction). An awareness of the differences between them will help the overall task of pastoral care to be better shaped and its tasks be more effectively focused.

Pastoral Counselling is not Spiritual Direction

The first difference between pastoral counselling and the spiritual direction tradition is the emotional and psychological state that is its focus. The pastoral counsellor tends to deal with people in distress, whereas the director works best with people who are in no particular crisis. Indeed, it is the continuing pastoral relationship that is the ground in which pastoral counselling can take place when and if crises occur, but the task of spiritual direction is continuous. There need be no previous relationship for a secular counsellor to work effectively: indeed, the absence of any previous relationship between counsellor and client is a positive advantage for many forms of counselling, and a necessity for psychodynamic counselling, where previous knowledge of the counsellor gets in the way of the transference. In spiritual direction, however, the relationship may well be that of pastor to church member before it takes the specific form of director to directee. 'The priest is primarily concerned with spirituality as the fundamental requirement of health. The therapist or counsellor is primarily concerned with sickness. They move within the same realm of reality, and so it is not surprising that there is considerable overlap.'[21]

Secondly, the context has historically been different. Spiritual direction has been located within the sacramental and liturgical framework of the Church, whereas pastoral counselling has been more rooted in the community. I would want to see this distinction reduced, with both spiritual direction and pastoral counselling rooted in the community of the Church, and both addressed not only to the Church community, but also to the wider world. Helping non-Churchgoing people make sense of their spiritual journey might be among the most creative ways of evangelism in a postmodern setting, as the Emmaus Project makes clear.

The third difference is in the goal or aim of the two disciplines. Pastoral counselling, with its therapeutic mindset, has seen the attainment of inner harmony, integration and freedom from anguish as its goals. It helps the client adjust their life to the environment they inhabit. However, the spiritual director will not want to reduce the spiritual life to one of simply peace and ease, for how can the Christian following Jesus not also weep over our Jerusalems and rage at our temple commerce. To grow spiritually is to become more angry at injustice and less at peace with the world as it is. To live a life open to Christ's love brings continual vulnerability to disappointment and loss as that love is expressed towards others. If pastoral counselling has as its focus the alleviation of psychological disease, spiritual direction has as one of its foci the sustenance of a holy dis-ease with the world.

The difference could be seen in the approach to that experience called the 'dark night of the soul'. A pastoral counselling approach, uninformed by spiritual wisdom, might seek to alleviate the distressing experience with consideration of its pathological roots. The aim would be to restore inner peace and a sense of God's presence. However, if the roots of the experience are not in a clinical depressive episode, or other psychiatric condition, then the spiritual director would want to affirm the appropriateness of the experience, not hurry the directee through it, but hold them prayerfully while the Spirit does his work. The director will recognise that 'the dark night is one of the ways God brings us to a hush, a stillness, so that he may work an inner transformation upon the soul,' and will encourage the directee to be 'grateful that God is lovingly drawing you away from every distraction so that you can see Him. Rather than chafing and fighting, become still and wait.'[22]

Similarly, when there is actual occultic or demonic oppression, which thankfully is rare (contrary to some opinions), the approach of the pastoral counsellor to effect the 'talking cure' will be misguided, and the discernment of the spiritual director will point to sources of the distress that are susceptible only to spiritual means, to prayer and exorcism. The pastoral carer needs to be at least versed in both disciplines, even if, as is likely, they will be better fitted to one or the other. Thankfully pastoral care is the ministry of the whole Church, and so there will be some who can excel where others are weak. The whole issue of cooperation and teamwork will be the theme of Chapter 13.

Within the overall aims of pastoral care, a wise and inclusive combination of the best of pastoral counselling and the best of spiritual direction by those 'who ground their care in the theological perspective of that faith tradition and who personally remain faithful to that faith through spiritual authenticity' seems to me the way to meet the challenges of pastoral care in a postmodern world.

At a biennial conference of pastoral counsellors and carers held at Swanwick, a broad range of traditions and disciplines are represented. I first attended in 1990 to lead the worship, and a strong theme at the close of that conference was a call to 'stop vandalising each other's trees'. Professional counsellors were tending to disparage pastoral carers, spiritual directors were looking askance at therapists and there were some who saw every problem in demonic terms, despairing of the 'lack of discernment' in everyone else. The Spirit of God was actually calling us to work together, to build up, not pull down, each other's ministries and ways of exercising pastoral care. I believe that call still rings true, and certainly it shaped the vision of the subsequent conferences in the series which I chaired. There is room for an eclectic mix in the work of pastoral care and much to learn from one another.

CHAPTER 12

Resources for Pastoral Care

Overview

With a demanding task to fulfil and continuing cultural change, the need for adequate resources by the pastoral carer has never been greater. Pastoral care is a long-term project. It embraces people at every stage of life and calls for wisdom, experience, understanding and courage from those who are particularly called to exercise pastoral care as a major role in life. I would argue for some expression of care to be expected of every normal, adult human being who wants to live a fulfilling life in society (even if that care is limited to family and friends), and particularly of every Christian who claims to follow in the way of Jesus of Nazareth. Thus some measure of resourcing is needed for everyone who wants to live in the nexus of giving and receiving of care that is implicit in family life. However, there are particular resources required for those whose primary ministry in Church and world is pastoral care, beyond the minimum expected of family life.

I want to categorise those resources under five headings: spirituality and liturgy, training, theology, the care of the carer and companionship. These resources overlap and interlock, and others might want to categorise them differently, but they seem to be the ways that I make most sense of the resources that keep me nourished in the journey of pastoral care.

Spirituality and Liturgy

Our working definition of pastoral care as stated in Chapter 1 emphasises an important element of personal discipleship or commitment to the faith tradition. For Christians this is often expressed in terms of personal commitment to the Father, the Son and the Holy Spirit, or a personal following of Jesus Christ, not just a commitment to the teachings of the Church. Spirituality is the expression of that relationship in prayerful, personal ways and the liturgy is the corporate way that the whole Christian community expresses its worship and devotion to God.

Kenneth Leech describes Christian spirituality as 'about a process of formation, a process in which we are formed by, and in, Christ . . . we come more and more to share the Christ nature'.[1] Leech identifies the Word of God and silence as the twin foci of that spiritual formation, and a profound confrontation with the prevailing cultural milieu, rather than an accommodation to it, as its consequence. There is immediately a contrast to much of the narcissism of postmodern culture, with its emphasis on that which makes me comfortable, feels good and acceptable, and its unrelenting search for inner peace. Genuine Christian spirituality can bring inner turmoil, distress and pain. Instead of a confident assertion of truth there might be only a tongue-tied confusion, instead of a mute acceptance of whatever is said by this spiritual guru or that international conference speaker, there is a weary wrestling with the truth. The essential narcissism of postmodern culture is also reflected in some parts of the Church, especially, but not exclusively, that part in which I find my roots, evangelicalism. Much of its message seems to emphasise the inner peace and joy of believing, and avoids the harsher realities of past and present experience. It is triumphalist and crusading towards the world, but in fact too readily absorbs the world's values and becomes content with a surface gloss of Christianity upon an untransformed framework.

Spirituality that engages with the Word and with silence is therefore important, if Christian pastoral care is not to be devalued to a secular caring with a little religion added to make it seem like the real thing. For pastoral care to remain genuine, its practitioners need to be pilgrims, not settlers; wrestlers themselves, not ringside cheerers of others' wrestling; listeners first, speakers second. Much second-rate pastoral care has been little more than a bastardised psychotherapy, neither good pastoral care nor effective therapy. The Scriptures, however, point to genuine pastoral care as having a goal, not of contentment and accommodation to the ills of this world, but of inner transformation, spiritual growth and conformity to Christ. Yes, it is concerned with the whole person, body, soul and mind, but it does not neglect the spiritual dimension; rather, that is its particular focus.

Sadly, some contemporary pastoral care has spiritual care and growth as an embarrassing afterthought. If that is to be changed and pastoral care is to recover its spiritual heritage and priority, then pastoral carers need to be willing to engage in the process of spiritual growth themselves. No self-respecting psychotherapist would ever practise without first having undergone therapy themselves, and quite possibly remaining in therapy throughout their practising career, for it is dangerous and hypocritical to call others to tread a path they have been unwilling to tread themselves.

Similarly practitioners of pastoral care need to be on the pathway of personal discipleship; of wrestling with faith, Scripture and prayer; of spiritual growth, if they are to call others to a similar pilgrimage and discovery. That is why on the 'Journey Through Life' course at St John's College, Nottingham, part of the professional training in pastoral counselling offered by the College, the students engage with Scripture in biblical meditation, to reflect upon their own spiritual journey and to integrate faith and practice. Training in pastoral counselling is not just the acquisition of skills in counselling, or understanding of psychological and developmental dimensions of the human condition. It calls for the continuing along the spiritual journey by those who practise it.

This may seem to be labouring the point, but necessarily so, I believe. In the technical characteristics of the postmodern age, where technique is paramount, pastoral care can so easily be reduced to the practice of techniques of caring, and particularly of counselling. But the quality of pastoral care is at least as dependent upon the integrity of its practitioners as upon their skilfulness in listening or interpretation, or their astuteness in negotiating the maze of social security entitlements in the benefits system. Having underlined its necessity, let us explore the resources for spiritual growth by the pastoral carer under three headings: Scripture, prayer and worship.

Scripture

First, I want to describe how the Scriptures should not be used as a resource for pastoral care. They are not a quarry to be dug into for instant answers to tricky pastoral situations, nor are they a prop to bolster our prejudices and disguise our blind spots. Crude fundamentalism, what James Barr calls 'a pathological condition of Christianity',[2] misuses Scripture in both of those ways. Nor is it to be used as an interesting, but optional, postmodern text, essentially unrelated to reality. If the fundamentalist's mistake is to enthrone Scripture where God should be, the postmodernist's mistake is to misunderstand the relationship between Scripture and the realities of life. Francis Watson argues against the postmodern absorption with the workings of the text to the exclusion of the relationship of that text to the rest of the world.

> An interpretative practice working within the world of the text may offer many insightful observations about the workings of that world. But it will tell us nothing at all about the one thing that actually matters, the relation of that imagined world to reality. If it wishes to engage responsibly in theological construction, biblical interpretation must abandon the myth of the self-enclosed text and learn to correlate the text with the reality to which it bears witness, understanding the text as located primarily within the Church which is itself located within the world. Interpretation must take the more demanding, but also more rewarding, way of seeking to discern the truth mediated in the texts of holy Scripture. And it must not be deterred by the scepticism that such a project is sure to evoke.[3]

If the proper use of Scripture is threatened by both fundamentalism and postmodernism, how is it to be an indispensable resource to the pastoral carer? Firstly, the Scriptures must be seen as the Word of God to the community of God, not just to individuals. Its interpretation is a communal affair, and wrestling with the Word of God as it addresses our world and its realities is also a communal affair. This is not to suppose that there is some universalist or ecumenical hermeneutic that is infallible. That would enthral the Word of God to the community, instead of the community being under the judgment of the Word.

However, the checks and balances of broad consensus over the interpretation of the Scriptures avoids the personal and cultural blind spots that keep us from hearing the whole counsel of Scripture. That broad consensus requires the voices of East and West, developed and developing worlds, African and Asian perspectives alongside European and North American; Catholic and Protestant, liberal and evangelical as well as charismatic and Pentecostal perspectives. The interpretation of the Scriptures is no longer the sole preserve of white, university-educated, male clerics . . . thank God!

The Scriptures also need to be personally appropriated by means of meditation and contemplation alongside the hermeneutical process, if they are to be a helpful resource for pastoral care. This focuses upon their transforming, disturbing and nourishing characteristics as the Holy Spirit applies them to the process of spiritual maturing. The Word is to dwell in us richly[4] and be on our lips and in our heart,[5] and it cuts through the defences that we erect to keep us from hearing God, being 'living and active. Sharper than any double-edged sword, it penetrates even to dividing soul and spirit, joints and marrow: it judges the thoughts and attitudes of the heart.'[6] This personal grappling with Scripture is the process whereby the Spirit speaks to the human heart and it is the process itself which is helpful, not just the interpretative outcome. It means engaging with God himself and allowing him to transform us. This personal appropriation involves contemplation and meditation of Scripture, not just its academic study (needful though that is). Deborah Seddon describes it as 'letting the Bible get "under our skin" so that we live it, breathe it and feel it,'[7] which involves finding 'a still point where individuals can find the space and solitude for the necessary inner creative brooding and prayerful reading'[8] of Scripture.

Third, the proper use of the Scriptures will inform and shape a world-view that contradicts the prevailing modernism and post-modernism. It creates a non-conformist mentality: 'Do not be conformed to this world, but be transformed by the renewing of your mind.'[9] This is vital in the process of remaining critical of the culture and sceptical about its certainties. Whereas modern culture sees pain and suffering as valueless and to be avoided at all costs, the Scriptures see it as having value, albeit limited and in an eternal perspective. 'Though outwardly we are wasting away, yet inwardly we are being renewed day by day. For our light and momentary troubles are achieving for us an eternal glory that far outweighs them all,' writes Paul to the Corinthians,[10] contradicting the current obsession with psychological painlessness at all costs. Jesus says that losing our grip on the self through self-forgetfulness is our only way of finding our selves, whereas much contemporary therapy calls for self-fulfilment to be realised at all costs, and often at great cost to others. The Scriptures help us to remain authentically disciples of Jesus Christ and breaks the tyranny of the contemporary.

Prayer

Prayer is such a varied thing that I hesitate to describe any norms for pastoral carers, but I do detect a trend. The more Christians wrestle with the demands and realities of others' lives in pastoral care, the less dogmatic they become about the patterns of God's dealings with human beings, and the more contemplative their prayers become. Prayer for those we care for pastorally becomes less a demanding of God that he do what we believe would be best for them (and ease our load into the bargain) and more a silent holding of them in prayer before God, knowing that he knows best anyway.

The stress on silence and solitude is well documented from the earliest times. The Desert Fathers valued it, while the orthodox spiritual community of Mount Athos, and the whole tradition that ensued from it, made the attainment of *hesychia*, inner silence and attentiveness to God, its central feature. Variously described as inner vigilance, the prayer of the heart, uninterrupted prayerfulness, or contemplative prayer, this quiet waiting upon God is the most powerful antidote to the restless, breathless round of pastoral encounters that can replace genuine pastoral care. Leech comments:

> Silence and solitude are important elements in pastoral practice. Nothing is more necessary in pastoral care and in spiritual direction than the ability to listen, an ability which is nourished in contemplation, stillness and inner silence. More than any other pastoral gifts, people are looking for pastors who are possessed of interior quietude. It is not a skill that can be learnt, nor can one take such a quality. It only comes as a by-product of a life in which silence and stillness have a major place.[11]

Those who have entered the barrenness of their own hearts and found a place in the inner desert for God to speak can then offer care to others on the way. The greater the pastoral task, the greater the urgency for that prayerful waiting upon God, that attentiveness to the silence in which God speaks beyond words and that stillness in which the still point of the turning world dances in eternity.

The pattern for this will vary, but there is an honourable tradition of a rule of life which embraces each day, week, season and year. Practitioners of pastoral care in a world which is falling apart need the glue of prayer each day to hold together faith and practice, life and ministry. In a world that spins out of control they need the discipline of a weekly sabbath rest for reorientation to God's compass. In a culture uprooted from history, they need the rhythm of season and feast, the penitential seasons of Lent and Advent, the celebrations of Christmas, Easter and Pentecost, the routine of that long season of Trinity to confirm their part in the long story of God's people and within each year some time to reflect is of great value.

Worship

The public liturgy of weekly or daily worship helps to root the disciplines of attentiveness to Scripture and attentiveness to God through prayer in the community of faith. Without that rootedness, spirituality can quickly become a specious form of piety, and a kind of conformity to the postmodern age that prevents the renewal of our minds that St Paul speaks of in Romans 12. As well as playing an indispensable role in the personal resourcing of the pastoral carer, it also has a vital role to play in the practice of pastoral care.

First, public worship is the place where the pastoral carer expresses their commitment to the Body of Christ and the community of faith. It celebrates the fact that they are not a lone ranger, but in relationship with others. In the reading and expounding of the Scriptures there is an attentiveness to God's Word; in praise and worship we affirm our creaturely dependence upon God; in prayer we lift the needs of the world to the God who acts; and in the Eucharist we participate in the benefits of the redeeming love of Christ. For the pastoral carer, as for every Christian, participation in public worship, probably on a Sunday, is a vital element in the maturing process.

However, there are dimensions to worship that are also part of the activity of pastoral care. Forrester, McDonald and Tellini argue not only for a pastoral dimension in worship (because the Church, the community which worships, is a pastoral fellowship, pastoral care should be the context, content and consequence of its worship), but also more significantly, I believe, a liturgical dimension to pastoral care.

> When worship and pastoral care become separated from one another, pastoral care easily becomes secular, theologically empty and rooted in the latest theories of psychotherapy without reference to Christian traditions. A kind of individualism takes over, [which we have seen is the spirit of the age in postmodern culture,] suggesting that pastoral care has nothing to do with the flock, but takes place in one-to-one therapeutic sessions or small encounter groups. The pastor becomes the expert whose skills disable mutual pastoral care within the fellowship.[12]

In place of such a disabling split, the liturgical dimension expresses the reality that the primary role in caring for people is God's, not ours, and that the whole community is involved in caring. Pastoral care within its liturgical expression prevents a new kind of sacerdotalism emerging, reducing the laity to the status of 'clients'. Just as worship is the activity of the whole people of God, so also a responsibility for care is laid upon all, although there will be those whose experience, gifting and training enable them to fulfil that function in a more extensive and fuller way – those we have been calling pastoral carers.

Public worship expresses three important themes of pastoral care. The first is fellowship and community. We have a sense of belonging, which is vital, and there is affirmation, enlightenment, forgiveness and hope expressed in that community. This up-building, nourishment and sustenance is found first of all in worship. As Barth says: 'It is not only in worship that the community is edified and edifies itself. But it is here first that this continuously takes place. And if it does not take place here, it does not take place anywhere.'[13] Since fellowship, *koinonia*, is not the normal state for humankind, but appears arising out of the redemptive purposes of God, it also speaks of restoration of relationship and the kingdom of God in the midst of history.

The second theme is wholeness, since in worship every aspect of the person is engaged: body, mind, spirit and emotions. The integration of the person is a task of pastoral care embodied in worship, with its joy and tears, body and mind, reason and emotion all engaged. It is not uncommon for those in the midst of distressing circumstances and personal discomfort to find the emotions they have kept under wraps for much of their life are given fuller expression in worship. Tears in particular are not an unfamiliar response in worship, and the pastorally sensitive fellowship will not make a big deal over the person quietly weeping in the service, but give them space and treat it as nothing strange. Forrester *et al.* continue with a third pastoral theme of liberation. The quest for freedom for the oppressed and persecuted is often sustained and foreshadowed in worship. It is not surprising that the Polish shipyard workers, striking for the right to a free trade union in the face of fierce opposition from the ruling Communist party, were sustained by the daily celebration of Mass in the yards. Where pastoral care is a sign of liberation from oppressive powers, not just those of a political kind, worship is the vehicle that expresses that freedom.

Finally, it is clear that in the celebration of rites of passage, public worship is an important element. At birth, coming of age, marriage and death, the Christian community celebrates these stages through infant dedication/baptism, confirmation, the wedding and the funeral. These are not just rituals expressing some deeper reality, but a part of the passage itself. Funerals help the bereaved to grieve, and weddings enable couples to publicly express their commitment to each other. These 'occasional offices' and their opportunities for pastoral care have been explored by Wesley Carr[14] and I commend his study of them.

I do not think that it is simply pious to say that these spiritual resources of Scripture, prayer and worship are paramount in the task of pastoral care. Where absent, that care becomes routine, joyless and burdensome. Where present, they sustain the pastor through the difficulties that will always be attendant on pastoral care, but by themselves they are inadequate to the task of sustenance. It is to other resources that we must now turn.

Training

We would not be at all confident if the new person at the doctor's surgery explained that they were the junior partner in the team and that their qualifications comprised a St John's Ambulance certificate in first aid and ready access to a copy of the *Reader's Digest Book of Family Health*! However, when I was nineteen and away, on holiday in Yorkshire with a group of fellow undergraduates, I was grateful for the first aid skills of a friend who studied engineering when I fell down a ravine, broke my arm and possibly fractured my skull. The three medical students on our party did not have a clue what to do! The skills needed to be appropriate to the context.

It is often assumed that pastoral care can be undertaken by any caring person, and I believe that the basic level of pastoral care should be performed by every Christian, whether or not they have any formal training in it. The initial discipleship training, be it in youth group, confirmation class or adult baptismal class, should encourage everybody to exercise responsible care for one another, and the routine of Sunday sermon and teaching should touch upon this responsibility. Writing an encouraging letter, telephoning a friend in need, sending a card expressing condolences to the recently bereaved, going shopping for the couple with a child in intensive care, mowing the lawn for the single person just back from skiing with the inevitable broken ankle – these are all expressions of care that everybody is capable of. They are the foundations of a hierarchy of care.

Other relatively straightforward expressions of care need a little guidance. A visit to a sick person in hospital might seem very ordinary, but guidance on how long to stay, how to listen and how to be supportive is often necessary. It is surprising how many people use a visit to the hospitalised as an opportunity for a captive audience to listen to their latest problem with the children, or the boring details of their holiday. Similarly, visiting the elderly in their homes is a commendable and fairly straightforward task that most are capable of, but some training in how long to stay, how frequently to visit, how to introduce a spiritual element to the conversation if appropriate and how to be sensitive to, say, a stroke victim, or someone in the early stages of dementia, are valuable. Others are gifted in the sensitive offering of prayer ministry to those who request it, but training is vital in listening skills, in the place of anointing with oil or the laying on of hands, or in the recognition (and referral) of deeper and more sinister spiritual conditions that might require the specialised ministry of deliverance.

Training ordinary members of the local Church in aspects of the pastoral care of their fellow Christians might not be difficult, but it is certainly preferable to the amateurish belief that these aspects of pastoral care will somehow just happen. At my present and former churches we have run 'Monday Training Schools' which have covered a wide range of themes for ordinary members of the church, from basic listening skills and introductions to pastoral counselling to leading small groups and understanding Christian doctrine. There is a place here for training at a basic level in pastoral skills. We recently ran one in Stevenage which covered introductions to pastoral care in general, the care of families, the elderly and those at critical life stages. We described what pastoral counselling is (though we did not attempt any training in it) and the place of prayer in pastoral care, and we held a conference on building a pastoral care team. Such an introduction is within the capabilities of most local pastors or other clergy.

There are those, however, whose tasks in pastoral care call for a more rigorous training beyond the capabilities of most local churches. Those training for the ordained ministry in any of the main denominations will undertake some pastoral training and cover, for instance, marriage preparation, bereavement visits, discipleship courses, human growth and development, some introduction to pastoral counselling, hospital chaplaincy and the care of the elderly. However, many are still trained before they have a great deal of experience (although so-called church-based training is increasingly popular), and there is a clear need for ongoing training, not only in the initial years of first pastorates or first curacies, but throughout ministry.

It could be argued that pastoral studies is a lifetime's study, so inexhaustibly fascinating is the human condition and so rapid is the cultural change taking place. I am well aware that qualifications can be unnecessary beyond a certain point, but more could be done to create an incentive to continue training, to continue to learn. The American system of transferable credits which can be accumulated from a wide variety of sources, for example (credit awarded for a suitably accredited day conference, and more credits for a course undertaken over a year), might be possible in Britain given the climate favourable to transferable credits in higher education. This could go some way to the awarding of, say, a Higher Diploma in Pastoral Studies, or be the foundation of an M.Div. degree. There is currently a proliferation of Masters degree courses in pastoral studies awarded by Theological Colleges, but their relation to other training agencies is very limited. Not every pastor wants, or is capable of, postgraduate study, but every pastor needs to keep growing, keep studying and keep up to date with the demands of ministry, and more could be done to encourage this.

At the highest levels of pastoral studies there is clearly a continuing need to rescue pastoral studies from its Cinderella status within the family of theological disciplines. Stephen Pattison argues for the centrality of pastoral studies within the theological enterprise. 'It is the place where religious belief, tradition and practice meets contemporary experiences, questions and actions and conducts a dialogue which is intellectually critical and practically transforming.'[15] However, he concludes that:

> The coronation of pastoral theology, like the *eschaton*, now seems to have been indefinitely postponed . . . It remains a minority concern . . . it is rare for a bright research student to opt for a topic in practical theology rather than in some better known academic theological discipline, however obscure or *recherché* its focus may be. Pastoral theology has failed to assert itself or to live up to its promise.[16]

At every level, from the local church initiative to the doctoral programme, from the day conference to the fully validated course, there is the need for more and better training of those who offer pastoral care.

But there is much that can be done individually. Those two commendable series *The New Library of Pastoral Care* (NLPC, published by SPCK) and *Handbooks of Pastoral Care* (HarperCollins) have much to commend them to the interested lay person as well as the professional. Similarly, Ballard and Pritchard's *Practical Theology in Action*[17] and Wesley Carr's *Handbook of Pastoral Studies*[18] in the NLPC Resources series are valuable resources for pastors and church libraries. At the Manna Counselling Services in South London, the library of books on counselling and pastoral care is heavily used and points to the interest in them by practitioners who want to improve their understanding and skills. I am sure this is repeated elsewhere, and could be repeated profitably much more widely. Let us not forget that most important of written resources in pastoral understanding: the novel. Writing of Hugh Maycock, Kenneth Leech says 'we need to read books which will nourish the human imagination, the total person, not just inform the ecclesiastical functionary. Through his novels and his music, Hugh became a very human kind of saint.'[19] The reading of novels, poetry or biographies is not some self-indulgence that keeps pastors from their proper work, but part of their proper work, if they are to be those who actually have something nourishing to offer the hungry soul.

Finally, in this section on training, I want to refer to probably the greatest training tool: the mentor. Pastoral care can be taught, but its passion is most effectively caught from observing and experiencing a passionate pastor. My first experience of pastoral care came from the church in which I was christened and confirmed, where I sang in the choir, was taught in Sunday School and then taught at Sunday School as a teenager, and in which I first sensed a call to pastoral ministry. All Saints, Patcham was a typical evangelical parish church of the 1960s and 1970s, with 1662 at 11.00 and 6.30, a weekly prayer meeting and Bible study and the usual youth activities. I only knew one vicar from as early as I can recall until leaving for University, a godly pastor and able preacher, who was nonetheless quite shy and a definite introvert. The Reverend Garston-Smith (no-one ever called him that, only 'Vicar', and certainly did not use his Christian name) took the trouble to talk with a rather bumptious sixteen-year-old who thought he might be called to the Anglican ministry, and was the model of quiet undramatic pastoral care.

At Lewin Road Baptist Church in Streatham, Douglas McBain demonstrated the indispensability and value of being there at times of crisis and family joy. Within hours of the birth of our first child in St Thomas's Hospital, Douglas and his wife, and all their Sunday lunch guests, crowded into the small side room where my wife had spent what remained of Saturday night with our newborn son. We so much valued the presence of our pastor at that time, to share in our joy and offer thanks to God. From my colleague and senior pastor at that same church some years later, by which time I was its associate pastor, I learnt the value of working with individuals in distress and need over a longer period of, say, months or years. These three pastors have been my mentors, and I have learnt more than I know from them.

The resources for training and equipping practitioners of all sorts of pastoral care are not difficult to find or to provide. How we value the quality of pastoral care we offer will determine whether we invest in those resources or not.

Theology

'The pastor's theological resource . . . is the whole Christian tradition, not only as it is (if ever there could be such a summary) but also as it is believed to be – a much more complex issue.' So writes Wesley Carr.[20] He identifies four different ways of doing theology for pastoral studies:

- The Bible and tradition, which asks the question 'what does the Bible (or tradition) have to say about this topic?' A simplistic answer may be forthcoming, especially if the one asking it is fundamentalist in outlook, but there are problems with this simple approach: the question asked of the tradition may be one which the tradition has not previously addressed, and it also ignores the developments in hermeneutical study which are sceptical of a simple interpretative approach.
- Narrative theology, which emphasises the importance of story. Here, the story from the pastoral context is brought alongside the biblical tradition used as an interpretative tool. There are dangers in the selection of biblical narrative which could become collusive with the pastoral story, rather than critical of it. Since the selection of biblical narrative is a subjective one, there needs to be the kinds of communal checks and balances which we referred to earlier to avoid accommodation to the status quo. However, this approach has much to be commended and is used creatively by students on the St John's College Diploma in Pastoral Counselling in their personal journey.
- The correlative approach, which was illustrated from the work of Don Browning earlier. It uses the human sciences to bring together – to correlate – the pastoral situation and the Christian tradition. 'Scripture, tradition and experience are thus brought together, coalescing around the presenting issue that the pastor is dealing with.'[21]
- The goal-oriented approach, which connects the theological reflection with wisdom and the experiential foundations of faith – prayer and worship. Here the goal of theological reflection is to connect the pastor with the community of faith and to result in a change in outlook or custom (Carr quotes Farley's term, derived from Bourdieu, of *habitus*[22]).

These differing modes of theological reflection utilise the various dimensions of the theological enterprise, biblical studies, systematic and historical theology, applied and philosophical theology. For instance, in helping a person with a burden of false guilt, the pastor brings to the encounter theological perspectives such as the insights of systematic theology concerning forgiveness and the atonement, psychological insights about the causes of that guilt, and perhaps biblical insights concerning freedom and enlightenment. These insights are correlated with the pastoral situation to enable growth and transformation.

It becomes clear, then, that theological resources are indispensable rather than a luxurious option for the leisured few. In fact, pastoral care is continually in dialogue with the community traditions, whether implicitly or explicitly, and pastoral carers need to become familiar with those theological traditions and able to interpret them in the pastoral context. Carr quotes Moody in summary of his exploration of theological resources.

> Pastors as watchers and explorers, bridge-builders and guardians of communal memories and vision, sharing and reflecting back to the rest of the *laos* its own ministry, have a special role in keeping the Church in the way of pilgrimage and in touch with its own nature as a sacrament of God-given humanity in Christ.[23]

Theological resources should enable at least some practitioners of pastoral care to be amongst the church's most creative theologians.

At the very least, pastors need to be able to hold clearly their view of 'the good life' if pastoral care is to have some coherence and clarity. When we encourage growth and transformation of life and outlook, what is the goal? We have seen that psychotherapy has often been obscure about those goals, yet every therapist implicitly holds a view of what the outcome of successful therapy might look like. Pastoral care needs to be clear in its articulation of what maturity in Christ means, if that is to be its overall goal. What does this mean for human freedom, conviviality, power and integrity? What shape does the holy life take in the midst of postmodern culture? Can we clearly differentiate between what is simply postmodern cultural gloss and what is authentic discipleship for a postmodern age? Does growth in godliness mean loss of humanity or its fulfilment? These are theological questions that pastoral care needs answers to as it follows its calling. Certainly, theological thinking is indispensable to the practice of pastoral care.

Care for the Carers

A recent study by the Evangelical Alliance Care for Pastors Partnership and the Claybury Trust highlighted some of the pressures upon pastoral ministry in the local church. The majority of church leaders consider themselves to be under significant stress from overwork. They have to function in a wide range of tasks, some of which they are singularly ill-equipped to fulfil. Few have training in team-building and teamwork, which if successfully implemented would go some way to easing the burden. Churches have high expectations of their pastors, and many pastors have even higher expectations of themselves. The study demonstrated the pressures upon family life, marriages and finances. Many leaders lacked clear lines of accountability and 65 per cent felt that their supervision was inadequate; 41 per cent felt less than adequately supported by their local church, while 75 per cent felt that preordination training was only adequate or worse. It is not surprising, then, that 28 per cent of all respondents to the research which underlies these results had felt for a prolonged period like leaving the ministry.

The results of the research formed the basis of a consultation which took place on 16 December 1996, and those present identified what they believed to be the three most significant factors which give rise to the excessive pressures and stress experienced by pastors:

(i) the causal reasons were identified as lack of self-awareness and understanding, unrealistic expectations and lack of accountability;

(ii) the cultural context, such as secular world views dictating pastoral demands, the accelerating pace of change leading to great uncertainties about the task and increased mobility; and

(iii) the inadequacy of leader training.

The consultation recommended the teaching of relational and self-awareness skills prior to ordination, greater accountability in ministry, greater emphasis upon boundary issues in counselling and sexuality, regular reviews of the role the pastor plays (appraisal) and greater consideration to post-ordination training.

I quote this research because it highlights the pressures that many in pastoral leadership labour under, and points to the vital need of care for those whose main task is to offer care to the Church, and wider community. Care for the carers is needed in four areas, I believe: self-acceptance, work ethic, family and friendship, and boundaries.

Self-acceptance of one's own limits, strengths and weaknesses, abilities and disabilities is vital in the practice of pastoral care, not only for the sake of its recipients, but also for the well-being of its practitioners. Too many succumb to the 'messiah syndrome', driven to greater and greater efforts in the belief that only they can solve this pastoral problem or care for those in a particular crisis. The roots of this lie in an inflated sense of their own importance, coupled with a low view of their own worth: a potent and deadly mixture. Such self-acceptance and self-awareness only comes from relationship, I believe. We have already touched upon the work ethic which makes some pastors workaholics unable to rest, grudging of any time taken off work, or holidays taken. Kenneth Leech, writing of Hugh Maycock, admires in him:

> the ability just to *be*. It is often said that priesthood is being, yet our behaviour contradicts it. We become slaves of the work ethic, slaves of the tyranny of time. Yet if we are to redeem time, that is, not to become its slave, or to escape it, we need to develop an eternal perspective, a way of co-operating with God in trust and hopeful optimism.[24]

This syndrome, inability to believe that others are capable in our absence, is common. It fails to see others as capable of caring for themselves, for a while at least, without constant attention from the parental pastor. Sometimes it comes from a compulsive repetition of a childhood of inadequate love or overly adult responsibilities placed upon a child, so that the compulsion to care is a way of trying to be parented in adult life, of winning people's affection and love through doing. Again, it is the care of others that loves enough to confront, rather than collude with, the neurosis which is a major part of the change that is needed.

The pastor's family should not be seen as an extension of the pastor's role, so that in calling a pastor, the church gains an unpaid spouse and model children into the bargain. Support and care is needed if the pastor seeks to change the pattern that some churches have grown used to in making uncalled-for demands upon the pastor's family.

Finally, care is needed if appropriate boundaries are to be maintained in the practice of pastoral care, whether they are boundaries between private and public life, working and non-working time, between appropriate love and affection and inappropriate sexual relationships, or between acceptable demands and the unacceptable. The maintenance of these boundaries is initially very dependent upon good supervision, though they may later be sufficiently internalised to require less supervisory oversight.

The tool which provides such care for the carers is adequate supervision by an outside person or group, just as any professional therapist or counsellor would expect. This should include good appraisal of the work done by the pastor, so that strengths can be honoured, weaknesses identified and growth encouraged. Proper appraisal procedures, now common in chaplaincy appointments, are still a rarity in church settings, although much is being done at the moment to improve upon this in the Methodist Church and among some Anglican dioceses. Proper accountability to some group or body is another important tool. For the professional pastor leading a local church, that accountability might be to the church authorities, such as the district superintendent or the archdeacon and bishop, whereupon adequate resources need to be developed to ensure the proper working of the accountability system. It might instead be to representative individuals within the local employing church, whereupon there need to be proper safeguards to ensure that their powers are not abused. Where the pastors are lay people working voluntarily within a local church, accountability might be to a team, or to a supervisory committee, or to the minister who leads the congregation. Again, adequate resources are needed to ensure that this is not accountability and support in name only, but has real substance and value.

Companionship

With all of the resources of spirituality, theological reflection, training and supervisory care, there is still nothing quite as encouraging as companions on the way. These companions range from the supportive and understanding spouse to colleagues on teams and friends in pastoral ministry whose journey we share. Of particular importance is the companionship of those who share a similar calling and who have pursued a similar journey, and so understand why we seem to see things differently to others in the Church. One such group of pastoral carers and counsellors which I belonged to in South London felt sufficiently alienated from the broader group of evangelical churches in which they served to call themselves 'the heretics'!

Pastoral counsellors can easily feel alone in their church setting: they adhere more strongly to boundaries of confidentiality than the general church member, and can seem aloof; they may be accused of failing to hold a moral line when they are seeking to be non-judgmental; pressure may be put upon them to be more 'evangelistic', if not more 'evangelical'. Finding the company of others who identify with those pressures is often difficult, and when found it is precious.

One of the great implicit values of the biennial Swanwick conference for pastoral care and counselling is the finding of companions on the way, and the setting up of local networks of people to meet more regularly for support and growth (the 'heretics' group in South London was one such group). I have experienced the value of two such groups in particular at different stages of pastoral ministry: the planning group of the Swanwick conference between 1988 and 1996, and my ongoing membership of the tutor group on the St John's College course in pastoral counselling. Those, along with a supportive wife and good supervision, have more than once been a lifeline through stormy and dark waters. Such companionship, where one can be truly one's self without being overly defensive, is a sure sign of the community of faith to which we belong. It shows us that the task of building community, which belongs in part to pastoral care, is not impossible, nor is it a pipe dream, but a living possibility pointing as a sign to the kingdom of God yet to come in all its fullness, but gloriously present in Jesus Christ.

CHAPTER 13

Building a Pastoral Care Team

Overview

It is unlikely that a superhuman pastor exists who is expert and accomplished at every aspect of pastoral care, and even more unlikely that they will be able to exist on an hour's sleep a day and thus give 23 hours a day to meeting the pastoral needs in the community. It is, however, all too common to discover pastors who think that is what they are called to be and do. Pastoral care located in the sole pastor, the lone ranger of the pastoral care world, is doomed to inadequacy and frustration.

The solution to this problem lies in that New Testament principle of shared leadership and ministry. What the individual is unlikely to accomplish on their own, the team might accomplish together. This closing chapter is perhaps more of an appendix, as we consider the principles and practicalities behind building a competent team of pastoral carers in the local church.

Creating the Team

The creation of a formal and organised, supervised and recognised pastoral team seems to me the most creative way forward. Other teams might be primarily composed of pastoral counsellors and be better described as counselling teams. The alternative is a spontaneous, unstructured and informal 'team' that relies upon ad hoc arrangements for pastoral care. This is probably the most widely adopted model, more by default, I fear, than by deliberate planning. We shall explore the formal and organised model.

There is a popular kind of armchair game much beloved of the newspapers at the moment, which involves fantasy teams. You can run your fantasy football team, cricket team and even Formula One motor racing team. The *New Statesman* runs a fantasy politics game, creating your own Cabinet. I want to play a version of this game called 'fantasy pastoral team'. Who would I have in a pastoral care team?

I must say that if I ever have the joy of leading a team such as the one I will outline, it will be the pastoral care equivalent of winning the lottery. However, this is a fantasy pastoral team, and here are the members:

- Pastoral leader
- Pastoral counsellors, trained and accredited
- Family therapist
- Marriage counsellors
- Bereavement counsellors and befrienders
- Care group leaders
- Spiritual directors
- Prayer counsellors
- Social and community workers
- Carer of elderly visitors and their carers
- Community mental health nurse
- Unlimited numbers of base level pastoral carers

In addition I would have access to those who could provide legal, financial and medical advice and support.

The composition of this team brings together professional and lay carers, i.e. a family therapist would be a professionally trained person, while the care of elderly visitors would be undertaken by an able and mature volunteer or lay person, under the overall leadership of a professionally trained pastor.

A word of explanation for some of the categories. Care group leaders, or house group leaders, are the first line of pastoral care, the generalists. They may work quite closely in regard to pastoral care with some members of their small groups, or they may 'refer' them on to more specialised carers, but they play a vital role in building community. Prayer counsellors are those whose care is typically expressed in prayer for the sick or the distressed. Social and community workers represent more specialised care for those whose social circumstances require support, and a community mental health nurse would represent the limit of psychiatric support appropriate to a local church, in support of local health professionals rather than in an autonomous way.

By base level pastoral carers I mean the many who, by virtue of a Christian faith and a sense of responsibility to live out the meaning of that faith, 'simply' befriend, care, support, babysit for the single mother, shop for the disabled neighbour, trim the hedge for the elderly person, etc., etc. This is by no means simple, for it requires skills in compassion, communication and availability that are not universally owned, but which can be learnt by most. They are often the Church's most widespread and obvious expression of pastoral care of an intensely practical kind. I have in mind a couple in my present church who by their cheerful and unsung caring for many others – visiting, shopping, transporting the elderly, offering of hospitality and so forth – are the church's pastoral care for many. They would probably understand it as doing simply what a Christian is called to do, unflattered by the grand title 'pastoral care', and they would be absolutely right.

So much for a 'dream team' in my fantasy pastoral team. The reality is that in my local church there are a few with a little counselling training, a prayer ministry group, some pastoral visitors of the elderly and home group leaders who offer good all-round basic pastoral care. I have no social and community workers on staff, although there are a couple in the church who work professionally in that way. There are no marital or family therapists, and no community mental health nurses, although I could easily use them if they were available. There is some informal spiritual direction, but no formal expression of that, and that is undertaken by older Christians who would not use that term to describe what they do. There are, however, plenty of people giving basic practical pastoral care, as I daresay there are in many churches.

The team I have is heavily weighted towards the 'lay' end of the spectrum, with little or none of the more specialised expressions of care, and I imagine that in that regard my church is fairly typical. For those areas not properly covered internally we refer on as best we can, to Relate or Cruse, or to counsellors or therapists elsewhere.

A prospective volunteer member of the team should be selected according to quite rigorous selection criteria. They need to be spiritually mature and reasonably self-aware. There needs to be proven integrity of lifestyle and character. They should be able to keep confidences and maintain a commitment. Above all they should be available. No matter how gifted and mature, if the volunteer can offer too limited a time to be useful they will be of little value to the team. They need to be growing in the three therapeutic qualities of accurate empathy, unconditional positive regard and genuineness.

How might such a team be developed?

Training

The first step seems to me to be the engendering of a sense of being team. Calling together the various existing pastoral carers to see their roles as part of a wider team is essential. The visitors of the elderly should be enabled to see their role in relation to care group leaders and the prayer ministry team; the counsellors should know they can look to the team for support in what can be a lonely ministry; the team should know that here are people in whom they can have confidence by virtue of supervision, training and professional boundaries; and the overall leader should know that the various groups and individuals are working in a more integrative way.

However, few churches would call or employ a minister without appropriate training, and it is no less important for the local church to invest time and finances in equipping the pastoral care team. Recently we ran a conference for our team led by a couple with wide experience of pastoral care. Later in this chapter, I shall describe in detail the team that Sonia Hall led at an Oxford parish church, but their experience of pastoral care both there, at the Oxford Christian Institute for Counselling, and professionally in training ordinands and in John Hall's job as a clinical psychologist at the Radcliffe Hospital in Oxford, enabled them to speak with authority and wisdom about the perils and opportunities of a pastoral care team. Other opportunities for training could include professionals addressing such themes as substance abuse, eating disorders, family systems, basic grief counselling or marriage preparation. The list is endless.

The basic syllabus for a course to train a pastoral care team would include: the rationale for Christian pastoral care; models of care; priorities in pastoral care; some basic counselling rules; the importance of boundaries and referral; confidentiality; practical and spiritual resources for the pastoral carer; some understanding of Christian ethics; working as a team; and the place of prayer in the practice of pastoral care.

Supervision

Perhaps the key boundary in pastoral care is that of supervision. It enables the team members, within appropriate bounds of confidentiality, to offload their pastoral burden, to be properly supported and to share the responsibility for the individuals in their care with their supervisor. That might be the minister, but not necessarily so. Indeed, there might be certain situations where the minister is not the most appropriate recipient of confidential information (where the client does not want their minister to know about a certain situation, for instance). It may be necessary to have a range of supervisors, including some from outside the local church (in a neighbouring church, for example). One hopes that such circumstances might be rare, but their possibility should be anticipated. The mechanics of this would include informing the client that the pastoral carer is supervised, and asking if there would be any objection to the normal supervisor, who would be a senior church member or minister, knowing about the information. The client's wishes must then be served. The situation might be clearer with pastoral counsellors, who might have their own external supervisor in any case.

In team meetings the issue of confidentiality becomes acute. How much information about those who are served by the pastoral carer can be shared with the wider team? Personal supervision rather than group supervision would be the best option for sensitive material, such as difficulties in a marriage which are not public news. Other items, such as the support of a recently bereaved widow, might be less sensitive, and could be supervised in the group setting, accompanied by prayer together for the individual in need and their carer(s).

Supervision of a pastoral care team helps to avoid similar dangers to those which pastoral counsellors are exposed to. These include over-involvement of the carer to the point where their own life seriously suffers and/or it becomes unhealthy for the client. The need to be needed, the danger of co-dependency, is something that pastoral carers are prone to. Christopher Perry, in his Jungian analysis of pastoral care[1] describes the findings of Hugh Eadie,[2] who observed a 'helping personality'. The profile of that personality breaks down into eight components:

1 idealised self-image: the appeal of love;
2 guilt: self-hate and self-criticism;
3 compulsive-obsessive characteristics;
4 affective controls on sexuality and aggression;
5 passivity, compliance and conformity;
6 attempts to resolve the conflicts;
7 intro-punitive hostility and self-hate; and
8 stress symptoms.

The pastor is beleaguered by moral imperatives which make their life patterned by 'shoulds' and 'should nots' and a conviction that self-denial is the way of expressing love to others. Feeding the pressure to love others is a fear of loneliness, and that isolation is reduced by exuding warmth and love to induce a corresponding lessening of aggression and increase of love. they become the indispensable pastor, always at others' beck and call, always denying their own needs (and where they are married or have children, denying their needs also), in order to subconsciously increase their acceptance by others. The result is over-involvement, an inability or unwillingness to step back and review, and the perception that others who might draw alongside to help share the load are potential rivals for the affection of the dependent group.

A second danger is sexual involvement. There need to be clear boundaries surrounding the pastoral relationship to avoid the destructive effects of a sexual relationship with the client. The transgressing of those boundaries and the public scandal and private grief that ensues can be avoided by adequate supervision and appropriate recognition of the dangers. It is foolish to presume that 'it cannot happen here' and an overt awareness of the sexual dimension to the caring relationship helps to keep it within proper bounds. The carer or client might not be able to prevent an element of sexual attraction between them, but the responsibility of the carer to maintain proper boundaries is aided by good supervision. To use the old adage, they might not be able to prevent the birds flying in the air, but it is possible to stop them nesting in their hair. Eadie suggests that the pastor retreats to the security of pulpit and study, and avoids intimacy by a wide range of pastoral relationships, all of which remain 'professional' or superficial. To cope with this conflict, the pastor either withdraws into a world of study, meditation and fantasy, or enacts rebellious and sexual impulses with disastrous consequences. 'The latter is simply a massive reinforcement of the pastor's tendency to punish himself and to turn his anger against himself.'[3]

Other dangers include a counselling elitism which pitches professional against lay person, counsellor against carer, and destroys the confidence in the competence of the less highly trained members of the team; the risks of voyeurism which wants to gain information for its own sake; and an inability to recognise the limits of competence of the individual team member. All of these can best be avoided by adequate supervision.

Maintenance

Some opportunity for mutual encouragement and fellowship is vital. This might be a monthly meeting for the whole team, or if the team is more highly focused and available, a weekly meeting. Other groups within the team, such as pastoral visitors of the elderly or pastoral counsellors, might also benefit from their own meeting to focus on specific issues. The team meeting should not only address issues of practice, but also be a means of spiritually supporting the team through prayer, fellowship and worship, perhaps including the Eucharist and prayer for healing.

The continuing need to integrate faith and practice, psychology and theology, is also a group activity, and needs to be undertaken at appropriate intellectual levels so as not to exclude those whose theological or psychological understanding is more limited. Similarly, issues of ethical controversy can be discussed in the group and a common policy hopefully achieved.

The group will need to support those whose experience is one of failure to care as thoroughly as they wish. Coming to terms with failure is an early lesson in pastoral care, but one which needs constantly to be renewed. The causes of failure will be manifold, but improvements in pastoral practice may lessen their impact.

Policies on payment of those professionals who earn their living from their caring role, such as therapists or counsellors in private practice, will need to be agreed. It may be that personal payment can be avoided in some instances, such as the church paying the fee, or it may be that a certain number of sessions are granted to the team *ex gratis*. In other circumstances, a payment, however small, by the client may be deemed to be part of the therapeutic exchange, and therefore to exclude all payment could hinder the therapy for some clients. At any rate, a clear policy should be agreed, albeit one which has some flexibility to it.

A Team in Action: St Andrew's, North Oxford

I mentioned earlier that in my own church, where the team is still in its infancy, we benefited from the help of Sonia Hall, who was a priest in the parish of St Andrew's, and prior to that was a pastoral worker in the same church, and her husband Dr John Hall. Their professional training is in clinical psychology. They were instrumental in founding the Oxford Christian Institute for Counselling. St Andrew's is a large evangelical Anglican parish in North Oxford with a full-time staff comprising the senior clergyman, the vicar of the parish, and his curates and administrative staff. With a large youth work, toddlers group and student members, it is a busy church with a congregation of over 600 members.

Sonia's task was initially to establish a pastoral team to assist the clergy in their pastoral task, particularly in the light of the priority they gave to the preparation for Sunday's sermons and the limits that placed upon their available time for one-to-one pastoral work. The model adopted was a small but highly committed team who gave extensively of their time. There were members from various professional backgrounds, such as clinical psychology, and some with more limited training, but the gift of simply being there and getting on with the task. In this way it was not an exclusively professional team.

They met weekly for support, training and prayer. Indeed, the priority of prayer in the team meetings gave it a profound spiritual dynamic. Members gave a commitment of at least six hours a week to the pastoral task, and it was deemed that this was inconsistent with a member caring for young children. Each member had one day a week off when they were unavailable for duty. Their mode of operation, therefore, echoed some of the terms of service of other professionals on the staff, enhancing the sense of valued service that they contribute to the life of this large congregation.

A Team in Action: Stoke Newington Baptist Church

Since the vast majority of clergy and pastors do not work in large suburban parishes with large pastoral care teams and what seems to the rest of us like unlimited resources, I want to also root this theme of building a pastoral team in a very different situation: an inner city, relatively small Baptist church in London.

Stoke Newington Baptist Church is only ten years old in its present form, but arose, phoenix-like, out of the ashes of London's oldest Baptist church, Devonshire Square. Originally located in the City, just south of Liverpool Street Station, Devonshire Square Baptist Church was started in 1638, but moved north to Stoke Newington in the nineteenth century (the equivalent of today's drift to the suburbs), where it flourished as a centre of non-conformity and local education.

Its more recent history can be picked up from the impact of the charismatic movement upon the Church in the 1970s and early 1980s. Under the influence of the more extreme elements in that movement, it had moved away from Sunday worship by 1985, meeting only in house groups, and to all intents and purposes, Stoke Newington (Devonshire Square) had ceased to exist as far as the London Baptist Association was concerned. However, they did not reckon with a 'retired' pastor, Humphrey Vellacott. In the mid-1980s he had restarted an almost redundant Baptist church in the inner city, Vernon Square at King's Cross. Humphrey sent Bob Stephens, his assistant, to Stoke Newington, and the 85 members of the Devonshire Square church of 1985 were replaced by the 15 members of Stoke Newington Baptist Church in 1987, with only two members belonging to both churches.

The majority of current members (there are around 60) have joined the church within the last ten years and have no previous church background, being new Christians. More recently there have been some more mature Christians joining the church, but despite the church being over 350 years old it is actually a very new congregation. The nineteenth-century building was mostly destroyed in the Second World War, and was rebuilt in the late 1950s, with only the Lecture Hall surviving. That 1950s building was sold in the late 1980s and replaced by flats, the church now meeting in a refurbished Lecture Hall (no longer called that, of course), which seats approximately 120 people. Its main morning congregation of 90 (including 20 children) comfortably fits into the building, and is mixed in both age and race, although its mainly working-class background is predominant.[4] Its current minister, John Taylor, who has been there since 1993, describes its morning congregation as 'more black than white', and its smaller evening congregation as 'more white than black'. African members come mainly from Nigeria, and Afro-Caribbean members from Jamaica.

In an inner-city, financially stretched church with a high turnover of members, the sophisticated pastoral team of my 'dream team', or even of St Andrew's, Oxford, is an impossibility. Yet, there are pastoral team structures in place at Stoke Newington that work for its social setting and context. With a high throughput of people it was proving difficult to get to know people and to keep tabs on them, so in the spring of 1997 a pastoral team of nine lay members was formed to do precisely that. After the morning service, they meet and check against a register those who are absent, who are then telephoned or visited the following week. This builds upon the work of the associate pastor, who worked with Bob Stephens. Brian followed up, and visited, everyone! If someone was not in church on Sunday, Brian wrote to them, or visited them by Tuesday, and more than anything else, that built the church during the early years of its new existence. The pastoral visiting team is a replacement for the work of that one man. Each member is willing to contact at least one person absent from church on the Sunday, and thus at a very basic level, everyone is made to feel that they matter and that they belong.

The pastoral care of those in need is also shared by the minister. With a team of three elders, including a husband and wife, Alan and Doris, the minister, John Taylor and his wife, Janet, comprise the pastoral care team. Alan and Doris were members of the old Devonshire Square church who were appointed pastoral leaders in the ten-month interregnum after Bob Stephens left. Both the elders have taken early retirement and so, while not full-time, they are able to offer considerably more than those who work. John therefore has a team of five who are all available during the daytime as well as the evening. They offer care, guidance and prayerful pastoring. The 'occasional offices' of weddings and funerals are John's province, while the routine pastoral care falls largely upon Alan and Doris's shoulders. Should any more complicated situations arise, they refer people on to John as the professional minister, and he likewise refers on to other agencies when the limits of his expertise are reached, although such situations have been rare over the past three years.

Pastoral Care Teams: An Urgent and Possible Priority

This situation demonstrates how much can be done with a large team of lay pastoral visitors (15 per cent of the membership) and those who are available for pastoral care by virtue of the blessed combination of availability and maturity. The potential for pastoral care teams comprised of those who have taken early retirement, or who on retirement are still fit and able and willing to start a new career in pastoral care, is vast. Perhaps in order for the Church to receive the pastoral care it deserves and so desperately needs, in its interface with its mission, ministers should be actively challenging older members to take early retirement, receive some appropriate training, and start a new and exciting life in pastoral care! Expenses incurred during that ministry could be reimbursed by the Church.

Instead of employing just full-time specialists, more diverse teams could be established which even the smaller and poorer churches could afford with little or no loss of effectiveness or value. Instead of employing another generalist but relatively highly trained minister and then expecting them to spend a large proportion of their time on routine visiting, they could function more as a specialist resource to a lay team of well-prepared and trained pastoral carers. It would seem a wise use of the scarce financial resources that every denomination in Britain is finding increasingly hard to find.

Of course, every minister and pastor, however specialist, cannot afford to become disconnected entirely from the day-to-day work of pastoral visiting. Our feet must remain planted in the soil of such routine pastoral care, but the degree to which churches expect all such visitation to be done by the minister must surely change if we are to meet the challenges of the postmodern world. New situations call for radical solutions, and teamwork must become the norm for pastoral care in churches large and small alike.

Postscript

In between the first and second drafts of this book, one of the most significant expressions of the postmodern turn that I have been attempting to describe and respond to took place in a motorway tunnel in Paris on the last day of August 1997. The death of Diana, Princess of Wales, and more particularly the response of the British public to it, and what that revealed about the changes taking place in our culture, was extraordinary.

The depth of shock and sadness, the response of the British people, the volume of newsprint and the sheer weight of flowers was overwhelming. As a nation we were surprised by ourselves, as if the changes that have crept up on us over the past decade suddenly jumped out from behind a wall and stood full face before us.

What was actually happening? I still do not know, but it was strange, and very profound. It has important consequences for the way we understand our society in transition, and how we make known the good news of the gospel in our day. It was much more than simply affection for a much-loved public figure.

I was not even sure what was happening to me. Standing at the morning service at Bunyan Baptist Church at 10.30 on 31 August to announce the death of Diana, Princess of Wales, and describe how we would mark that, moved me more than I would ever have imagined. I was more deeply affected at the announcement of that death than most of the announcements that I have made over the years. I was as cynical as most people about the story of Diana and Dodi al Fayed and the photos taken of them on Mediterranean yachts. I was saddened at the break-up of Charles and Diana's marriage, but it seemed with hindsight to be almost inevitable given the two dysfunctional families they came from, and I have never bought a paper simply because it had news or photos of Diana in it. I am not really that interested in Royalty, and probably would not shed any tears if we became a Republic. But this death touched me, and more than that, the response of a nation famed for its 'stiff upper lip' has been so bewildering, so unexpected that I feel I do not quite know who we are any more as a British people. Bryan Appleyard put it like this:

> In one short, fevered week the entire national culture seemed to have performed a somersault. A sort of magic seems to have gripped the nation.[1]

Actually, there were not a lot of tears, and little hysteria. Her funeral was not the scene of the surging and emotional crowds of, say, the funeral of the Ayatollah Khomeini in Teheran. But the sense of loss was true, spontaneous and intense: it was not media hype, nor media-generated, although ironically, without the media reporting her death around the globe instantly, and the complex and ambiguous relationship that she had with the media, she would not have been mourned as she is. No, this was a powerful sign that we are no longer the deferential, emotionally cautious society we were even ten years ago. We are more post-modern than we ever realised, and it was the unwitting genius of Diana to encapsulate those changes. Here was a woman who thought with her heart, not her head, who was more honest about her struggles and failings than most Christians dare to be, despite our belief in the forgiveness and grace of God. Here was a woman who was able to reinvent herself and her story as life dealt its blows: from shy young woman to fashion icon, from divorced wife to campaigner for justice.

What Does it Say About our Society?

That over-used word 'icon' refers to the way that she encapsulated so many of the trends and changes that are changing modernism into postmodernism.

She somehow represented through her interests those parts of our society that have often felt left out and oppressed. Black and Asian people were there at the gates of the Palaces, alongside homeless people, women and gay men. But most of all, women. One British writer who has lived in New York for much of the past 12 years says he 'felt like a foreigner in my own country':

> Walking around Kensington Gardens last week, I was shocked at the number of blacks, Asians and gays who were there laying flowers. Even more surprising . . . how well these minorities seemed to be getting on with the blue-rinse and leisure-wear brigades. Diana, however she did it, was able to transcend differences of race, sexuality and social background in a way that even American presidents find hard to copy.[2]

She represented a new liberal, fluid, cosmopolitan and informal society: the same society that embraced New Labour in electing a Labour government, but much more Tony Blair himself, to power. Her use of touch symbolised this. It is ironic that something as embodied as touch should have been her tool, for it often seemed that she was obsessed with her body, awkward about it: the bulimia, the fitness clubs, the clothes, all seemed to suggest someone who was not comfortable with her self, yet it was her willingness to touch others that struck a chord. She knew the importance of touch.

The response of those at the flower strewn gates in the week between death and funeral echoed this. Complete strangers hugged one another and held one another. This was more than shared grief for a decent woman trying her best under difficult circumstances. It echoes the shifts in society that she did not create, but which she somehow understood. Pain today is not hidden away, but can be expressed, and can be shared with others. Diana was, after all, a child of the therapy age and herself a famous consumer of it. Maybe we *were* mourning all sorts of other losses, not only of close friends or family, but also of the hope that we might belong to a compassionate and just society, or just *belong*, but this death has allowed people to acknowledge death and live with it, rather than the usual shying away from it. I wonder whether we will mourn more openly for others now? What changes might there be in the way people approach the funeral?

Postmodernists know the importance of style and image. Indeed, their detractors complain that that is all there is, just a veneer of style and image. Diana knew a good image when she saw one! We are left with many powerful images of her: sitting alone before the Taj Mahal just before her separation, walking amidst landmine fields, holding the hand of an AIDS victim, or touching the leper. The cynics might comment that this was all media manipulation on her part, and certainly she knew how to work the media, even if ultimately it proved impossible to control.[3] However, those in the know say that a great deal went on unannounced and out of the limelight. There is every reason to believe that her innate compassion was real, and that she did more than was required by the mere need to project a saintly image. Maybe this too is something that has struck a chord: nothing is so despised in our postmodern age as hypocrisy and sham. Actions must at least match words, if not speak louder than them. Coupled with the very public way we knew about her mistreatment and failings, this increasingly important part of her life endeared her to the popular imagination and to those who knew her well.

The final aspect of this whole sad and fascinating episode is its unmistakably religious dimension. I was struck at once by the language being used: a 'shrine' was proposed to Diana; Althorp was described as a place of 'pilgrimage'. The canonisation of Diana as a modern secular saint is well underway, with ridiculous calls for a national Bank Holiday in her honour: Diana Day! There is no doubt that we are in the midst of a religious phenomenon, with Diana as a contemporary Christ-like figure, touching the leper, comforting the sick, worshipped for her iconic beauty, yet also somehow accessible because of her acknowledged failings, the marital infidelity and unsuitable choice of male companions in latter years.

'She has given expression to a basic form of religious fervour that most of us thought had vanished', says Bryan Appleyard, 'a marginal phenomenon in the world of late liberal capitalism'.[4] All the ingredients are there: flowers, candles, offerings (teddy bears and the like), petitions and adoration. This is natural religion, 'popular religion without benefit of clergy', as Clifford Longley puts it.[5] It demonstrates the depth of longing for meaning, for transcendence, for belonging, in our fragmented and alienated culture. Diana's life and death struck the popular psyche with the story of our redemption that it does not remember from its authentic setting and ultimate significance, but which echoes down the centuries in ways that cannot be ignored. The one who suffers on behalf of all, who shows us what we are like, whose influence in death transcends that of life. This is popular religion. What do we make of it as Christians? Is it blasphemous, pitiable, dangerous? Or just another pointer to the real longings of men and women, longings which most feel are unlikely to be met in organised religion, be it High Anglican pomp and reserve, or mundane and embarrassing 'happy clappy bappy'?

What Does this Mean for Christian Pastoral Care?

In our Protestant, coolly cerebral worship, with its over-reliance on words, we do well to remember the power of symbol. The messages on the thousands of cards were, in the main, short, but accompanied by symbols – flowers, teddies (for comfort?), even champagne. The public have returned to pagan instincts as well as the instincts of pilgrimage (queuing for hours outside St James's Palace) and worship at the shrine. We may dismiss these as abuses of religion (and there were plenty of appeals to God in the books of condolence and the messages on the £25 million worth of flowers left at the shrines, but few to Jesus: there are not Christian sentiments here, perhaps not even sub-Christian ones), but we must not ignore them. We need to find a new place for the symbolic in worship whenever it has been rejected as either 'mystical' or 'popish'. The style of worship of the Taizé and Iona Communities point the way here. Equally, we must ensure that the message that it is Jesus Christ who is Saviour be communicated.

Most of the thousands who went to London or Althorp and who will continue to do so, never met Diana, or if they did, only briefly. There was no personal relationship there. This may be a tribute to the skills of the modern media to convey a person through photographs and television interviews, but more likely it points to how far we have travelled down the postmodern road. The boundary between reality and fiction has become so blurred that we feel with more clarity and power the loss of someone we never met than the real people we knew and now miss. When we talk of a personal relationship with Jesus Christ in our post-modern world, we have to know how easy it is for people to misunderstand what we mean. When people feel they have more of a personal relationship with the cast of *Neighbours* than they have with their next-door neighbour, what on earth do they understand by our pastoral and gospel emphasis upon a personal relationship with Jesus? Just another fictional character, perhaps. Pastoral care must be rooted in the flesh and blood of genuine relationship. It is there that a transforming relationship with Jesus Christ might be glimpsed and hoped for.

Cant, hypocrisy, denial of reality (especially of the reality of emotional distress) and cold formality are rightly rejected by ordinary men and women. Too often those qualities are precisely what they encounter in church life. No wonder they reject expressions of the Christian faith whenever they fall short of God's glorious liberty and grace. The stench of double standards and a concern for British reserve too often replace honesty in things intellectual and emotional. We can ill afford to tolerate such shortcomings, let alone celebrate them, any more than we can be communities which exclude blacks, Asians, women and gay people from roles of influence simply because they have traditionally been subservient or invisible.

How we offer pastoral care to a culture like this is one of the great challenges of our day, if not the greatest challenge facing the Church of Jesus Christ. There is no doubt that our culture is changing fast. What is less certain is the capacity of the Church to respond to those changes. That it has a key role is sure, as shown by the fact that among those in the lost and grieving crowds in the Mall and around the Palaces some turned instinctively to anyone with a clerical collar, just as they did at Dunblane, and will do so again wherever genuine pastoral care is offered with sensitivity to the culture and truthfulness of the Christian hope.

Notes

PART ONE – PATTERNS IN POSTMODERN CULTURE

Chapter 1 – Holding Ministry Together in a World that is Falling Apart

1 *Alternative Service Book*, pp. 370–372.
2 *Patterns and Prayers for Christian Worship*, Oxford, Oxford University Press, 1991, p. 184.
3 Charles Forder, *The Parish Priest at Work: An Introduction to Systematic Pastoralia*, London, SPCK, 1947.
4 S. K. Knight, *Fulfilling the Ministry*, Cambridge Pastoral Theology Lectures of 1925–1926, Cambridge, Cambridge University Press, 1933.
5 Richard Baxter (1615–1691) was an Anglican pastor of strongly Puritan sympathies. He served the parish of Kidderminster from 1641 to 1660, where he sought to implement a thorough pastoral ministry, and which provided the practical experience of ministry about which he wrote in *The Reformed Pastor* (1656). He was a man of broad sympathies, rejecting the extremes of both sides of the ecclesiastical debates of the day, but found himself excluded from the Church of England after the 1662 Act of Uniformity. Continuing to preach, however, he found himself imprisoned for doing so in 1685 and 1686.
6 R. E. O. White, *A Guide to Pastoral Care*, London, Pickering and Inglis, 1976.
7 W. A. Clebsch and C. R. Jaeckle, *Pastoral Care in Historical Perspective*, New York, Aronson, 1975.
8 Stephen Pattison, *A Critique of Pastoral Care*, 2nd edition, London, SCM Press, 1993.
9 Pattison, ibid.
10 Rodney Hunter (ed.), *Dictionary of Pastoral Care and Counselling*, Nashville, Abingdon, 1990.
11 Alasdair MacIntyre, *After Virtue*, London, Duckworth, 1985.
12 Alasdair MacIntyre, *Whose Justice? Whose Rationality?*, London, Duckorth, 1988.
13 Amitai Etzioni, *The Spirit of Community*, London, Fontana Press, 1995.
14 Graham Ward, *Theology and Contemporary Critical Theory*, Basingstoke, Macmillan Press, 1996.
15 Peter Brierley and Heather Wraight (eds.), *UK Christian Handbook 1996–97 Edition*, London, Christian Research, 1996, p. 739.

16 Kenneth Leech, *Spirituality and Pastoral Care*, London, Sheldon Press, 1986.
17 Eugene Peterson, *Working the Angles: The Shape of Pastoral Integrity*, Grand Rapids, William Eerdmans, 1987.
18 Bernice Martin, *A Sociology of Contemporary Cultural Change*, Oxford, Blackwells, 1981, p. 197.
19 Stephen Pattison and James Woodward, 'A Vision of Pastoral Theology: In Search of Words that Resurrect the Dead', *Contact*, Pastoral Monograph No. 4, 1994.
20 Pattison and Woodward, *op. cit.*

Chapter 2 – A History of Pastoral Care in the Late-Modern Period

1 See Pattison, *A Critique of Pastoral Care*; Alistair Ross, *An Evaluation of Clinical Theology*, Oxford, Clinical Theology Association, 1994; and Derek Tidball, *Skilful Shepherds: An Introduction to Pastoral Theology*, Leicester, InterVarsity Press, 1986, ch. 11.
2 See Forder, *The Parish Priest*.
3 Ernest Jones, *Psycho Analysis*, London, Ernest Benn Ltd, 1928.
4 Ross, *op. cit.*, p. 150.
5 F. Barry, *Christianity and Psychology*, revised edition, London, SCM Press, 1933, p. 264.
6 J. C. M. Conn, *The Menace of the New Psychology*, London, InterVarsity Fellowship (IVF), 1939.
7 'We believe wholeheartedly that for the minister of the religion to do his work in a truly evangelical way, the knowledge which psychology and psychotherapy can give him is essential.' J. G. McKenzie, *Psychology, Psychotherapy and Evangelicalism*, London, George Allen and Unwin, 1940.
8 J. T. McNeill, *A History of the Cure of Souls*, London, SCM Press, 1952, p. 320.
9 E. E. Thornton, 'Clinical Pastoral Education', in Hunter (ed.), *Dictionary of Pastoral Care and Counselling.*
10 Robert Lambourne, 'Objections to a National Pastoral Organisation', *Contact*, 35, 1971.
11 Thomas Oden, *Kerygma and Counselling*, Philadelphia, Westminster Press, 1966.
12 Tidball, *op. cit.*, p. 229.
13 Don Browning, *Atonement and Psychotherapy*, Philadelphia, Westminster Press, 1966.
14 Thomas Oden, *Care of Souls in the Classic Tradition*, Philadelphia, Fortress Press, 1984, p. 24.
15 See Don Browning, *The Moral Context of Pastoral Care*, Philadelphia, Westminster Press, 1976; *Religious Ethics and Pastoral Care*, Philadelphia, Fortress Press, 1983; 'Ethics and Pastoral Care' in Hunter (ed.), *op. cit.*, pp. 364-6.
16 See Donald Capps, *Biblical Approaches to Pastoral Counselling*, Philadelphia, Fortress Press, 1981; *Life Cycle Theory and Pastoral Care*,

Philadelphia, Fortress Press, 1983; 'Pastoral Use and Interpretation of the Bible' in Hunter (ed.), *op. cit.*, pp. 82–5.

17 Pattison, *op. cit.*

18 Elaine Graham, *Transforming Practice: Pastoral Theology in an Age of Uncertainty*, London, Mowbray, 1996.

19 George Mulrain, 'Bereavement Counselling Among African-Caribbean People in Britain', *Contact*, 118, 1995.

20 Robert Beckford, 'Do the Masai Have a Point?: Black Sexual Representations and Pastoral Care', *Contact*, 118, 1995.

21 John Swinton, 'A Question of Values: People with Learning Difficulties, Society and the Church', *Contact*, 117, 1995.

22 Pattison, *op. cit.*, p. 215.

Chapter 3 – Fragments and Fragility

1 I am indebted to Derek Tidball for the structure of these categories.

2 David Harvey, *The Condition of Postmodernity*, Oxford, Blackwell, 1989, p. 101.

3 Harvey, *op. cit.*, p. 102.

4 Louis Wirth, 'Urbanisation as a Way of Life', *American Journal of Sociology*, Vol. 44, 1938. Wirth argues that urbanisation leads to social heterogeneity and an attendant alienation as kinship ties break down and are replaced by new allegiances to diverse groups. Instability becomes the norm and there is a retreat into the private world.

5 The American Declaration of Independence.

6 Colin Gunton, *The One, the Three and the Many: God, Creation and the Culture of Modernity*, Cambridge, Cambridge University Press, 1993, p. 12.

7 John Henry Newman, *The Grammar of Assent*, 1870, quoted in David Atkinson, *The Message of Ruth*, Leicester, InterVarsity Press, 1983, p. 15.

8 Robert Pippin, *Modernism as a Philosophical Problem*, Oxford, Blackwell, 1990, p. 22.

9 Harvey, *op. cit.*, p. 240.

10 Gunton, *op. cit.*, p. 99.

11 Jeremiah 17:9.

12 Matthew 15:19.

13 Richard Middleton and Brian Walsh, *Truth is Stranger Than it Used to be*, London, SPCK, 1995, p. 25.

14 Langdon Gilkey, *Reaping the Whirlwind: A Christian Interpretation of History*, New York, Seabury Press, 1976, p. 16.

15 Gunton, *op. cit.*, p. 124.

16 Harvey, *op. cit.*, p. 42.

17 David Lyon, 'Anything in the Post?', *Third Way*, April 1996.

18 Charles Jencks, 'The Rise of Postmodern Architecture', *Architecture Association Quarterly*, No. 4, 1975.

19 Charles Jencks, 'What is Postmodernism?', *Art and Design*, 1986.

20 Michel Foucault, *Folie et déraison: Histoire de la folie à l'âge classique*, Paris, Plon, 1961.

21 Jean-François Lyotard, *The Postmodern Condition: A Report on Knowledge*, trans. Geoff Bennington and Brian Massumi, Minneapolis, University of Minneapolis Press, 1984.
22 David Aaronovitch, 'The Sunday Review', *Independent on Sunday*, 29 September 1996.
23 Martin Redfern, 'The Sunday Review', *Independent on Sunday*, 6 October 1996.
24 ibid.
25 Quoted in Jock MacGregor, 'The Mask, Madonna and Postmodernism', *Ministry Today*, 4, June 1995.
26 Walter Truett Anderson, *Reality Isn't What it Used To Be: Theatrical Politics, Ready to Wear Religion, Global Myths, Primitive Chic and Other Wonders of the Postmodern World*, San Francisco, Harper and Row, 1990.
27 Middleton and Walsh, *op. cit.*, p. 25.
28 *South Bank Show*, November 1996.
29 Middleton and Walsh, *op. cit.*, p. 51.
30 Turning and turning in the widening gyre
The falcon cannot hear the falconer;
Things fall apart; the centre cannot hold;
Mere anarchy is loosed upon the world,
The blood-dimmed tide is loosed, and everywhere
The ceremony of innocence is drowned;
The best lack all conviction, while the worst
Are full of passionate intensity.
W. B. Yeats, *The Second Coming*, 1921
31 Mark 5:9.
32 Genesis 11:1–9.
33 Middleton and Walsh, *op. cit.*, p. 43.
34 R. Hooykas, *Religion and the Rise of Modern Science*, Edinburgh, Scottish Academic Press, 1972.
35 Arthur Jones, 'Whose Side is Science On?', *Third Way*, April 1996.
36 Michael Polanyi, *Personal Knowledge: Towards a Post-Critical Philosophy*, London, Routledge and Kegan Paul, 1958.
37 Thomas Kuhn, *The Structure of Scientific Revolutions*, Chicago, 1962.
38 A. Huyssens 'Mapping the Postmodern', *New German Critique*, 33, 1984. Quoted in Harvey, *op. cit.*

Chapter 4 – What do we Think of Humpty Dumpty?

1 Colossians 1:16.
2 Hebrews 1:3b.
3 Genesis 1:27–28.
4 Romans 23:23–4.
5 Colossians 1:21.
6 Romans 8:20.
7 Romans 8:2–4.
8 Ephesians 2:19–22.
9 Ephesians 4:22–4.

10 For a more detailed exposition, see Stanley Grenz, *Theology for the Community of God*, Carlisle, Paternoster Press, 1994; Alistair McGrath, *Christian Theology: An Introduction*, Oxford, Blackwell, 1994.

11 For instance, in the writings of Don Cupitt, including: *Taking Leave of God*, London, SCM Press, 1980; *The Long Legged Fly: A Theology of Language and Desire*, London, SCM Press, 1987.

12 'Each human being is a superbly constructed, astonishingly compact, self-ambulatory computer': Carl Sagan, cited in Dennis McCallum (ed.), *The Death of Truth*, Minneapolis, Bethany House Publishers, 1996, p. 24.

13 Gunton, *The One, the Three and the Many*, p. 129.

14 *Idem.*

15 The Cappadocian Fathers were all bishops of the places that feature in their names: Basil of Caesarea (c. 330–379), Gregory of Nazianzus, later of Constantinople (329–389) and Gregory of Nyssa (c. 330–395). They became the leaders of a reaction to those who opposed the position of the Council of Nicea (AD 325) on the Trinity, and their formulation was legitimised by the Council of Constantinople (AD 381). In opposing the Arians' premise that the Father alone was God, they used the logical distinction between universals and particulars: the universal of the Trinity was uncreatedness and Godhead, while the particulars, or differentiating particularities, of generacy, generation and procession were the modes of being of Father, Son and Spirit. Against the Pneumatomachi, they brought the doctrine of the Holy Spirit to a new confidence in his deity, of the same substance, ομοουσιος, *homoousios*. Their starting point of the three Hypostases, persons, of the Trinity united in a single substance was the exact opposite to the Western tradition of Augustine, who starts from a single unity and works out to the three persons. Where the Cappadocians, in their clarity and metaphysical logic, have to work hard to preserve the unity of the Godhead, but amply defend the distinctives of the persons, Augustine, from the mysticism of love, finds himself in difficulty over the status of the persons.

16 Gregory of Nazianzus, *Oration*, 40.41.

17 Hilary of Poitiers, *De Trinitate*, 3.24.3f.

18 Richard of St Victor, *De Trinitate*, 3.19.

19 Gunton, *op. cit.*, p. 163.

20 That is, to do with the Church Fathers, the theologians of the first 800 years of the Church.

21 Alastair Campbell, *Paid to Care? The Limits of Professionalism in Pastoral Care*, London, SPCK, 1985, p. 1.

22 Romans 1:20.

23 John Macmurray, *Persons in Relation*, London, Faber, 1961.

24 John Aves, 'Persons in Relation: John Macmurray', in Christoph Schwobel and Colin Gunton (eds.), *Persons, Divine and Human*, Edinburgh, T&T Clark, 1991, p. 136.

25 Being as communion is John Zizioulas' phrase. See *Being as Communion: Studies in Personhood and the Church*, London, Darton, Longman and Todd, 1985.

26 Nick Fox, 'Roosting Chicken . . .', *Third Way*, April 1996.

27 Karl Barth, *Church Dogmatics* Vol. 1, Part I, Edinburgh, T&T Clark, 1936, ch. 4.
28 Jean Calvin, *Institutes of the Christian Religion*, 1, IX, 3 ed. J. T. McNeill, Philadelphia, Westminster Press, 1960.
29 1 Corinthians 12:12–26.
30 John 14:6.

Chapter 5 – Pastoral Care and Postmodern Ethics

1 Michael Jacobs, *Swift to Hear: Facilitating Skills in Listening and Responding*, London, SPCK, 1985, pp. 61–2.
2 Gerard Egan, *The Skilled Helper*, 5th edition, Pacific Grove, Brooks/Cole Publishing Company, 1994, p. 179.
3 Don Cupitt, *Creation out of Nothing*, London, SCM Press, 1990, p. 77.
4 Nigel Biggar, *Good Life: Reflections on What we Value Today*, London, SPCK, 1997, p. 1.
5 Gunton, *op. cit.*, p. 106.
6 Gunton, *op. cit.*, p. 124.
7 Philip Goodchild, 'Christian Ethics in the Postmodern Condition', *Studies in Christian Ethics*, Vol. 8(1), pp. 20–32.
8 David Wells, *God in the Wasteland: The Reality of Truth in a World of Fading Dreams*, Leicester, InterVarsity Press, 1994, p. 219.
9 MacIntyre, *After Virtue*.
10 ibid., p. 8.
11 ibid., p. 70.
12 MacIntyre, *Whose Justice? Whose Rationality?*, p. 352.
13 *Phronesis* is reasoned and true state of capacity to act with regard to human goods (*Ethics* 1140, 20–5). John Casey calls it moral imagination, an ability to see 'what is at stake where the application of rules may not be at all obvious, and to know how to respond' (*Pagan Virtue*, Oxford, Oxford University Press, 1990, p. 146).
14 Fergus Kerr, 'Moral Theology after MacIntyre', *Studies in Christian Ethics*, Vol 8 (1).
15 MacIntyre, *op. cit.*, p. 240.
16 MacIntyre, *op. cit.*, p. 263.
17 Andrew Jones, 'Difficult Encounters: Christian Ethics and Pastoral Care', *Contact*, 117, 1995.
18 Quoted in Jones, ibid.
19 John Hoffman, *The Ethical Confrontation in Counselling*, Chicago, Chicago University Press, 1979, p. 5.
20 Alan Storkey, *A Christian Social Perspective*, Leicester, InterVarsity Press, 1979, p. 198.
21 Ephesians 5:25.
22 See *The Moral Context of Pastoral Care*, Philadelphia, Westminster Press, 1976; *Religious Ethics and Pastoral Care*, Philadelphia, Fortress Press, 1983; and 'The Pastoral Counsellor as Ethicist', *Journal of Pastoral Care*, 1988.
23 Graham, *Transforming Practice*, p. 84.

24 J. Sandler and A. U. Dreher, *What Do Psychoanalysts Want? The Problem of Aims in Psychoanalytical Therapy*, London, Routledge, 1996.
25 Sigmund Freud, *Analysis Terminable and Interminable*, Standard Edition Vol. 23, London, The Hogarth Press, 1937.
26 Ernest Jones, 'The Attitude of the Psychoanalytical Physician Towards Current Conflicts', in *Papers on Psychoanalysis*, 2nd edition, London, Bailliere, Tindall and Cox, 1918.
27 Karen Horney, 'Ziele Der Psychoanalytischen Therapie' Psyche 5, 1951, pp. 463–77. Cited in Sandler and Dreher, *op. cit.*, p. 63.
28 David Tracy, *The Analogical Imagination*, London, SCM Press, 1981, pp. 79–80.
29 Trevor Hart, *Faith Thinking: The Dynamics of Christian Theology*, London, SPCK, 1995, pp. 73–4.
30 Similar concerns are implicit in both Pannenberg and Schillebeeckx in Europe. Pannenberg sees faith as something grounded on public, historical knowledge, crucially of the resurrection of Jesus Christ. Thus, theology cannot be a private, sheltered sphere of life. Theological affirmations must be subject to the rigour of critical enquiry concerning the historical reality on which they are based. He has something of the postmodern condition in mind, perhaps, when he contends that 'consensus alone is not a sufficient criterion of truth' (*Systematic Theology*, Vol. 1, Edinburgh, T&T Clark, 1991, p. 13).
31 George Lindbeck, *The Nature of Doctrine*, London, SPCK, 1984.
32 Tracy, *op. cit.*, p. 78.
33 Graham, *op. cit.*, p. 93.
34 Karl Barth, *Fides Quaerens Intellectum: Anselm's Proof of the Existence of God in the Context of His Theological Scheme*, Virginia, Richmond, 1960.
35 Anselm of Canterbury, *Proslogion*, in E. R. Fairweather (ed.) *Library of Christian Classics*, Vol. X: *A Scholastic Miscellany*, Philadelphia, Westminster Press, 1956.
36 Polanyi, *Personal Knowledge*.
37 Hart, *op. cit.*, p. 97.
38 Thomas Oden, *Systematic Theology*, Vol. 1: *The Living God*, San Francisco, Harper & Row, 1987, p. 323.
39 Robert Lambourne, 'Counselling for Narcissus or Counselling for Christ', in M. Wilson (ed.), *Explorations in Health and Salvation*, Birmingham, University of Birmingham Press, pp. 135–61.
40 Gordon Lynch, 'Moral Reflection and the Christian Pastoral Counsellor', *Contact*, 117, 1995.
41 Carl Rogers, 'A Therapist's View of the Good Life: The Fully Functioning Person', *The Humanist*, Vol. 17, 1957, expanded in *On Becoming a Person*, Boston, Houghton Mifflin, 1961, pp. 184–96.
42 ibid., p. 8.

Chapter 6 – Community

1 Glenda Cooper, 'Britain in 2020'; John Tusa, 'The Price of Separation from the Good Society', *The Independent*, 30 January 1997.
2 John 10:10.
3 Biggar, *Good Life*, p. 16.
4 Speech to Labour Party Conference, Blackpool, 4 October 1994.
5 Etzioni, *Spirit of Community*, p. 54.
6 ibid., p. 24.
7 ibid., p. 1.
8 Roger Scruton, *The Times*, 7 December 1995.
9 Stephen Holmes, cited by Samuel Brittan, 'Tony Blair's Real Guru', *New Statesman*, 7 February 1997.
10 Etzioni, *op. cit.*, p. 52.
11 John Milbank, 'Postmodern Critical Augustinianism: A Short Summa in 42 Responses to Unasked Questions', *Modern Theology*, 7 (3), April 1991, No. 11.
12 This section was first explored in 'The Church as Sign and Agent of the Kingdom', a paper in Steve Finnamore (ed.), *On Earth as in Heaven: A Theology of Social Action for Baptist Churches*, Baptist Union Publications, 1996.
13 Colossians 1:14.
14 Philippians 2:4.
15 John Swinton, 'Friendship in Community', *Contact*, 122, 1997.
16 Blake Morrison, *As If*, London, Granta Books, 1997.
17 Suzanne Moore, 'Are You Just One of Myra's Lynch Mob?', *The Independent*, 7 February 1997.
18 Luke 7:47.
19 Milbank, *op. cit.*, No. 25.

PART TWO – PRIORITIES IN PASTORAL CARE

Introduction

1 1 Kings 19:3–5.

Chapter 7 – Metaphors for Pastoral Care

1 Eberhard Jungel, 'Metaphorical Truth: Reflections on the Theological Relevance of Metaphor as a Contribution to the Hermeneutics of Narrative Theology', in J. Webster (trans.) *Theological Essays*, Edinburgh, T&T Clark, 1989.
2 Psalm 23:1.
3 Isaiah 53:6.
4 John 10:11.
5 1 Peter 5:2.
6 Eberhard Jungel, *God as the Mystery of the World: On the Foundation of*

the Crucified One in the Dispute Between Theism and Atheism, trans. D. L. Guder, Edinburgh, T&T Clark, 1983.

7 John 10:14–15.

8 John 1:11–12.

9 Acts 2:38.

10 1 Thessalonians 5:18.

11 Romans 12:6, 8.

12 John 17:3.

13 John Milbank, 'Can a Gift be Given? Prologemena to a Future Trinitarian Metaphysic', *Modern Theology*, 11:1, January 1995.

14 See 1 John 4:10.

15 Milbank, *op. cit.*, p. 150.

16 1 John 3:16–17.

17 2 Corinthians 1:3–5.

18 παρακλεσις, *paraklesis*, is a key word controlling the discussion in this section of Paul's letter, and a key term for pastoral care. It is variously translated as comfort (in the sense of *cum fortis*, with strength), consolation and encouragement. It is the action, in John, of the Comforter, the *paraclete*, the Holy Spirit. In Paul's writings, it has a particular nuance taken from the messianic role of comfort in Isaiah 40:1, 'Comfort, comfort my people, says your God,' and is linked to the proclamation of salvation and deliverance (cf. Isaiah 51:3, 12, 19; 52:9–10). On the proclamatory role of pastoral care, see below.

19 Milbank, *op. cit.*, p. 121.

20 ibid., p. 125.

21 Ephesians 4:8; Psalm 68:18.

22 Ephesians 4:11–12.

23 For a full discussion of the difficulties in the exposition of these verses, see Andrew Lincoln, *Word Biblical Commentary: Ephesians*, Vol. 42, Dallas, Word Books, 1990, pp. 66–82.

24 John 10:11, Hebrews 13:20 and 1 Peter 2:25.

25 Acts 20:28.

26 1 Peter 5:1–4.

27 Philippians 1:1.

28 See Acts 14:23 and the Pastoral Epistles.

29 Hêlên Cixous, 'Sorties', in H. Cixous and C. Clement, *The Newly Born Woman*, Manchester, Manchester University Press, 1990.

30 Nicholas Fox, *Postmodernism, Sociology and Health*, Buckingham, Open University Press, 1993.

31 Robert Warren, *Being Human, Being Church*, London, Marshall Pickering, 1995.

32 Campbell, *Paid to Care?*, p. 59.

33 Richard Holloway and Brice Avery, *Churches and How to Survive Them*, London, HarperCollins, 1994.

34 James Dunn, *Word Biblical Commentary: Romans 9–16*, Vol. 38B, Dallas, Word Books, 1988.

35 Edward Schillebeeckx, *Church: The Human Story of God*, London, SCM Press, 1990, p. 13.

36 Peter Hodgson and Robert Williams (eds.), *Christian Theology: An Introduction to its Tradition and Tasks*, London, SPCK, 1982, p. 245.
37 *Lumen gentium*, 1, 9, 48; *Sacrosanctum concilium*, 5, 26; *Gaudium et spes*, 42, 45.
38 *Lumen gentium*, 5.
39 cf. 1 Corinthians 2:1, 7; Ephesians 1:9, 3:9; Colossians 1:26.
40 *Gaudium et spes*, 22.
41 Walter Kasper, *Theology and Church*, London SCM Press, 1989, p. 121.
42 Karl Rahner, 'Considerations of the Active Role of the Person in the Sacramental Event', *Theological Investigations*, XIV, London, Darton, Longman and Todd, 1976, pp. 169ff.
43 *Lumen gentium*.
44 Colin Gunton, 'The Church on Earth: The Roots of Community', in Colin Gunton and Daniel Hardy (eds.), *On Being the Church: Essays on the Christian Community*, Edinburgh, T&T Clark, 1989, p. 60.

Chapter 8 – The Urgent Tasks of Pastoral Care: Building Christian Community

1 Deuteronomy 26:12.
2 Isaiah 1:14–17.
3 See Amos 5.
4 Deuteronomy 24:7.
5 Deuteronomy 24:14–15.
6 Deuteronomy 25:13–16.
7 Matthew 5:38–42. Here quoted from Exodus 21:24–5; Leviticus 24:20; Deuteronomy 19:21.
8 Jürgen Moltmann, *The Way of Jesus Christ: Christology in Messianic Dimensions*, London, SCM Press, 1990, p. 125.
9 Galatians 6:2.
10 Matthew 18:21–35.
11 Luke 10:25–37.
12 Jeremiah 31:31; Ezekiel 36:26–7.
13 Romans 13:10.
14 Romans 12:9–10.
15 Romans 13:8.
16 Galatians 5:6.
17 Philippians 2:1–11.
18 Colossians 3:14.
19 Colossians 3:12–13.
20 Ephesians 2:11–22.
21 1 Corinthians 11:18–22.
22 1 Corinthians 5:1–2, 6:12–20.
23 Philippians 4:2.
24 2 Thessalonians 3:6–15.
25 Ephesians 5:25.
26 1 Corinthians 1:9.
27 2 Corinthians 13:13.

28 Philippians 1:5.
29 Philemon 6.
30 Moltmann, *op. cit.*, p. 230.
31 Irenaeus iii, 24, 1: 'Ubi Ecclesia, ibi te Spiritus Sanctus, et ubi Spiritus Dei, illic Ecclesia et omnis gratia: Spiritus autem Veritas.' Where the Church is, there the Holy Spirit is too, and where the Spirit of God is, there is the Church and all grace: for the Spirit is Truth.
32 Moltmann, *op. cit.*, p. 231, echoing Jean Calvin's doctrine of Word and Spirit.
33 Baptist, Methodist and United Reformed Churches.
34 E. H. Erikson, *Childhood and Society*, London, Paladin, 1963.
35 Eric Rayner, *Human Development: An Introduction to the Psychodynamics of Growth, Maturity and Ageing*, 3rd edition, London, Unwin Hyman, 1986, p. 68.
36 Brice Avery, *The Pastoral Encounter: Hidden Depths in Human Contact*, London, Marshall Pickering, 1996, p. 137.
37 John 15:15.
38 Moltmann, *op. cit.*, p. 255.
39 Alistair Ross, *Understanding Friends: How to Get the Best Out of Relationships*, London, Triangle, 1993, p. 5.
40 Moltmann, *op. cit.*, p. 256.
41 Aristotle, *Nicomachean Ethics* VIII.
42 Darrel Bock, *The IVP New Testament Commentary: Luke*, Downers Grove, InterVarsity Press, 1994, p. 143.
43 Moltmann, *op. cit.*, pp. 263–4.
44 See Romans 16:16; 1 Corinthians 16:20; 2 Corinthians 13:12.
45 The conflict arising over the distribution to the widows in Acts 6, Paul and Barnabas' scrap over John Mark in Acts 15, and the place of the Jewish law for gentile Christians, only partly resolved at the Jerusalem Council (also in Acts 15), figure in the Early Church. The disciples' arguments over who was greatest seems most poignant, as it takes place on the road to Jerusalem and the death of Jesus (Matthew 20:20–28).
46 See: David Augsburger, *Caring Enough to Confront*, Scottdale, Herald Press, 1973; David Augsburger, *When Caring is not Enough: Resolving Conflicts Through Fair Fighting*, Ventura, Regal Books, 1983; David Cormack, *Peacing Together: From Conflict to Resolution*, Crowborough, MARC Monarch, 1989; Justin Dennison, *Team Ministry: A Blueprint for Christian Leadership*, London, Hodder and Stoughton, 1997.
47 Leonardo Boff, *Ecclesiogenesis: The Base Communities Reinvent the Church*, Maryknoll, NY, Orbis Books, 1986.

Chapter 9 – The Urgent Tasks of Pastoral Care: Creating Relational Health

1 In 1990 there were 318,000 marirages contracted in England and Wales, compared to 404,000 in 1971, and by 1995 this had dropped to 283,000.
2 Paul Beasley-Murray, *Happy Ever After? A Guide to the Marriage Adventure*, Didcot, Baptist Union Publications, 1997.

3 Church Pastoral Aid Society, *Marriage in Mind*, Warwick, 1993.
4 Sue Walrond-Skinner, *The Fulcrum and the Fire: Wrestling with Family Life*, London, Darton, Longman and Todd, 1993, p. 158.
5 A Christian version that has been acclaimed is *Your Marriage* by Michael and Myrtle Baughen, London, Hodder and Stoughton, 1994.
6 Walrond-Skinner, *op. cit.*, p. 118.
7 Bruce and Mary Reddrop, *For Better, For Worse: A Guide to Contemporary Marriage Counselling*, London, HarperCollins, 1995, pp. 236–7.
8 D. J. Dormer, *The Relationship Revolution*, London, One Plus One, 1992.
9 Mark Bonnington and Bob Fyall, *Homosexuality and the Bible*, Grove Biblical Series 1, Cambridge, Grove Books, 1996.
10 A recent symposium, *The Way Forward*, edited by Timothy Bradshaw, would be a good place to begin wider reading on this dilemma.
11 See Romans 1:24–32; 1 Corinthians 6:9–11; and 1 Timothy 1:10–11.
12 See Martin Hallett, *I am Learning to Love*, Basingstoke, Marshall Pickering, 1987.
13 Bonnington and Fyall, *op. cit.*, p. 25.
14 Hebrews 12:2.
15 Stephen Covey, *The Seven Habits of Highly Effective People*, London, Simon and Schuster, 1992, p. 199.

Chapter 10 – The Urgent Tasks of Pastoral Care: Healing the Wounded Soul

1 Pattison, *Critique of Pastoral Care*, p. 26.
2 David Atkinson and Francis Bridger, *Counselling in Context: Developing a Theological Framework*, London, HarperCollins, 1994, p. 36.
3 Roger Hurding, 'Christian Counselling: An Overview', in *The Bible and Counselling*, London, Hodder & Stoughton, 1992, ch. 9. See also his *Roots and Shoots: A Guide to Counselling and Psychotherapy*, London, Hodder and Stoughton, 1986.
4 Kirk Farnsworth, *Wholehearted Integration: Harmonising Psychology and Christianity Through Word and Deed*, Grand Rapids, Baker Book House, 1985.
5 Atkinson and Bridger, *op. cit.*, p. 49.
6 ibid., p. 50.
7 Charles Truax and Robert Carkhuff, *Towards Effective Counselling and Psychotherapy: Training and Practice*, Chicago, Aldine, 1967.
8 Thomas Oden, *Pastoral Counsel*, New York, Crossroad, 1989, p. 7.
9 Petrüska Clarkson, *The Therapeutic Relationship in Psychoanalysis: Counselling Psychology and Psychotherapy*, London, Whurr Publishers, 1995.
10 ibid., p. viii.
11 J. Holmes and R. Lindley, *The Values of Psychotherapy*, Oxford, Oxford University Press, 1989, p. 3.
12 Clarkson, *op. cit.*, p. 15.
13 ibid., p. 19.
14 Eric Berne, *Principles of Group Treatment*, New York, Grove Press, 1966, p. 63.

15 Brian Thorne, *Person-centred Counselling: Therapeutic and Spiritual Dimensions*, London, Whurr Publishers, 1991, p. 180.
16 Clarkson, *op. cit.*, p. 25.
17 These are the words of 1 John 1:8–9, found in the *Book of Common Prayer.*
18 Lewes Smedes, *Shame and Grace: Healing the Shame we don't Deserve*, London, Triangle, 1993, p. 4.
19 Paul Ricoeur, *Hermeneutics and the Human Sciences: Essays on Language, Action and Interpretation*, trans. J. B. Thompson, Cambridge, Cambridge Unversity Press, 1981.
20 Jurgen Habermas, *Knowledge and Human Interests*, London, Heinemann, 1972.
21 Abraham Maslow, 'Self-actualisation and Beyond', in J. F. T. Bugental (ed.), *Challenges of Humanistic Psychology*, New York, McGraw Hill, 1967, p. 284.
22 Phil Mollon, *Multiple Selves, Multiple Voices: Working with Trauma, Violation and Dissociation*, Chichester, John Wiley and Sons, 1996, p. 184.
23 2 Corinthians 4:7.

Chapter 11 – The Urgent Tasks of Pastoral Care: Nurturing and Sustaining Faith

1 Richard Foster, *Celebration of Discipline: The Path to Spiritual Growth*, London, Hodder and Stoughton, 1980.
2 Joyce Huggett, *Listening to God*, London, Hodder and Stoughton, 1986.
3 Brother Ramon SSF, *Deeper Into God*, Basingstoke, Marshall Pickering, 1987; and *Soul Friends*, Basingstoke, Marshall Pickering, 1989.
4 Anne Townsend, *Faith Without Pretending*, London, Hodder and Stoughton, 1990.
5 Sister Margaret Magdalen CSMV, *Jesus – Man of Prayer*, London, Hodder and Stoughton, 1987; and *A Spiritual Checkup*, Crowborough, Highland Books, 1990.
6 Joyce Huggett, *Listening to Others*, London, Hodder and Stoughton, 1985.
7 Peterson, *Working the Angles.*
8 Leech, *Spirituality and Pastoral Care*, pp. 78–9.
9 Peterson, *op. cit.*, p. 3.
10 ibid., p. 151.
11 ibid., p. 162.
12 1 Corinthians 4:15.
13 Leech, *op. cit.*, p. 48.
14 ibid., p. 51.
15 ibid., p. 67.
16 ibid., p. 72.
17 ibid., pp. 73–4.
18 cf. Malcolm Goldsmith and Martin Wharton, *Knowing Me, Knowing You*, London, SPCK, 1993.

19 Gordon Jeffs, *Spiritual Direction for Every Christian*, London, SPCK, 1987, p. 19.
20 Kenneth Leech, *Soul Friend: A Study of Spirituality*, London, Sheldon Press, 1977, pp. 88–9.
21 ibid., p. 101.
22 Foster, *op. cit.*, pp. 90–1.

Chapter 12 – Resources for Pastoral Care

1 Leech, *Spirituality and Pastoral Care*, p. 5.
2 Cited in Leech, *Spirituality and Pastoral Care*, p. 7.
3 Francis Watson, *Text, Church and World: Biblical Interpretation in Theological Perspective*, Edinburgh, T&T Clark, 1994, p. 292.
4 Colossians 3:16.
5 Romans 10:8.
6 Hebrews 4:12.
7 Deborah Seddon, 'Meditating on Scripture', in Ian Bunting (ed.), *Closer to God: Practical Help on Your Spiritual Journey*, London, Scripture Union, 1995, p. 156.
8 Leech, *op. cit.*, p. 16.
9 Romans 12:2.
10 2 Corinthians 4:16–17.
11 Leech, *op. cit.*, p. 21.
12 Duncan Forrester, Ian McDonald and Gian Tellini, *Encounter with God: An Introduction to Christian Worship and Practice*, 2nd edition, Edinburgh, T&T Clark, 1996, p. 192.
13 Karl Barth, *Church Dogmatics*, IV/2, Edinburgh, T&T Clark, 1958, p. 638.
14 Wesley Carr, *Brief Encounters: Pastoral Ministry Through the Occasional Offices*, London, SPCK, 1985.
15 Pattison and Woodward, 'A Vision of Pastoral Theology'.
16 ibid.
17 Paul Ballard and John Pritchard, *Practical Theology in Action: Christian Thinking in the Service of Church and Society*, London, SPCK, 1996.
18 Wesley Carr, *Handbook of Pastoral Studies*, London, SPCK, 1997.
19 Leech, *op. cit.*, p. 112.
20 Carr, *op. cit.*, p. 94.
21 Carr, *op. cit.*, p. 96.
22 P. Bourdieu, *Outline of a Theory of Practice*, Cambridge, Cambridge University Press, 1977.
23 Chris Moody, *Eccentric Ministry: Pastoral Care and Leadership in the Parish*, London, Darton, Longman and Todd, 1992, p. 133, cited in Carr, *op. cit.*, p. 110.
24 Leech, *op. cit.*, p. 114.

Chapter 13 – Building a Pastoral Care Team

1 Christopher Perry, *Listen to the Voice Within: A Jungian Approach to Pastoral Care*, London, SPCK, 1991, pp. 17ff.
2 Hugh Eadie, 'Clergy Stress', *Contact*, Summer 1975.
3 Perry, *op. cit.*, p. 18.
4 There are some professional middle class members, but there is high unemployment and those in work are often poorly paid or working part-time.

Postscript

1 Bryan Appleyard, 'Diana, First Lady of the Global Village', *Sunday Times*, 7 September 1997, Part 4.
2 John Cassidy, 'Back to Blighty, and a Vision of a Ruling Class on the Run', *Sunday Times*, 7 September 1997, Part 4.
3 The editorial in *Le Monde* on Tuesday after her death observed that 'the Princess grew up in the global media village in which celebrities are by turn victims, accomplices and manipulators of the Press, in games more complex and more multilayered than those who now send the paparazzi to perdition suspect'. Cited by John Lloyd in *New Statesman*, 5 September 1997.
4 *op. cit.*
5 Clifford Longley, 'Religion Without Benefit of Clergy', *Daily Telegraph*, 12 September 1997.

Bibliography

Anderson, Walter Truett, *Reality Isn't What it Used to Be: Theatrical Politics, Ready to Wear Religion, Global Myths, Primitive Chic and Other Wonders of the Postmodern World*, San Francisco, Harper and Row, 1990

Anselm of Canterbury, 'Proslogion' in Fairweather, E. R. (ed.), *Library of Christian Classics* Vol. X *A Scholastic Miscellany*, Philadelphia, Westminster Press, 1956

Atkinson, David and Bridger, Francis, *Counselling in Context: Developing a Theological Framework*, London, HarperCollins, 1994

Augsburger, David, *Caring Enough to Confront*, Scottdale, Herald Press, 1973

Augsburger, David, *When Caring is not Enough: Resolving Conflicts Through Fair Fighting*, Ventura, Regal Books, 1983

Avery, Brice, *The Pastoral Encounter: Hidden Depths in Human Contact*, London, Marshall Pickering, 1996

Aves, John, 'Persons in Relation: John Macmurray' in Schwobel, Christoph and Gunton, Colin (eds.), *Persons, Divine and Human*, Edinburgh, T&T Clark, 1991

Ballard, Paul and Pritchard, John, *Practical Theology in Action: Christian Thinking in the Service of Church and Society*, London, SPCK, 1996

Barry, F., *Christianity and Psychology*, revised edition, London, SCM Press, 1933

Barth, Karl, *Church Dogmatics* Vol I, Part 1, Edinburgh, T&T Clark, 1936

Barth, Karl, *Church Dogmatics* Vol IV, Part 2 Edinburgh, T&T Clark, 1958

Barth, Karl, *Fides Quaerens Intellectum: Anselm's Proof of the Existence of God in the Context of His Theological Scheme*, Virginia, Richmond, 1960

Baughen, Michael and Myrtle, *Your Marriage*, London, Hodder and Stoughton, 1994

Bauman, Zygmunt, *Intimation of Postmodernity*, London, Routledge, 1992

Bauman, Zygmunt, *Postmodern Ethics*, Oxford, Blackwell, 1993

Beasley-Murray, Paul, *Happy Ever After? A Guide to the Marriage Adventure*, Didcot, Baptist Union Publications, 1997

Beckford, Robert, 'Do the Masai Have a Point? Black Sexual Representations and Pastoral Care', *Contact*, 118, 1995

Berne, Eric, *Principles of Group Treatment*, New York, Grove Press, 1966

Biggar, Nigel, *Good Life: Reflections on What we Value Today*, London, SPCK, 1997

Bock, Darrel, *The IVP New Testament Commentary: Luke*, Downers Grove, Illinois, InterVarsity Press, 1994

Boff, Leonardo, *Ecclesiogenesis: The Base Communities Reinvent the Church*, Maryknoll, NY, Orbis Books, 1986

Bonnington, Mark and Fyall, Bob, *Homosexuality and the Bible*, Grove Biblical Series 1, Cambridge Grove Books, 1996

Bourdieu, P., *Outline of a Theory of Practice*, Cambridge, CUP, 1977

Bradshaw, Timothy (ed.), *The Way Forward? Christian Voices on Homosexuality and the Church*, London, Hodder and Stoughton, 1997

Brierley, Peter and Wraight, Heather (eds.), *UK Christian Handbook 1996–7 Edition*, London, Christian Research, 1996

Brittan, Samuel, 'Tony Blair's Real Guru' *New Statesman*, 7 February 1997

Browning, Don, *Atonement and Psychotherapy*, Philadelphia, Westminster Press, 1966

Browning, Don, *The Moral Context of Pastoral Care*, Philadelphia, Westminster Press, 1976

Browning, Don, *Religious Ethics and Pastoral Care*, Philadelphia, Fortress Press, 1983

Browning, Don, 'The Pastoral Counsellor as Ethicist', *Journal of Pastoral Care*, 1988

Calvin, Jean, *Institutes of the Christian Religion*. 1, IX, 3 ed. J. T. McNeill Philadelphia, Westminster Press, 1960

Campbell, Alastair, *Paid to Care? The Limits of Professionalism in Pastoral Care*, London, SPCK, 1985

Capps, Donald, *Biblical Approaches to Pastoral Counselling*, Philadelphia, Fortress Press, 1981

Capps, Donald, *Life Cycle Theory and Pastoral Care*, Philadelphia, Fortress Press, 1983

Carr, Wesley, *Brief Encounters: Pastoral Ministry Through the Occasional Offices*, London, SPCK, 1985

Carr, Wesley, *Handbook of Pastoral Studies*, London, SPCK, 1997

Casey, John, *Pagan Virtue*, Oxford, Oxford University Press, 1990

Cixous, Hêlên, 'Sorties' in Cixous, H. and Clement, C. *The Newly Born Woman*, Manchester, Manchester University Press, 1990

Clarkson, Petrüska, *The Therapeutic Relationship in Psychoanalysis, Counselling Psychology and Psychotherapy*, London, Whurr Publishers, 1995

Clebsch, W. A. and Jaekle, C. R., *Pastoral Care in Historical Perspective*, New York, Aronson, 1975

Conn, J. C. M., *The Menace of the New Psychology*, London, InterVarsity Fellowship, 1939

Cormack, David, *Peacing Together: From Conflict to Resolution*, Crowborough, MARC Monarch, 1989

Covey, Stephen, *The Seven Habits of Highly Effective People*, London, Simon and Schuster, 1992

Cupitt, Don, *Taking Leave of God*, London, SCM Press, 1980

Cupitt, Don, *The Long Legged Fly: A Theology of Language and Desire*, London, SCM Press, 1987

Cupitt, Don, *Creation out of Nothing*, London, SCM Press, 1990

Dennison, Justin, *Team Ministry: A Blueprint for Christian Leadership*, London, Hodder and Stoughton, 1997

Dunn, James, *Word Biblical Commentary: Romans 9–16*, Vol. 38B, Dallas, Word Books, 1988

Eadie, H., 'Clergy Stress', *Contact*, Summer 1975

Egan, Gerard, *The Skilled Helper*, 5th edition, Pacific Grove, Brooks/Cole Publishing Company, 1994

Erikson, Erik H., *Childhood and Society*, London, Paladin, 1963

Etzioni, Amitai *The Spirit of Community*, London, Fontana Press, 1995

Farnsworth, Kirk, *Wholehearted Integration: Harmonising Psychology and Christianity Through Word and Deed*, Grand Rapids, Baker Book House, 1985

Flanagan, Kieran and Jupp, Peter C. (eds.), *Postmodernity, Sociology and Religion*, Basingstoke, Macmillan Press, 1996

Forrester, Duncan, McDonald, Ian and Tellini, Gian, *Encounter With God: An Introduction to Christian Worship and Practice*, 2nd edition, Edinburgh, T&T Clark, 1996

Foster, Richard, *Celebration of Discipline: The Path to Spiritual Growth*, London, Hodder and Stoughton, 1980

Foucault, Michel, *Folie et déraison: Histoire de la folie à l'âge classique*, Paris, Plon, 1961

Fox, Nicholas, *Postmodernism, Sociology and Health*, Buckingham, Open University Press, 1993

Freud, Sigmund, *Analysis Terminable and Interminable*, Standard Edition, Vol. 23, London, The Hogarth Press, 1937.

Gilkey, Langdon, *Reaping the Whirlwind: A Christian Interpretation of History*, New York, Seabury Press, 1976

Gill, Robin, *Moral Communities*, Exeter, Exeter University Press, 1992

Goldsmith, Malcolm and Wharton, Martin, *Knowing Me, Knowing You*, London, SPCK, 1993

Goodchild, Philip, 'Christian Ethics in the Postmodern Condition', *Studies in Christian Ethics*, Vol. 8(1)

Goodliff, Paul, 'The Church as Sign and Agent of the Kingdom', in Finnermore, Steve (ed.), *On Earth as in Heaven: A Theology of Social Action for Baptist Churches*, Didcot, Baptist Union Publications, 1996

Graham, Elaine, *Transforming Practice: Pastoral Theology in an Age of Uncertainty*, London, Mowbray, 1996

Grenz, Stanley, *Theology for the Community of God*, Carlisle, Paternoster Press, 1994

Gunton, Colin, 'The Church on Earth: The Roots of Community', in Gunton, Colin and Hardy, Daniel (eds.), *On Being the Church: Essays on the Christian Community*, Edinburgh, T&T Clark, 1989

Gunton, Colin, *The One, the Three and the Many: God, Creation and the Culture of Modernity*, Cambridge, Cambridge University Press, 1993

Habermas, Jurgen, *Knowledge and Human Interests*, London, Heinemann, 1972

Hallett, Martin, *I am Learning to Love*, Basingstoke, Marshall Pickering, 1987

Hart, Trevor, *Faith Thinking: The Dynamics of Christian Theology*, London, SPCK, 1995

Harvey, David, *The Condition of Postmodernity*, Oxford, Blackwell, 1989

Hodgson, Peter and Williams, Robert (eds.), *Christian Theology: An Introduction to its Tradition and Tasks*, London, SPCK, 1982

Hoffman, John, *The Ethical Confrontation in Counselling*, Chicago, Chicago University Press, 1979

Holloway, Richard and Avery, Brice, *Churches and How to Survive Them*, London, HarperCollins, 1994

Holmes, J. and Lindley, R., *The Values of Psychotherapy*, Oxford, Oxford University Press, 1989

Hooykas, R., *Religion and the Rise of Modern Science*, Edinburgh, Scottish Academic Press, 1972

Huggett, Joyce, *Listening to Others*, London, Hodder and Stoughton, 1985

Huggett, Joyce, *Listening to God*, London, Hodder and Stoughton, 1986

Hunter, Rodney (ed.), *Dictionary of Pastoral Care and Counselling*, Nashville, Abingdon, 1990

Hurding, Roger, *Roots and Shoots: A Guide to Counselling and Psychotherapy* London, Hodder and Stoughton, 1986

Hurding, Roger, *The Bible and Counselling*, Hodder and Stoughton, 1992

Huyssens, A., 'Mapping the Postmodern', *New German Critique*, 33, 1984

Jacobs, Michael, *Swift to Hear: Facilitating Skills in Listening and Responding*, London, SPCK, 1985

Jeffs, Gordon, *Spiritual Direction for Every Christian*, London, SPCK, 1987

Jencks, Charles, 'The Rise of Post-modern Architecture', *Architecture Association Quarterly*, No.4, 1975

Jencks, Charles, 'What is Postmodernism?', *Art and Design*, London, Academy Editions, 1986

Jones, Andrew, 'Difficult Encounters: Christian Ethics and Pastoral Care', *Contact*, 117, 1995

Jones, Arthur, 'Whose Side is Science on?', *Third Way*, April 1996

Jones, Ernest, 'The Attitude of the Psychoanalytical Physician Towards Current Conflicts', in *Papers on Psychoanalysis*, 2nd edition, London, Bailliere, Tindall and Cox, 1918

Jones, Ernest, *Psycho Analysis*, London, Ernest Benn Ltd, 1928

Jungel, Eberhard, *God as the Mystery of the World: On the Foundation of the Crucified One in the Dispute Between Theism and Atheism*, trans. D. L. Guder, Edinburgh, T&T Clark, 1983

Jungel, Eberhard, 'Metaphorical Truth: Reflections on the Theological Relevance of Metaphor as a Contribution to the Hermeneutics of Narrative Theology', in *Theological Essays*, trans. J. Webster, Edinburgh, T&T Clark, 1989

Kasper, Walter, *Theology and Church*, London, SCM Press, 1989

Kearney, Richard and Rainwater, Mara (eds.), *The Continental Philosophy Reader*, London, Routledge, 1996

Kerr, Fergus, 'Moral Theology After MacIntyre', *Studies in Christian Ethics*, Vol 8 (1)

Knight, S. K., *Fulfilling the Ministry*, Cambridge Pastoral Theology Lectures of 1925–1926, Cambridge, Cambridge University Press, 1933

Kuhn, Thomas, *The Structure of Scientific Revolutions*, Chicago, Chicago University Press, 1962

Lambourne, Robert, 'Objections to a National Pastoral Organisation', *Contact*, 35, 1971

Lambourne, Robert 'Counselling for Narcissus or Counselling for Christ', in Wilson, M. (ed.), *Explorations in Health and Salvation*, Birmingham, University of Birmingham Press, 1983

Leech, Kenneth, *Soul Friend: A Study of Spirituality*, London, Sheldon Press, 1977

Leech, Kenneth, *Spirituality and Pastoral Care*, London, Sheldon Press, 1986

Lincoln, Andrew, *Word Biblical Commentary: Ephesians*, Vol. 42, Dallas, Word Books, 1990

Lindbeck, George, *The Nature of Doctrine*, London, SPCK, 1984

Lynch, Gordon, 'Moral Reflection and the Christian Pastoral Counsellor', *Contact*, 117, 1995

Lyon, David, 'Anything in the Post?', *Third Way*, April 1996

Lyotard, Jean-François, *The Postmodern Condition: A Report on Knowledge*, trans. Bennington, Geoff and Massumi, Brian, Minneapolis, University of Minneapolis Press, 1984

MacGregor, Jock, 'The Mask, Madonna and Postmodernism', *Ministry Today*, 4, June 1995

MacIntyre, Alasdair, *After Virtue*, 2nd edition, London, Duckworth, 1985

MacIntyre, Alasdair, *Whose Justice? Whose Rationality?*, London, Duckworth, 1988

Macmurray, John, *Persons in Relation*, London, Faber, 1961

McCallum, Dennis (ed.), *The Death of Truth*, Minneapolis, Bethany House Publishers, 1996

McGrath, Alistair, *Christian Theology: An Introduction*, Oxford, Blackwell, 1994

McKenzie, J. G., *Psychology, Psychotherapy and Evangelicalism*, London, George Allen and Unwin, 1940

McNeill, J. T., *A History of the Cure of Souls*, London, SCM Press, 1952

Magdalen, Sister Margaret, CSMV, *Jesus – Man of Prayer*, London, Hodder and Stoughton, 1987

Magdalen, Sister Margaret, CSMV, *A Spiritual Check-up*, Crowborough, Highland Books, 1990

Martin, Bernice, *A Sociology of Contemporary Cultural Change*, Oxford, Blackwell, 1981

Maslow, Abraham, 'Self-actualisation and Beyond', in Bugental, J. F. T. (ed.), *Challenges of Humanistic Psychology*, New York, McGraw Hill, 1967

Middleton, Richard, and Walsh, Brian, *Truth is Stranger Than it Used to be*, London, SPCK, 1995

Milbank, John, 'Postmodern Critical Augustinianism: A Short Summa in 42 Responses to Unasked Questions,' *Modern Theology*, 7(3), April 1991

Milbank, John, 'Can a Gift be Given? Prologemena to a Future Trinitarian Metaphysic', *Modern Theology*, 11:1, January 1995

Mollon, Phil, *Multiple Selves, Multiple Voices: Working With Trauma, Violation and Dissociation*, Chichester, John Wiley & Sons, 1996

Moltmann, Jürgen, *The Way of Jesus Christ: Christology in Messianic Dimensions*, London SCM Press, 1990

Montefiore, Hugh (ed.), *The Gospel and Contemporary Culture*, London, Mowbray, 1992

Moody, Chris, *Eccentric Ministry: Pastoral Care and Leadership in the Parish*, London, Darton, Longman and Todd, 1992

Moore, Suzanne, 'Are You Just One of Myra's Lynch Mob?' *The Independent*, 7 February 1997

Morrison, Blake, *As If*, London, Granta Books, 1997

Mulrain, George, 'Bereavement Counselling Among African-Caribbean People in Britain', *Contact*, 118, 1995

Newman, John Henry, *The Grammar of Assent*, 1870. Quoted in David Atkinson, *The Message of Ruth*, Leicester, Intervarsity Press, 1983

Oden, Thomas, *Kerygma and Counselling*, Philadelphia, Westminster Press, 1966

Oden, Thomas, *Care of Souls in the Classic Tradition*, Philadelphia, Fortress, 1984

Oden, Thomas, *Systematic Theology* Vol 1 *The Living God*, San Francisco, Harper & Row 1987

Oden, Thomas, *Pastoral Counsel*, New York, Crossroads, 1989

Osborne, Lawrence, *Restoring the Vision: Gospel and Modern Culture*, London, Mowbray, 1995

Pannenberg, Wolfhart, *Systematic Theology*, Vol 1, Edinburgh, T&T Clark, 1991

Pattison, Stephen, *A Critique of Pastoral Care*, 2nd edition, London, SCM Press, 1993

Pattison, Stephen, and Woodward, James, 'A Vision of Pastoral Theology: In Search of Words that Resurrect the Dead', *Contact*, Pastoral Monograph No.4, 1994

Perry, Christopher, *Listen to the Voice Within: A Jungian Approach to Pastoral Care*, London, SPCK, 1991

Peterson, Eugene, *Working the Angles: The Shape of Pastoral Integrity*, Grand Rapids, William Eerdmans, 1987

Pippin, Robert, *Modernism as a Philosophical Problem*, Oxford, Blackwell, 1990

Polanyi, Michael, *Personal Knowledge: Towards a Post-Critical Philosophy*, London, Routledge and Kegan Paul, 1958

Rahner, Karl, 'Considerations of the Active Role of the Person in the Sacramental Event', in *Theological Investigations* XIV, London, Darton, Longman and Todd, 1976

Ramon, Brother, SSF, *Deeper into God* Basingstoke, Marshall Pickering, 1987

Ramon, Brother, SSF, *Soul Friends*, Basingstoke, Marshall Pickering, 1989

Rayner, Eric, *Human Development: An introduction to the Psychodynamics of Growth, Maturity and Ageing*, 3rd edition, London, Unwin Hyman, 1986

Reddrop, Bruce and Mary, *For Better, For Worse: A Guide to Contemporary Marriage Counselling*, London, HarperCollins, 1995

Ricoeur, Paul, *Hermeneutics and the Human Sciences: Essays on Language, Action and Interpretation*, trans. J. B. Thompson, Cambridge, Cambridge University Press, 1981

Rogers, Carl, 'A Therapist's View of the Good Life: The Fully Functioning Person', *The Humanist*, Vol 17, 1957

Rogers, Carl, *On Becoming a Person*, Boston, Houghton Mifflin, 1961

Ross, Alistair, *Understanding Friends: How to Get the Best out of Relationships*, London, Triangle, 1993

Ross, Alistair, *An Evaluation of Clinical Theology*, Oxford, Clinical Theology Association, 1994

Sandler, J. and Dreher, A. U., *What do Psychoanalysts Want? The Problem of Aims in Psychoanalytical Therapy*, London, Routledge, 1996

Schillebeeckx, Edward, *Church: The Human Story of God*, London, SCM Press, 1990

Seddon, Deborah 'Meditating on Scripture', in Bunting, Ian (ed.), *Closer to God: Practical Help on your Spiritual Journey*, London, Scripture Union, 1995

Smedes, Lewes, *Shame and Grace: Healing the Shame we don't Deserve*, London, Triangle, 1993

Storkey, Alan, *A Christian Social Perspective*, Leicester, InterVarsity Press, 1979

Swinton, John, 'A Question of Values: People with Learning Difficulties, Society and the Church', *Contact*, 117, 1995

Swinton, John, 'Friendship in Community', *Contact*, 122, 1997

Tidball, Derek, *Skilful Shepherds: An Introduction to Pastoral Theology*, Leicester, InterVarsity Press, 1986

Thorne, Brian, *Person-centred Counselling: Therapeutic and Spiritual Dimensions*, London, Whurr Publishers, 1991

Townsend, Anne, *Faith Without Pretending*, London, Hodder and Stoughton, 1990

Tracy, David, *The Analogical Imagination*, London, SCM Press, 1981

Truax, Charles and Carkhuff, Robert, *Towards Effective Counselling and Psychotherapy: Training and Practice*, Chicago, Aldine, 1967

Tusa, John, 'The Price of Separation from the Good Society', *The Independent*, 30 January 1997

Walrond-Skinner, Sue, *The Fulcrum and the Fire: Wrestling with Family Life*, London, Darton, Longman and Todd, 1993

Ward, Graham, *Theology and Contemporary Critical Theory*, Basingstoke, Macmillan Press, 1996

Wara, Graham, *The Postmodern God: A Theological Reader*, Oxford, Blackwell, 1997

Warren, Robert, *Being Human, Being Church*, London, Marshall Pickering, 1995

Watson, Francis, *Text, Church and World: Biblical Interpretation in Theological Perspective*, Edinburgh, T&T Clark, 1994

Wells, David, *God in the Wasteland: The Reality of Truth in a World of Fading Dreams*, Leicester, InterVarsity Press, 1994

White, R. E. O., *A Guide to Pastoral Care*, London, Pickering and Inglis, 1976

Wirth, Louis, 'Urbanisation as a Way of Life', *American Journal of Sociology*, Vol. 44, 1938

Young, Frances (ed.), *Dare we Speak of God in Public?*, London, Mowbray, 1995

Zizioulas, John, *Being as Communion: Studies in Personhood and the Church*, London, Darton, Longman and Todd, 1985

Index